The Economics of Conflict

CESifo Seminar Series

Edited by Hans-Werner Sinn

See http://mitpress.mit.edu for a complete list of titles in this series.

The Economics of Conflict

Theory and Empirical Evidence

edited by
Karl Wärneryd

CESifo Seminar Series

The MIT Press
Cambridge, Massachusetts
London, England

MIT Press books may be purchased at special quantity discounts for business or sales promotional use. For information, please email special_sales@mitpress.mit.edu.

This book was set in PalatinoLTStd by Toppan Best-set Premedia Limited, Hong Kong. Printed and bound in the United States of America.

Library of Congress Cataloging-in-Publication Data

The economics of conflict : theory and empirical evidence / edited by Karl Wärneryd.
    pages cm. – (CESifo seminar series)
    Includes bibliographical references and index.
    ISBN 978-0-262-02689-5 (hardcover : alk. paper) 1. Insurgency–Economic aspects.
2. War–Economic aspects. 3. Economic development–Political aspects. I. Wärneryd, Karl Erik, 1927-
    HB195.E3524 2014
    330–dc23
                            2013027452

10 9 8 7 6 5 4 3 2 1

Contents

Series Foreword

This book is part of the CESifo Seminar Series. The series aims to cover topical policy issues in economics from a largely European perspective. The books in this series are the products of the papers and intensive debates that took place during the seminars hosted by CESifo, an international research network of renowned economists organized jointly by the Center for Economic Studies at Ludwig-Maximilians-Universität, Munich, and the Ifo Institute for Economic Research. All publications in this series have been carefully selected and refereed by members of the CESifo research network.

Preface

This book collects a selection of papers presented at a CESifo Summer Institute workshop that took place on the island of San Servolo in the Venetian Lagoon in July of 2011. I thank Arye Hillman, Dan Kovenock, Johannes Münster, and Alberto Vesperoni, who acted as discussants at the workshop, and the anonymous referees of the book, for their comments and suggestions for improvement, John Covell, Emily Taber, and Dana Andrus of the MIT Press for their editorial work, and CESifo for providing financial and human resource support for the entire project.

Stockholm, April 2013
Karl Wärneryd

Introduction

Karl Wärneryd

According to Pinker (2011), the world has recently become a much less violent place, at least in proportional terms. One of the explanations he suggests for this development is the impact of Enlightenment moral philosophy and classical liberalism on the average Western person's attitude toward violence. In short, people realized that peaceful exchange in a market is a nicer and more efficient way of allocating goods than is war.

Perhaps this explains why modern economics, which also has its origin in the Enlightenment and is directly related to classical liberal political philosophy, has largely ignored the issue of outright conflict as an alternative to market exchange. Although there are isolated examples, such as Pareto (1971) and Haavelmo (1954), of authors discussing coercion and conflict explicitly, throughout the history of economics, most of economic theory has taken the existence of well-defined property rights, enforced by some shadowy, benevolent third party, as given.

Nevertheless, even though war may affect a smaller share of the world's population today, as Pinker convincingly argues, it is still an ongoing concern, and an economically important one. This in itself would justify economists taking an interest in the study of conflict. But there is also an additional reason. Even ostensibly peaceful, cooperative transactions do take place in the shadow of conflict as an outside option. This outside option may constrain the outcomes that can be reached through voluntary agreement. Hence an understanding of conflict from a theoretical perspective is needed also to understand what happens in the absence of outright conflict.

Consider, for example, two parties who have entered into a trade contract specifying, say, that one of them should deliver a particular good to the other, and that the latter should pay a certain sum of money in return. Suppose that the seller has accepted the money but has nevertheless failed to deliver, or has delivered something the buyer feels is not what was specified in the contract. In the world assumed by the standard economics model, it is implicit that if the buyer complained the original terms of the contract would immediately and costlessly be enforced. It is as if the formal legal system is assumed to already know every relevant detail of the situation. In reality, of course, if there is disagreement one of the parties has to take the other to court. The court knows nothing about the particular contract, and listens to the cases presented by the two parties in order to collect information on which to base its decision. A party that presents no evidence for its case is sure to lose. Hence litigation consumes resources, for example, in the form of fees paid to lawyers, and may have the character of a contest where the party that presents the best evidence is most likely to win. This also implies that even in cases where contracting does not end in ex post disagreement, the fact that all contracting takes place in the shadow of costly litigation nevertheless puts restrictions on which contracts will be possible. Similarly peace between nations cannot be understood without taking into account that outright warfare is always available as an option, and democratic politics within a nation is restricted by the outside option of political violence on the part of disgruntled groups.

The present volume aims at presenting a spectrum of recent economic research on conflict, broadly interpreted.

Contests

The theoretical analysis of conflict using the tools of economics, such as game theory, is a rather recent phenomenon. A few examples from this nevertheless already quite voluminous literature are Schelling (1960), Hirshleifer (2001), Brito and Intriligator (1985), Skaperdas (1992), Garfinkel (1994), Bueno de Mesquita and Lalman (1992), and Dixit (2004).

A common model of the technology of conflict in the theoretical literature is the *contest success function*, so called because it gives the probability of players winning given the expenditures (e.g., on arms) or efforts of all. The contest perspective offers at least two advantages over other approaches:

· It makes the strategic nature of conflict explicit, as opposed to models of response to an external threat that is taken as fixed, and

- it helps avoid the frequently simplistic conclusions from 2×2 games, such as the Prisoner's Dilemma (e.g., that all-out conflict is inevitable in the absence of third-party enforcement of agreements).

Let x_1 and x_2 be the efforts (expenditures on arms, sizes of armies, etc.) of two parties involved in outright conflict. An influential paper by Skaperdas (1996) axiomatizes a ratio-form class of contest success functions where the probability of player $i \in \{1, 2\}$ winning is

$$p_i(x_1, x_2) = \frac{f(x_i)}{f(x_1) + f(x_2)},$$

with f a positive, increasing function.

In the context of the study of rent seeking, Tullock (1980) proposed a ratio-form contest success function that has become a de facto standard also for modeling conflict more generally. The simplest form of the Tullock function gives the probability of player i winning as

$$p_i(x_1, x_2) := \begin{cases} x_i / (x_1 + x_2) & \text{if } x_1 + x_2 > 0 \\ 1/2 & \text{otherwise.} \end{cases}$$

Although Haavelmo (1954) had already proposed this technology as relevant for the study of international conflict, he did not solve such a model for equilibrium. Suppose that the players are risk neutral, have strictly positive valuations of winning equal to v_1 and v_2, respectively, and that conflict efforts come at unit cost. Then player i's expected utility is

$$u_i(x_1, x_2) := p_i(x_1, x_2)v_i - x_i.$$

Note that it cannot happen in equilibrium that no one expends anything. For suppose that one party expended nothing on conflict. Then, if the other party also did so, it would win with probability $\frac{1}{2}$. But an arbitrarily small positive expenditure would raise the winning probability to one. Hence it cannot be a best reply to also expend nothing.

The best reply of player i given the effort of player $j \neq i$ is therefore given by the first-order condition

$$\frac{\partial u_i}{\partial x_i} = \frac{x_j}{(x_1 + x_2)^2} v_i - 1 = 0.$$

That is, player i's *best reply function* is

$$x_i = \sqrt{x_j v_i} - x_j.$$

In equilibrium both players must be playing best replies, so we must have that

$$x_1 = \frac{v_1^2 v_2}{(v_1 + v_2)^2}$$

and

$$x_2 = \frac{v_1 v_2^2}{(v_1 + v_2)^2}.$$

Hence player 1's equilibrium probability of winning is

$$p_1(x_1, x_2) = \frac{x_1}{x_1 + x_2} = \frac{v_1}{v_1 + v_2}.$$

A central result is therefore that the player with the higher valuation wins with a greater probability. Another important observation about this simple model is the effect of asymmetry of valuation on equilibrium efforts. Specifically, the greater is the difference in valuation of winning between the players, the lower is aggregate equilibrium effort. Let $v_1 = v - \delta$ and $v_2 = v + \delta$ for some v and some $\delta > 0$. Aggregate expenditure is then

$$x_1 + x_2 = \frac{v_1^2 v_2 + v_1 v_2^2}{(v_1 + v_2)^2} = ((v - \delta) + (v + \delta)) \frac{(v - \delta)(v + \delta)}{((v - \delta) + (v + \delta))^2} = \frac{v^2 - \delta^2}{2v},$$

which declines in δ. (Also see Konrad 2009.) Intuitively, the greater incentive to win of the player with the higher valuation makes it more costly for the low-valuation player to participate. More generally, asymmetries between the participants, not just with regard to valuations of winning, but abilities, information, and the like, tend to lower equilibrium efforts. (For a survey of the case of informational asymmetries, see Wärneryd 2012.)

In the present volume, four largely theoretical chapters (by Konrad, Cubel, Fiaschi, and Jia and Liang) and one largely empirical (by Evia, Laserna, and Skaperdas) use contest success functions to model conflict.

Theory

Konrad (in chapter 1) uses the contest approach to study the scope for alliance formation in conflict. An early economic literature on alliances, started by Olson and Zeckhauser (1966), treats the threat of conflict as exogenously given and focuses on defense as a public good for the members of the alliance. Explicitly modeling conflict as a strategic game, however, raises some questions about how military alliances might come about in the first place.

In line with the close connection between the analysis of rent seeking and that of conflict more broadly conceived, Cubel (in chapter 2) considers conflict under fiscal federalism. A central government provides transfers to two regions. A region that is dissatisfied with its outcome may decide to engage in conflict (e.g., through lobbying) over its share of the total transfer, if doing so would be profitable. Cubel shows that whether conflict will happen or not depends on the degree of publicness of regional budgets, and on the similarity between regions.

That an abundance of natural resources can be a "curse" for a nation, in the sense of being correlated with low growth rates, is a phenomenon that has recently attracted much attention. Sachs and Warner (1997) provide a "Dutch disease" argument to explain why resource-rich nations on average grow slower than nations with less resources. Mehlum et al. (2006), however, point out that there are nations with abundant natural resources that also do well on growth. Whether natural resource abundance is a problem or not has to do with institutional quality, they argue. Specifically, the resource curse may be due to imperfectly enforced property rights, which creates incentives for costly appropriation activity.

Fiaschi (in chapter 3) constructs an explicitly dynamic model of growth and conflict over resouces. He considers how low initial per capita income, high population growth, and high natural resource rents, through their effects on the likelihood and intensity of conflict, could lock a nation into permanent underdevelopment.

Jia and Liang (in chapter 4) formulate a model of the relationship between decentralization of government and political stability and test it on data on *coups d'état* in developing countries. In their model, citizens can choose between subordinating themselves to a central government or plotting a *coup*. Following ideas articulated already by Machiavelli, but hitherto largely ignored, they consider the role of the internal organization of government in enabling commitment to non-aggression.

Empirics

The study of civil war and insurgency, rather than international conflict, has been a recent concern of empirical research in the economics of conflict, led by contributions such as Collier and Hoeffler (2004). The empirical papers in the present volume follow this trend.

Caruso, Costa, and Ricciuti (in chapter 5) relate income, ethnic fractionalization, and external threat levels to the probability of military coups in Africa. Per capita income is shown to have a negative effect on the probability of military rule, offering support for the "modernization" theory of democracy. Fractionalization also lowers the probability of military rule, while external threats have a lagged positive effect.

Evia, Laserna, and Skaperdas (in chapter 6) discuss the effect of social conflict on economic performance in Bolivia. The authors distinguish between economic growth due to external factors and that due to productive investment. They find a positive correlation between externally induced growth and conflict, and a negative one between investments and conflict.

Bove and Elia (in chapter 7) examine the link between occupational opportunities and antigovernment activity in Afghanistan. In particular, they focus on the link between opium prices and the level of insurgent violence. It is found that whereas opium prices do not drive conflict, increased conflict leads to increased supply and lower opium prices.

Stroup and Zissimos (in chapter 8) investigate why IMF's Structural Adjustment Program (SAP) sometimes seems to provoke social unrest. The idea is that an SAP involves liberalization and a scaling-down of government employment. Liberalization of trade in a nation with a comparative advantage in primary products will benefit the elite owners of the land used for their production, and hence increase income inequality. In the absence of an SAP, the elite would be able to appease the losers by expanding government employment, but when they are unable to do so, outright conflict may ensue.

The final chapter 9, by Cassar, Grosjean, and Whitt, uses experimental methods to study the effect on cooperation and trust of having been exposed to the civil war in Tajikistan. Ex-combatants are shown to exhibit much less trust toward, and willingness to cooperate with, anonymous strangers than non-combatants do, in contrast with an existing literature that suggests that exposure to violence may increase pro-social behavior. The authors argue that conflict may sharpen the difference in attitudes toward in-group and out-group members, respectively.

Concluding Remarks

As argued previously, economics needs a theory of conflict, since, even when they are not outright conflictual, economic transactions necessarily take place in the shadow of conflict. But the study of conflict also needs economics. At its worst, the earlier political science literature discusses the origins of war in terms of national "destinies" and other vague superindividual driving forces. In contrast, the more hard-nosed methodological individualism of economics stresses that conflictual action, like any human action, can fruitfully be viewed as undertaken by rational actors who frequently have short-term material gains in mind. Second, the study of models of conflict more sophisticated than the Prisoner's Dilemma shows that the conclusions drawn from too simple games are often misleading.

The present volume aims to provide a collection of important new contributions, but also a bird's-eye view of the field of the economics of conflict as it currently stands. It brings together a variety of approaches, from the purely game-theoretical to the experimental, that all have in common a rational-choice perspective on conflict, a topic that often in the past has been thought to involve the inherently irrational. We hope it will serve not only to enlighten readers new to the field, but also to stimulate new research.

References

Dagobert L Brito and Michael D Intriligator. 1985. Conflict, war, and redistribution. *American Political Science Review* 79: 943–57.

Collier, Paul, and Anke Hoeffler. 2004. Greed and grievance in civil war. *Oxford Economic Papers* 56: 563–95.

Bueno de Mesquita, Bruce, and David Lalman. 1992. *War and Reason: Domestic and International Imperatives*. New Haven: Yale University Press.

Dixit, Avinash K. 2004. *Lawlessness and Economics: Alternative Modes of Governance*. Princeton: Princeton University Press.

Garfinkel, Michelle R. 1994. Domestic politics and international conflict. *American Economic Review* 84:1294–1309.

Haavelmo, Trygve. 1954. *A Study in the Theory of Economic Evolution*. Amsterdam: North-Holland.

Hirshleifer, Jack. 2001. *The Dark Side of the Force: Economic Foundations of Conflict Theory*. Cambridge, UK: Cambridge University Press.

Konrad, Kai A. 2009. *Strategy and Dynamics in Contests*. Oxford: Oxford University Press.

Mehlum, Halvor, Karl Ove Moene, and Ragnar Torvik. 2006. Institutions and the resource curse. *Economic Journal* 116: 1–20.

Olson, Mancur, and Richard Zeckhauser. 1966. An economic theory of alliances. *Review of Economics and Statistics* 48: 266–79.

Pareto, Vilfredo. [1927] 1971. *Manual of Political Economy.* Ann S. Schwier, trans. London:Augustus M. Kelley

Pinker, Steven. 2011. *The Better Angels of Our Nature: Why Violence Has Declined.* New York: Viking.

Jeffrey D Sachs and Andrew M Warner. 1997. Natural resource abundance and economic growth. Working paper. Harvard University.

Schelling, Thomas C. 1960. *The Strategy of Conflict.* Cambridge: Harvard University Press.

Skaperdas, Stergios. 1992. Cooperation, conflict, and power in the absence of property rights. *American Economic Review* 82: 720–39.

Skaperdas, Stergios. 1996. Contest success functions. *Economic Theory* 7: 283–90.

Tullock, Gordon. 1980. Efficient rent seeking. In James M Buchanan, Robert D Tollison, and Gordon Tullock, eds., *Toward a Theory of the Rent-Seeking Society.* College Station: Texas A&M University Press, 269–82.

Wärneryd, Karl. 2012. Informational aspects of conflict. In Michelle R Garfinkel and Stergios Skaperdas, eds., *The Oxford Handbook of the Economics of Peace and Conflict.* Oxford: Oxford University Press, Oxford, 23–42.

1 Strategic Aspects of Fighting in Alliances

Kai A. Konrad

But the strong man is strongest when alone.
—Friedrich Schiller, *Wilhelm Tell*

1.1 Introduction

Players who have a common goal often form alliances. In many instances there are multiple rival alliances, with the success of one alliance ruling out the success of the other alliances, and military alliances, political parties, R&D alliances, and team competition in sports are some of the most salient examples for this type of competition. It has been pointed out by economists for a long time that such alliances have to bridge two potentially important disadvantages compared to standalone players: a free-rider problem and a holdup problem.

The free-rider problem results because alliance members, when contributing effort to the success of the alliance as a whole, make a contribution to a group public good. If one alliance member contributes more effort to the common goal of the alliance, this player bears the cost of this effort, but the effort typically benefits other members of the alliance as well. In the absence of cooperation or enforceable contracts, the contributions to this public good are made voluntarily. The principle that governs contributions hence is simple: each member of an alliance makes a contribution to the alliance's public good such that a marginal increase in a player's contribution has a marginal cost for this player that is equal to this player's own benefit from the increased winning probability of the alliance that is caused by it. Olson and Zeckhauser (1966) were the first to draw attention to this free-rider problem in alliances. An implication of this general insight is that the members of an alliance who contribute the lion's share to the success of the alliance are members who have higher than average total benefits if the alliance

achieves its goals, and who have a cost advantage in making contributions to the alliance.[1] Considering the expenditure of the different
members of the North Atlantic Treaty Organization (NATO), they
found patterns that are in line with these predictions. The military
expenditure as a percentage of GNP was highest for the United States,
with 9.0 percentage points of GNP, whereas Luxembourg, being the
smallest member of NATO, expended a share of only 1.7 percentage
points.[2] Their analysis led to a considerable amount of further theoretical work that partially refined some of the arguments and looked at
various modifications.[3] They also inspired a considerable stock of
further empirical analyses on this topic.

Alliances may also suffer from a holdup problem. If the alliance is
victorious, this may create rivalry within the alliance, depending on
the goal. A defense alliance may aim at the preservation of peace and
territorial protection for its member states, such that all member states
participate in the benefits of achieving this goal in a nonrival and non-
exclusive way; in particular, they need not struggle internally about
how to distribute the peace and security benefits. This, however, is not
true for all types of alliances. Alliances in an actual military conflict
may win something that is not a group public good. If an alliance
defeats its rival enemy, the members of the alliance may have to divide
the spoils of victory among its members. In this situation a second
strategic problem emerges within alliances. The players who have formerly been members of the alliance may start quarrelling about obtaining a larger share in these spoils, and this quarrel may easily end up
in a fight. The Second World War is an illustrative example. During the
war a number of military powers including the United States, the
United Kingdom, France, and the Soviet Union formed the Great Alliance with the defeat of Nazi Germany and its allies as its common
objective. However, the spoils of this victory were not a pure public
good. Instead, it became clear even while Germany was not finally
defeated that the Great Alliance would split into at least two major
groups that would fight about how to divide the spoils of victory
between them. This fight became known as the cold war. It took about
forty years, and the arms races that took place between the rivals dissipated an enormous amount of resources that could have been used
peacefully instead.

Historians document that the struggle over the spoils of victory
among the players who had been members of the winning alliance is
a rather common phenomenon. O'Connor (1969) documents this

outcome for the Napoleonic wars: "The conflicting ambitions of the allies were subdued so long as the military danger was paramount; when the enemy weakened perceptibly, the concept of victory embraced by each member of the alliance either changed or became more distinctive. . . . A quarrel over the spoils need not await the end of hostilities, and the form of victory envisioned by the participants may vary accordingly" (O'Connor 1969, p. 369). Similar outcomes are reported about the aftermath of the First World War: "The British also disagreed with the French over economic policy. To be sure, the two Allies cooperated on economic matters during most of the War, and they were the principal sponsors of the Paris Economic Resolutions. However, their cooperation dissolved as victory became certain and reparation and indemnity replaced other wartime planning. Thereafter, they became the principal competitors for shares of compensation from Germany" (Bunselmeyer 1975, p. 15).[4] For the Second World War: "The fact that victory was finally in sight in 1944 thus had a double and contradictory effect on the alliance. On the one hand, the removal of mortal danger made them less inclined to subordinate individual aims to the need for hanging together and hence a greater willingness to disregard the susceptibilities of allies. On the other hand, the imminence of victory and the obvious desperation of the Germans suggested that this was a poor time to allow divergent views of policy and strategy to break up a winning coalition and thereby risk all that had already been attained at huge cost in lives and treasure" (Weinberg 1994, p. 736).

If members of a victorious alliance break up and fight over the spoils of victory, this should reduce the value that the now former members of an alliance attribute to the victory of their alliance. This then creates a holdup problem with regard to a member's decision about how much effort to invest or contribute to increase the probability that the alliance is victorious. The first to formally analyze this holdup problem in the context of alliances were Katz and Tokatlidu (1996) and Wärneryd (1998). Later Esteban and Sákovics (2003) considered a two-stage contest in which players A and B are teamed up in an alliance in a contest against player C. Should C win, C receives the full prize and the game ends. Should the alliance win, the alliance members have to fight over which player receives the prize, in a contest that follows similar rules to those of the contest in the first stage. They compare this game with a symmetric, one-stage contest among the three players A, B, and C, and find that under rather general conditions, players A and

B are better off in the symmetric, one-stage contest. The combined strategic disadvantages of the holdup problem and the free-riding problem inside the alliance make the formation of an alliance fairly unattractive. Their result points to what could be called an "alliance puzzle": the formation of an alliance actually weakens the members of the alliance, in comparison to a situation where they would act as stand-alone players.

The insights of Esteban and Sákovics (2003) contrast with the major role that alliances play in military conflict, in politics, in business, and in daily life. This suggests that there must be other aspects and considerations in the formation of alliances that more than offset the strategic disadvantages. In this chapter, I study some of these offsetting effects and the environments where the strategic disadvantages of alliance formation do not play a big role. In particular, in the next sections I consider (1) supermodularity in alliance members' efforts, (2) budget constraints that are sufficiently tight to remove the strategic problems of free-riding and holdup, (3) the potentially beneficial role of a threat of internal conflict, as an incentive for overcoming the free-riding problem in making contributions to the alliance effort, (4) possible benefits from information transfers among members of an alliance, (5) the role of multiple fronts if alliance members are resource constrained and can mutually support each other by resource transfers, and (6) evolutionary forces that generate in-group favoritism and spiteful behavior toward the out-group.

There are evidently many strategic aspects of alliances that are not considered here. For instance, the formation and the breakup of alliances typically take place voluntarily and in the absence of property rights or binding contracts. This requires alliances to be self-enforcing. Considerations 1 through 6 may explain why the formation of an alliance can be mutually beneficial and self-enforcing. But I do not directly address the dynamics of formations and dissolutions and re-arrangements of alliances. Political scientists have studied the sequential process of the formation and re-grouping of countries in different alliance networks over time. They have also emphasized the different types and functions of alliances. These include the role of alliances as means to prevent conflict (e.g., see Wagner 2009 for a discussion). Economists who have studied the process of endogenous alliance formation focus on situations in which the conflict takes place. Their analysis of coalition formation shows that much depends on the assumptions about the rules that apply if members of an alliance disagree or find it advantageous to leave and join another alliance, on how far-sighted they are (e.g., for further references, see Bloch, Sán-chez-Pagés, and Soubeyran 2006; Bloch 2009).

1.2 The Baseline Model

The game considered by Esteban and Sácovics (2003) is a generic frame-work for analyzing the alliance puzzle. The game is as follows: There is a set of three players, $N = \{A, B, C\}$. All three players compete for a prize of a given size that is normalized to a monetary value $v = 1$. Player C is a stand-alone player who chooses an effort $x_C \geq 0$ that has a cost $C(x_i) = x_i$. Players A and B are members of an alliance. They also choose efforts $x_A \geq 0$ and $x_B \geq 0$, and have costs $C(x_A) = x_A$ and $C(x_B) = x_B$.[5] All effort choices take place independently and simultaneously. A contest success function determines the allocation of the prize as a random function of the effort choices. In general terms, the probability for the alliance to win is $p(x_A, x_B, x_C)$, and the probability for C to win is $1 - p(x_A, x_B, x_C)$, where p is a probability and will be specified in more detail. In the baseline framework, $p(x_A, x_B, x_C) = p(x_A + x_B, x_C)$; that is, the effort choices of alliance members simply add up to the total effort of the alliance, making their efforts perfect substitutes. Should C win the prize, the game ends and the payoffs of players are $\pi_C = 1 - x_C$ for player C and $\pi_A = -x_A$ and $\pi_B = -x_B$ for player B. If the alliance wins, then the alliance members must determine how to allocate the prize between them. Taking the behavior of victorious war alliances as the role model, they start another fight about the prize. Players A and B expend intra-alliance efforts $y_A \geq 0$ and $y_B \geq 0$, and a contest success function $q(y_A, y_B)$ that may be of similar nature as p determines the win probabilities of A and B under these circumstances. Accordingly, the payoffs of members of a winning alliance in this subgame are $1 - y_i - x_i$ for the winner and $-y_j - x_j$ for the loser. All this is common knowledge among the players.

We can solve this game by backward induction, starting with stage 2, for different types of contest success functions p and q. Figure 1.1 shows the equilibrium results for three cases.

The first row in the table in figure 1.1 shows the case where winning is determined by pure luck ($p = q \equiv 1/2$). In this case the disadvantage of alliance players is smallest, and is essentially induced by the specific choice of the exogenous win-probabilities.

	p	q	$x_A + x_B$	x_C	$Ey_A (= Ey_B)$	$E\pi_A (= E\pi_B)$	$E\pi_C$
Lottery	$\dfrac{1}{2}$	$\dfrac{1}{2}$	0	0	0	$\dfrac{1}{4}$	$\dfrac{1}{2}$
Lottery contest	$\dfrac{x_A + x_B}{x_A + x_B + x_C}$	$\dfrac{y_A}{y_A + y_B}$	$\dfrac{1}{25}$	$\dfrac{4}{25}$	$\dfrac{1}{4}$	$\dfrac{3}{100}$	$\dfrac{16}{25}$
All-pay auction without noise	1 if $x_A + x_B > x_C$ 0 if $x_A + x_B \leq x_C$	1 if $y_A > y_B$ $\dfrac{1}{2}$ if $y_A = y_B$ 1 if $y_A < y_B$	0	0	$\dfrac{1}{2}$	0	1

Figure 1.1
Equilibrium strategies and payoffs for the alliance game in the baseline model for three different contest success functions

The second row in figure 1.1 shows the case where winning or losing follows the Tullock (1980) lottery contest success function, namely $p = (x_A + x_B)/(x_A + x_B + x_C)$, where $x_A + x_B + x_C > 0$, and $p = 1/2$ otherwise, and $q = y_A/(y_A + y_B)$ where $y_A + y_B > 0$, and $q = 1/2$ otherwise. In this case the internal fight between former alliance members A and B reduces the value that each member attributes to winning the contest from $1/2$ (if they just shared the prize equally) to $1/4$. Accordingly, the stage-1 contest between the alliance and player C is highly asymmetric in the values attributed to winning. This also makes the equilibrium contributions and the equilibrium payoffs asymmetric.

The third row in figure 1.1 shows the case where, at both stages, the party that wins the contest expends the higher effort. The contest success functions are those of an all-pay auction without noise in this case.[6] Here the holdup problem is at a maximum: players A and B know that they will dissipate the full value of the prize in their internal fight, should their alliance win against player C.[7] Hence, even if they win, they win nothing. Each attributes a value of zero to the victory of the alliance, whereas player C attributes the full value of the prize to winning against the alliance, as this player receives this prize without any further fighting. In this asymmetric contest between the alliance and C, the players A and B do not have an incentive to expend positive effort in stage 1, and this explains the outcome in the third line of figure 1.1.

While it is difficult to test how alliances cope with the problem of free-riding and with the holdup problem caused by an internal distributional conflict, experimental work by Ke, Konrad, and Morath (2013) tests these predictions. According to their findings, alliances are sometimes able to cope with the free-riding problem and to mobilize considerable resources. More generally, alliances do suffer, however, from such internal conflict, and this likely reduces the effectiveness of the alliance. In what follows, I consider several departures from the baseline model for which alliances are less disadvantaged from a strategic point of view.

1.3 Complementarities in Fighting Power

A first modification from the baseline model is discussed by Skaperdas (1998). He points out that alliance members' effort choices need not be perfect substitutes, and that the impact of efforts x_A and x_B may simply be much higher than the sum of these efforts. The reasons behind this may be manifold. The alliance may make the sum of their efforts more powerful as the alliance may allow for a reallocation of efforts in a way that is unavailable in the absence of an alliance. Or the separate efforts of alliance members may be complementary such that one player's effort x_A makes the effort of player x_B more valuable.

Note that this effect needs to be considerable if the contest between former alliance members dissipates a large share of the prize. In particular, if this contest is described by a symmetric all-pay auction without noise, the incentive for players A and B to contribute a positive effort in stage 1 is zero, regardless of how strong the synergies between A's and B's efforts are.

1.4 Tight Budget Caps

An alliance between players A and B can be attractive for their purposes if both players have tight budgets, even if the contest success functions are those of an all-pay auction without noise. This case is analyzed by Konrad and Kovenock (2009). They consider the baseline framework where the contest success functions p and q are all-pay auctions without noise, as in the third line in figure 1.1. Let the prize be normalized to 1, and assume that players face budget constraints, with $x_i \in [0, m_i]$ for $i \in \{A, B, C\}$, and $y_i \in [0, m_i]$, for $i \in \{A, B\}$.[8] They show that

$$m_A = m_B \equiv m \in \left(\frac{m_C}{2}, \frac{1}{2} - \frac{m_C}{2} \right) \tag{1.1}$$

is a sufficient condition for the existence of a subgame-perfect equilibrium in which A and B benefit from forming an alliance. Their payoffs increase from zero in a contest among three stand-alone players to $1 - m_C - 2m$. At the same time, the formation of the alliance reduces the payoff of player C to zero. To illustrate, consider $m_A = m_B = 0.1$, and $m_C = 0.15$. In this example, should C win in stage 1, this player takes home the full prize $v = 1$. This determines C's valuation of winning in stage 1. If the alliance wins, both players have to fight over the prize. Since both have the same budget, and this budget is very small, they both expend the whole budget in stage 2, namely $y_A = y_B = 0.1$, and each player wins with probability $1/2$.[9] As a result each attributes a value to the outcome where the alliance wins that is equal to $1/2 - m = 0.4$. Both the continuation value for C and the continuation values for A and B are higher than the respective budgets of the players. Accordingly, the players A and B are also budget constrained in stage 1.

In the absence of an alliance, the fact that $m_C = 0.15 > 0.1 = m$ implies that player C can always outcompete both stand-alone players A and B. And while $x_C = m + \varepsilon$ is not the equilibrium outcome, it determines C's payoff in the equilibrium in absence of an alliance, as $1 - m = 0.9$. And the equilibrium payoffs of players A and B are zero in this case.

If A and B form an alliance, they can jointly outcompete C, as their joint resources exceed the joint resources of player C. This potentially shifts the rent from player C to the players A and B, should they manage to make clever joint bids. Konrad and Kovenock (2009) show that they can use a stochastic coordination mechanism (only observable to them) that makes their joint contributions follow the equilibrium bidding strategies of a single player with budget $2m$ who plays against C.

1.5 Overcoming Free-Riding by a Threat of Internal Conflict

In the framework that is analyzed by Esteban and Sákovics (2003), the free-rider problem and the holdup problem inside an alliance add or even compound. There is hope, however, that the two problems interact in a more constructive way. Konrad and Leininger (2011) analyzed an inter-alliance conflict in which the holdup problem of possible internal fighting can be used to incentivize the members of an alliance and thereby overcome the free-rider problem of making contributions to the total fighting effort of the alliance.

A modified and simplified version of their mechanism can be described as follows: The alliance consists of n players, numbered by $1, \ldots, n$. For simplicity, unlike Konrad and Leininger (2011), let us consider a symmetric set of players. The players contribute efforts x_i to the total alliance effort X that is the sum of these contributions. The group fights against an outside group that may consist of several players or a stand-alone player, and the alliance wins this fight with a probability $p(X, Y)$, where Y is the aggregate effort generated by the outside group, and p is a contest success function, as in the baseline model. In order to stay close to the baseline model, assume that the opposing group is a stand-alone player. If that stand-alone player wins, the prize goes to that player and the game is over. If the alliance wins, then they have to find a way to divide their gain among themselves.

As regards this division of the prize, we can simplify the analysis compared to that of Konrad and Leininger (2011) without a major change in the qualitative results. We assume that the subgame played by the members of the victorious alliance is a Nash division game.[10] This subgame is described as follows: each of the n former members of the victorious alliance chooses a share $\alpha_i \geq 0$. If all shares α_i sum up to less or equal to 1, then each player receives his share in the prize, and what is not claimed by the players is costlessly disposed. If, however, the sum of shares claimed exceeds 1, then the whole prize is lost for the members of the alliance. The Nash division subgame has multiple equilibria. Any set of $\alpha_i < 1$ that sums up to 1 also constitutes an equilibrium of this subgame, and in each of these equilibria the full prize is peacefully allocated to members of the alliance. Let us denote a representative of this class of equilibria as $\boldsymbol{\alpha}^* = (\alpha_1^*, \ldots, \alpha_n^*)$. However, a whole further set of equilibria exists which has the property that $\Sigma_{j \neq i} \alpha_j > 1$ for all $i = 1, \ldots n$.[11] One element of this set is $\boldsymbol{\alpha}^0 = (1, 1, \ldots, 1)$.[12] All players who have been members of the alliance receive a zero payoff in any of these equilibria for which $\Sigma_{j \neq i} \alpha_j > 1$ in the internal distribution subgame.

The multiplicity of equilibria can now be used to implement alliance members' effort choices in the inter-alliance fight as follows. Suppose that the combination of contributions to be implemented is $\mathbf{x}^* = (x_1^*, \ldots, x_n^*)$. Suppose further that players have the following beliefs about the equilibrium that is played in case the alliance wins the prize: they believe that one specific $\boldsymbol{\alpha}^* = (\alpha_1^*, \ldots, \alpha_n^*)$ is chosen if all players behave according to **x***, and α^0 is selected if at least one of the alliance players deviates from **x***. In this case, for a given aggregate effort choice Y^* of the enemy, (**x***, α^*) can be the outcome of selfish, individually rational interaction among the alliance members if

$$\alpha_i^* p(\Sigma_{i=1}^{i=n} x_i^*, Y^*) - x_i^* \geq 0 \quad \text{for all } i = 1, \ldots, n. \tag{1.2}$$

The left-hand side in (1.2) is the expected equilibrium payoff of player i if player i makes an effort choice in accordance with x_i^*, and this is followed by the peaceful sharing outcome in case the alliance is victorious.

Konrad and Leininger (2011) consider a distribution game within the alliance that has considerably more structure and is closer to the structure of the baseline model. In their framework, one of the alliance members receives all the winnings and makes (unconditional) payments or gifts to the members of his group. And the members of the group are either satisfied both with their own and other members' contributions to the alliance effort, and with what they received from the prize, or they are displeased with one or several of these items. As a result of their satisfaction with these choices they either choose a noncooperative interaction that is peaceful, or they choose to fight among themselves, in which case a large share of the winner prize is dissipated. This more complex structure serves a very similar purpose as a Nash division game does.

1.6   The Role of Information

An alliance may provide benefits to its members that are not accounted for in the baseline model or by the variants analyzed so far. As has been discussed by Bearce, Flanagan, and Floros (2006), alliances may serve the purpose of information exchange. They consider some military alliances, including the North Atlantic Treaty Organization (NATO) and argue that such alliances may facilitate the flow of information among its members. Such an information flow may be beneficial for its members, may facilitate coordination, and may help increasing the efficiency of use of their fighting resources. One of many of such aspects is addressed in a study by Konrad (2011).

This study considers n players and starts with assuming that these players may be partitioned arbitrarily into subsets $A_1, \ldots, A_r$ of alliances that consist of one or several players. Each player chooses his or her effort $x_i \in [0, m_i]$, where m_i is the player's budget limit, which is assumed to be small in comparison to the size of the prize that is again normalized to 1. A contest success function allocates the prize to one of the n players as a probabilistic function of all players' effort choices $x_1, \ldots, x_n$, where $p_i(x_1, \ldots, x_n)$ denotes the win probability for player i. This latter assumption removes one of the most salient features of alliances from the picture on purpose: efforts of alliance members do not add or compound in this framework, and it is not the alliance that wins the prize, but the prize is appropriated directly by one of the players in the set of players, even if this player is a member of an alliance that consists of several players. In this way a possible holdup problem from intra-alliance fights and the free-rider problem of making contributions to total alliance effort that benefits also the other members of the alliance are both removed from the picture. The framework also does not allow for effects of supermodularity of alliance members' contributions (as in Skaperdas 1998), nor for the possibility that players can overcome budget limits by way of forming an alliance (as in Konrad and Kovenock 2009). Instead, the framework focuses on a specific aspect of information exchange: it assumes that players' budget limits m_i are their private information. These limits are random draws from a commonly known distribution $F(m)$ with support $[0, b]$, but the actual realizations of these random choices are observed only by the player himself, and by all co-players who are in the same alliance as this player.

Konrad (2011) analyzes first the Bayesian Nash equilibrium in the case in which all alliances consist of single players ($r = n$) and derives a condition for $F(m)$, which makes sure that it is a dominant strategy for each player to simply expend his whole budget in the fight of all-against-all. Intuitively, expending the whole military capacity available to one player is a worthwhile strategy if the likely distribution of budgets of all other players is such that the player would even like to expend more than he has, even if he anticipates that all other players will expend their full budgets. For instance, if the contest success function is the all-pay auction without noise, then a sufficient condition for $x_i = m_i$ to constitute an equilibrium is shown in Konrad (2011) to be

$$(n-1)(F(m))^{n-2} F'(m) \geq 1 \qquad \text{for all } m \in (0, b). \tag{1.3}$$

Condition (1.3) states that for any level m, the marginal increase in win-probability from expending one additional marginal unit more effort (left-hand side of condition 1.3) is at least as high as the marginal cost of this additional unit of effort (right-hand side of 1.3).

This expenditure $x_i = m_i$ is worthwhile for player i under this condition only in the absence of information about the actual resources expended by other players. If a player i has a small budget and knows that one or several other players can and will expend more effort, player i may want to withdraw. This is particularly true if the contest success function is highly discriminatory, for instance, for the all-pay auction without noise. Two players i and j would generally benefit if they could truthfully exchange information about their budget limits m_i and m_j. If p is the contest success function of the all-pay auction, the player with the higher budget may then still want to continue to expend some more, given that there are other players who are expected to expend their whole budget. But the player i who learns that his budget falls short of the budget of j may withdraw from the competition to save his resources, instead of burning them up in a competition that is impossible to win. The information exchange is then beneficial for both players in expectation. This mutual benefit of information explains why players benefit from forming alliances in this framework, even if the only implication of being in an alliance with another player is the exchange of information about their budget limits. Based on this principle, the formation of information alliances is always beneficial for the members of such an alliance, and the merger of two alliances to an even larger alliance is also beneficial. Accordingly, with other aspects being absent, a process of alliance formation comes to an end in this framework only if the smallest number of alliances that is possible has been reached, namely if a further merger between existing alliances is no longer feasible.

1.7   Multiple Fronts and Resource Transfers

A further important reason why the formation of an alliance can be advantageous is provided by Kovenock and Roberson (2012). Their analysis departs from the baseline model along several dimensions. First, players have exogenously given amounts of military resources. These resources are used up in the military contest, because they have no use for the resources other than in the military competition. Second, players fight against each other at several fronts simultaneously, with a competition for a single prize at each front. Their main concern is therefore not about the choice of the total quantity of effort, but about how to use the given capacity of effort along different fronts. They consider alliances that allow players to transfer military resources among themselves within an alliance.

An important result is that alliances may increase all alliance members' payoffs, compared to a situation where players stand alone. Even the player who transfers military resources to another player and is left with a lower stock of military resources may himself gain from the transfer.

To give a simplified example of the type of situation that has a similar flavor, consider a military conflict among three players. Say these players are countries A, B, and C. Let country C have common frontiers with countries A and B, as in figure 1.2, and let C fight two wars simultaneously, one at its common frontier with country A, another at the common frontier with country B. By assumption, in each of the two conflicts a prize of size 1 is at stake, which is appropriated by the winner of the respective conflict. Consider next the respective conflicts and the rules that apply more specifically. Each country has a given endowment of military resources, denoted as m_A, m_B, and m_C. Recall that the military resources have no value or use other than in

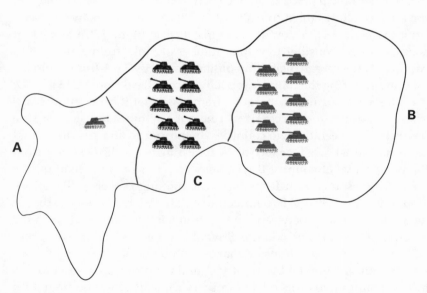

Figure 1.2
Two-front war with very unequal alliance partners: the initial distribution of military capacity

the military conflict. Let $x_{ij} \geq 0$ denote the military resources used by country i in the direct conflict with country j. By definition, $x_{AB} = x_{BA} = 0$, as these countries have no common frontier. Let country C's probability of winning the respective conflict at its frontiers with A and B be defined by the lottery contest: that is, $p_{Cj}(x_{Cj}, x_{jC}) = x_{Cj}/(x_{Cj} + x_{jC})$ if $x_{Cj} + x_{jC} > 0$, and equal to $1/2$ otherwise. Of course, the respective win probabilities for A and for B are $p_A = 1 - p_{CA}$ and $p_B = 1 - p_{CB}$.[13]

In the absence of an alliance between A and B, we require that $x_{AC} \in [0, m_A]$, $x_{BC} \in [0, m_B]$, and $x_{CA} + x_{CB} \in [0, m_C]$. Consider now the equilibrium choices of efforts. As p_A and p_B are increasing in x_{AC} and x_{BC}, we can safely assume that $x_{AC} = m_A$ and $x_{BC} = m_B$. Moreover $x_{CA} + x_{CB} = m_C$ in the equilibrium will hold, given that military effort within the given capacity limits has no opportunity cost. The problem therefore reduces to the optimal division of m_C between the two fronts. The (interior) solution for an optimum requires that military effort have the same marginal impact at both fronts, that is,

$$\frac{\partial p_{CA}}{\partial x_{CA}} = \frac{m_A}{(m_A + x_{CA})^2} = \frac{m_B}{(m_B + (m_C - x_{CA}))^2} = \frac{\partial p_{CB}}{\partial x_{CB}}. \tag{1.4}$$

Consider now a possible alliance between A and B, and assume that the alliance allows them to reallocate military capacity between them, prior to the two actual conflicts. For instance, in figure 1.2, assume that country B may consider to ship a number of tanks from country B to country A, hence enhancing the military capacity in A from m_A to $m_A + D$, and reducing the military capacity in country B from m_B to $m_B - D$. As it fits with our noncooperative framework, let this be an unconditional transfer of resources; let us rule out any other transfers or side payments between the two countries, both prior to and past the actual conflicts. We ask whether such a resource transfer can be desirable from the perspective of country B. The answer is less obvious than it may seem. The resource transfer reduces the fighting power of B. Considered in isolation, this is bad for country B. If country C were to divide its military capacity between the two fronts in the same way as in the absence of the transfer, country B would simply reduce its win probability. However, the transfer makes country A a stronger military power. This is observed by country C, and country C may react to this fact and shift more of its overall military capacity from the front with country B to the front with country A. This relocation of military resources by country C is advantageous for player B. Whether or not

m_A	m_B	m_C	x_{CB}	x_{CA}	π_B	π_A
1	11	10	5.8	4.2	0.65076	0.19621
2	10	10	5.2	4.8	0.65782	0.29419

Figure 1.3
Payoffs in the numerical example on two-front war

an unconditional resource transfer from B to A can improve B's payoff then depends on whether the effect of directly weakening own military power is stronger or weaker than the strategic effect that is caused by the relocation of military resources away from the front between B and C.

The answer about the relative size of the direct effect and the strategic effect generally depends on the type of contest success functions that apply for the two fronts, and on the military endowments that are at the command of the three countries. A simple example can illustrate, however, that the strategic effect can be stronger than the direct effect of weakening own military power. Figure 1.3 gives a specific numerical example. The first row shows the initial distribution of military capacities, the division of m_C between the two fronts as an optimal reply by C for this given distribution, and the resulting payoffs for A and B. The second line shows the reallocation of military capacity between A and B, the optimal division of m_C as a reply to this changed allocation, and the resulting payoffs. Note that the payoffs of both countries B and A are increased due to the shift of one unit of military capacity from country B to country A. This describes how such a transfer can be self-enforcing in a fully noncooperative framework.

One of the properties of this example is that the transfer is made from a comparatively well-endowed country to a country with very little military resources. Intuitively, the alliance allows the countries to reallocate their fighting capacity to where it generates higher gains. This, in isolation, increases the sum of their payoffs. Moreover the reallocation of one unit has a very large marginal impact on the military threat that C encounters at the border with country A. This is why C relocates considerable resources away from the border with B and to the border with A, and this makes such a transfer beneficial for country B.

1.8   In-Group Favoritism and Out-Group Spite

Much of the historical evidence on the eventual breakup of victorious alliances may be conceptually in line with the holdup problem of military and other alliances. Psychological studies suggest some points about the formation of an alliance and the existence of an enemy that are not captured in the baseline model. There is considerable evidence that members of a group develop what is called in-group favoritism: members of a group such as an alliance tend to choose actions that benefit the whole group, even if these actions are based on narrowly defined selfish material interest (Brewer 1979). They also showed that what is needed in terms of an institutional setup, shared history, and so forth, to generate such in-group behavior is extremely little (Tajfel and Turner 1979). This is referred to as the minimal group paradigm. And there is also evidence that in-group favoritism becomes stronger if there is a conflict between this group and another group, referred to as the out-group (e.g., Sherif et al. 1961).

Eaton, Eswaran, and Oxoby (2011) and Konrad and Morath (2012) address this phenomenon. They ask whether in-group altruism and spiteful actions toward the out-group and its members can be rationalized on the basis of evolutionary arguments in the context of small or finite populations. Eaton et al. (2011) consider a framework in which players can observe the behavioral preferences of their co-players. Konrad and Morath (2012) consider a framework in which such behavioral preferences can emerge without observability of the co-players' types. They analyze a framework in which two symmetric groups, A and B, interact in a static game. Each group consists of n members. The two groups fight in a standard Tullock (1980) contest for a prize that is allocated to the members of the winning group and yields a value of Q to each member of the winning group.[14] Each individual i provides some nonnegative effort x_i to the total effort of the own group. Let X_K denote the sum of efforts of members of group $K \in \{A, B\}$ and X_{-K} the sum of efforts in the respective other group, with $\mathbf{x}_{-i}$ as the vector of contributions of all other players. Then the monetary payoff of member i of group K is

$$\pi_i(x_i, \mathbf{x}_{-i}) = \frac{X_K}{X_K + X_{-K}} Q - x_i \tag{1.5}$$

if $X_A + X_B > 0$, and equal to $Q/2$ if $X_A + X_B = 0$. This problem constitutes the "state game" of an evolutionary game in which each single generation of players interacts in one such state game, but where there is a series of nonoverlapping generations and a series of such state games.

In order to find the evolutionarily stable strategies in this context, first a set of possible types of players has to be defined. We may define this type space as the interval $[0, \infty)$, where a player of type t is a player who chooses effort $x_i \equiv t$. We can apply Schaffer's (1988) concept of evolutionary stability; that is, a population that consists of players of type t^* is a monomorphic equilibrium in evolutionarily stable strategies if t^* is a solution to

$$\max_{x_i}[\pi_i(x_i, \mathbf{x}_{-i}) - \pi_{-i}(x_i, \mathbf{x}_{-i})] \tag{1.6}$$

for $\mathbf{x}_{-i} = (t^*, \ldots, t^*)$ being the vector of the efforts t^* chosen by all $2n - 1$ other players. This notion of evolutionary stability compares the monetary payoff of a player who has a possibly different type x_i and who interacts with $2n - 1$ players who all are of the same equilibrium type t^*, with the expected monetary payoff of each of these $2n - 1$ players if they interact with $2n - 2$ players of type t^* and one player of type x_i. A strategy t^* is evolutionarily stable according to this condition, if there is no other (mutant) strategy that, if used by a single player in an otherwise homogeneous population of type t^*, yields a higher payoff to this mutant strategy than to the average nonmutant player.

The Schaffer (1988) definition of evolutionary stability in finite populations as in (1.6) has an interesting feature: a player who adopts a mutant strategy can do well in this population not only if this mutant strategy yields a higher payoff to this player but also if this mutant strategy yields a lower average payoff to the other, nonmutant players. A player can therefore improve his evolutionary fitness by adopting actions that harm others, even if these actions do not benefit the player directly, and a player harms himself if he adopts actions that benefit others, even if these actions do not harm the player directly (in terms of monetary payoff). Applied to the inter-alliance conflict, this feature has interesting implications. Consider a player i who contributes more effort to his own alliance. Apart from the direct implications for the player's monetary payoff, this affects both the payoffs of other group members, and the payoffs of members of the out-group. Higher effort by i benefits the members of the in-group, as this higher effort by i increases the win probability for the players in i's alliance. Also higher effort by i reduces the win probability for the rival alliance; hence it harms the members of the out-group.

As shown by Konrad and Morath (2012), the evolutionarily stable strategies involve higher effort than the effort emerging in a Nash equilibrium with payoff functions as in (1.5). Intuitively, let us start at a situation that is an interior Nash equilibrium for players who maximize their material payoffs (1.5). Consider player i who thinks about increasing his effort just above the equilibrium effort level. This increase has a zero first-order effect for the player's own material payoff—due to the fact that this increase happens at Nash equilibrium levels. However, the increase has two other first-order effects. The additional effort benefits co-players from the same group as i, and it harms players from the rival group, as it makes the own group more likely to win, and reduces the win probability of the other group. From an evolutionary point of view, the first effect is a disadvantage for i, the second effect is an advantage for i. Overall, starting from a Nash equilibrium, the beneficial effect for i from an increase in own effort dominates.

They also consider the evolutionarily stable preferences that can implement these higher efforts as mutually optimal replies to each other for individuals who maximize these preferences by their choices of effort. They find that a combination of in-group altruism and spiteful preferences vis-à-vis members of the out-group is suitable for inducing such effort choices as Nash equilibrium choices. And an interpretation of these findings is in line with the in-group favoritism found by psychologists.

1.9 Conclusions

Alliances are very common, despite the potential for free-riding inside the alliance and the holdup problem due to fighting and rivalry inside the alliance. This suggests that there are benefits of alliance formation that counterbalance these strategic disadvantages, or reasons why these strategic disadvantages do not have strong effects. This chapter has highlighted some of the reasons that have been put forward on why the strategic disadvantages may be less strong than in a benchmark model of alliances. One mechanism that overcomes both problems simultaneously is based on the idea that internal rivalry and fighting may be triggered by a lack of contributions to the total alliance effort. The threat of internal conflict may then fully eliminate the strategic disadvantages. Also, even if the strategic disadvantage from a possible holdup problem exists, it need not dominate the benefits from joint action if players' budgets are small in comparison to the stakes they are fighting about. The survey also highlighted a number of potential benefits of fighting within an alliance. Among these are the possible synergies between alliance players' efforts. What they expend individually may have a total impact that is higher than the sum of their individual efforts if the alliance gives them the means to use their military capacity in a superior fashion. On the general level, there are many reasons for why this may be the case. The survey also highlighted one instance in which this may be due to multiple fronts and the possibility to optimally use a given military capacity inside an alliance. Information exchange inside the alliance was identified as another benefit from alliance formation that is absent in the baseline model. Finally, the chapter touched on the literature pertaining to the role of group spirit, the in-group favoritism and the negative attitudes toward members of other groups, particularly if the own group competes with these out-groups. In a fight between groups, in-group favoritism and out-group spite can be based on evolutionary grounds and may allow players to overcome the free-riding problem and induce them to make high effort.

Acknowledgments

This chapter was prepared for the workshop on *The Economics of Conflict—Theory and Policy Lessons* at the CESifo Venice Summer Institute 2011. Part of my analysis draws on chapter 9 in Konrad (2009). I thank the participants of the workshop for helpful comments and Bernhard Enzi for research assistance. The usual caveat applies.

Notes

1. For a formal analysis of the model of voluntary contributions to a group public good see the seminal work by Bergstrom, Blume, and Varian (1986) and by Esteban and Ray (2001).

2. The ranking in economic size and the ranking in military expenditure as a percentage of the GNP are not perfectly correlated, but their table 1 (p. 267) shows that the two rankings follow each other fairly closely.

3. These include, for instance, Baik, Kim, and Na (2001), Baik and Lee (1998), Davis and Reilly (1999), Esteban and Ray (2001), Katz, Nitzan, and Rosenberg (1990), Lee (1995), Nitzan (1991a), Nitzan (1991b), Nitzan and Ueda (2008), Rapoport and Amaldoss (1997), Sandler (1993), and Ursprung (1990).

4. See also Kent (1989).

5. Esteban and Sákovics (2003) assume convex cost functions. This has the advantage of making interior equilibrium outcomes more likely, but also introduces notation that we do not need in what follows.

6. Note that different tie-breaking rules are applied in the inter-alliance contest and in the intra-alliance contest in this case, in order to avoid an openness problem for the equilibrium in the inter-alliance conflict.

7. This equilibrium outcome is well known from work by Hillman and Riley (1989) and by Baye, Kovenock, and de Vries (1996).

8. Note that this assumes that players face the same budget constraint in the inter-alliance contest as in the intra-alliance contest, and that their effort choices in the inter-alliance contest do not affect their budgets in the intra-alliance contest. Of course, many variations of these assumptions that are also plausible are possible, and can lead to different results.

9. Note that it is assumed here that the budgets of A and B that are available for fighting internally against each other do not depend on the players' effort choices in the fight between player C and the alliance of A and B.

10. This simplification has been suggested to me by James Fearon. I am grateful for this suggestion. The usual caveat applies.

11. If this condition is fulfilled for player i, the player knows that the full prize is wasted in any case, regardless of his own choice α_i. Accordingly the player can make a claim that is sufficiently high to support this equilibrium and to help this condition be fulfilled by other players.

12. To be precise, for $n = 2$, there is only one inefficient equilibrium, $\alpha^0 = (1, 1)$ but a continuum of efficient equilibria. For $n > 2$, the set of inefficient equilibria is a continuum as well.

13. Here the example departs from Kovenock and Roberson (2012), as they consider a Colonel–Blotto game in which the conflict at each front is determined by the rules of an all-pay auction without noise. Also they consider a framework with many players and battle fronts, allowing for much richer combinations of resource transfers.

14. Their framework therefore includes cases where the prize is a public good for the members of the group as well as the cases where the prize is a private good, and players have to fight internally about its distribution.

References

Baik, Kyung Hwan, In-Gyu Kim, and Sunghyun Na. 2001. Bidding for a group-specific public-good prize. *Journal of Public Economics* 82 (3): 415–29.

Baik, Kyung Hwan, and Sanghack Lee. 1998. Group rent seeking with sharing. In Michael R. Baye, ed., *Advances in Applied Microeconomics*, vol. 7. Stamford, CT: JAI Press, 75–85.

Baye, Michael R., Dan Kovenock, and Casper G. de Vries. 1996. The all-pay auction with complete information. *Economic Theory* 8 (2): 291–305.

Bearce, David H., Kristen M. Flanagan, and Katharine M. Floros. 2006. Alliances, internal information, and military conflict among member-states. *International Organization* 60 (3): 595–625.

Bergstrom, Ted, Larry Blume, and Hal R. Varian. 1986. On the private provision of public goods. *Journal of Public Economics* 29 (1): 25–49.

Bloch, Francis. 2009. Endogenous formation of alliances in conflicts. Unpublished manuscript. Ecole Polytechnique, Palaiseau.

Bloch, Francis, Santiago Sánchez-Pagés, and Raphaël Soubeyran. 2006. When does universal peace prevail? Secession and group formation in conflict. *Economics of Governance* 7 (1): 3–29.

Brewer, Marilynn B. 1979. In-group bias in the minimal intergroup situation: A cognitive-motivational analysis. *Psychological Bulletin* 86 (2): 307–24.

Bunselmeyer, Robert E. 1975. *The Cost of the War 1914–1919*. Hamden, CT: Archon Books.

Davis, Douglas D., and Robert J. Reilly. 1999. Rent-seeking with non-identical sharing rules: An equilibrium rescued. *Public Choice* 100 (1–2): 31–38.

Eaton, B. Curtis, Mukesh Eswaran, and Robert J. Oxoby. 2011. Us and them: The origin of identity, and its economic implications. *Canadian Journal of Economics. Revue Canadienne d'Economique* 44 (3): 719–48.

Esteban, Joan M., and Debraj Ray. 2001. Collective action and the group size paradox. *American Political Science Review* 95 (3): 663–72.

Esteban, Joan M., and József Sákovics. 2003. Olson vs. Coase: Coalitional worth in conflict. *Theory and Decision* 55 (4): 339–57.

Hillman, Arye L., and John G. Riley. 1989. Politically contestable rents and transfers. *Economics and Politics* 1 (1): 17–39.

Katz, Eliakim, Shmuel Nitzan, and Jacob Rosenberg. 1990. Rent-seeking for pure public goods. *Public Choice* 65 (1): 49–60.

Katz, Eliakim, and Julia Tokatlidu. 1996. Group competition for rents. *European Journal of Political Economy* 12 (4): 599–607.

Ke, Changxia, Kai A. Konrad, and Florian Morath. 2013. Brothers in arms: An experiment on the alliance puzzle. *Games and Economic Behavior* 77 (1): 61–76.

Kent, Bruce. 1989. *The Spoils of War: Politics, Economics, and Diplomacy of Reparations, 1918–1932*. Oxford: Oxford University Press.

Konrad, Kai A. 2009. *Strategy and Dynamics in Contests*. Oxford: Oxford University Press.

Konrad, Kai A. 2011. Information alliances in contests with budget limits. *Public Choice* 151 (3–4): 679–93.

Konrad, Kai A., and Dan Kovenock. 2009. The alliance formation puzzle and capacity constraints. *Economics Letters* 103 (2): 84–86.

Konrad, Kai A., and Wolfgang Leininger. 2011. Self-enforcing norms and efficient non-cooperative collective action in the provision of public goods. *Public Choice* 146 (3–4): 501–520.

Konrad, Kai A., and Florian Morath. 2012. Evolutionarily stable in-group favoritism and out-group spite in intergroup conflict. *Journal of Theoretical Biology* 306 (1): 61–67.

Kovenock, Dan, and Brian Roberson. 2012. Coalitional Colonel Blotto games with application to the economics of alliances. *Journal of Public Economic Theory* 14 (4): 653–76.

Lee, Sanghack. 1995. Endogenous sharing rules in collective-group rent-seeking. *Public Choice* 85: 31–44.

Nitzan, Shmuel. 1991a. Collective rent dissipation. *Economic Journal* 101 (409): 1522–34.

Nitzan, Shmuel. 1991b. Rent-seeking with nonidentical sharing rules. *Public Choice* 71 (1–2): 43–50.

Nitzan, Shmuel, and Kaoru Ueda. 2008. Collective contests for commons and club goods. Mimeo. Bar-Ilan University.

O'Connor, Raymond G. 1969. Victory in modern war. *Journal of Peace Research* 6: 367–84.

Olson, Mancur, and Richard Zeckhauser. 1966. Economic theory of alliances. *Review of Economics and Statistics* 48 (3): 266–79.

Rapoport, Amnon, and Wilfred Amaldoss. 1997. Social dilemmas embedded in between-group competitions: Effects of contest and distribution rules. Unpublished manuscript. Hong Kong University of Science and Technology.

Sandler, Todd. 1993. The economic theory of alliances. *Journal of Conflict Resolution* 37 (3): 446–83.

Schaffer, Mark E. 1988. Evolutionary stable strategies for a finite population and a variable contest size. *Journal of Theoretical Biology* 132 (4): 469–78.

Sherif, Muzafer, O. J. Harvey, B. Jack White, William R. Hood, and Carolyn W. Sherif. 1961. The Robbers Cave experiment: Intergroup conflict and cooperation. Norman, OK: University Book Exchange.

Skaperdas, Stergios. 1998. On the formation of alliances in conflict and contests. *Public Choice* 96 (1–2): 25–42.

Tajfel, Henri, and John Turner. 1979. An integrative theory of inter-group conflict. In William G. Austin and Stephen Worchel, eds., *The Social Psychology of Intergroup Relations*. Monterey, CA: Brooks/Cole Publishers, 33–48.

Tullock, Gordon. 1980. Efficient rent seeking. In James M. Buchanan, Robert D. Tollison, and Gordon Tullock, eds., *Toward a Theory of the Rent-seeking Society*. College Station: Texas A&M University Press, 97–112.

Ursprung, Heinrich W. 1990. Public goods, rent dissipation, and candidate competition. *Economics and Politics* 2: 115–32.

Wagner, R. Harrison. 2009. *War and the State: The Theory of International Politics*. Ann Arbor: University of Michigan Press.

Wärneryd, Karl. 1998. Distributional conflict and jurisdictional organization. *Journal of Public Economics* 69 (3): 435–50.

Weinberg, Gerhard L. 1994. *A World at Arms: A Global History of World War II*. Cambridge, UK: Cambridge University Press.

2   Fiscal Equalization and Political Conflict

Maria Cubel

2.1   Introduction

Fiscal equalization is a redistribution device that serves to correct vertical fiscal unbalances and to diminish horizontal inequity between regions. According to the Canadian Constitution Act, 1982, Section 36 (2), the purpose of equalization is to ensure "that provincial governments have sufficient revenues to provide reasonably comparable levels of public services at reasonably comparable levels of taxation." It also works as an insurance (risk-sharing)[1] mechanism. Fiscal equalization schemes are used in many countries: two well-documented examples are the systems in place in Canada and in the German Länder.[2]

The level of fiscal equalization determines the degree of solidarity among regional governments. In this sense, an *excessive* level of redistribution would be perceived as unfair, by the contributing regions, especially if they end up losing positions in the final (per capita resource) ranking. In fact the literature on income distribution considers the reranking effect due to progressive transfers as undesirable. Moreover the Pigou–Dalton condition (Pigou 1912; Dalton 1920) establishes that any small transfer from a relatively *richer* individual to a relatively *poorer* individual that does not alter the order (ranking) in the income distribution is inequality reducing. Notice, though, that the preservation of the original ranking is a necessary condition.[3] Therefore it seems reasonable that the same principle should also be applied when redistributing resources between regional governments in order to secure horizontal equity.

My objective in this chapter is to analyze the political viability of fiscal equalization using a model of conflict directly inspired by Esteban and Ray (1999, 2001a, b). I analyze the circumstances under which one region would be inclined to initiate political conflict when by doing so it would obtain a higher share of resources than under full equalization. I show how political conflict affects fiscal redistribution across regions and thus sometimes violates the Pigou–Dalton principle.

Political conflict, in a broad sense, includes mass rallies, protests, boycott to the approval of central laws in the Parliament, secession demands, and lobbying. These confrontations are costly because they use up time and money, reduce economic activity of businesses and sales in the areas where the protests take place, engender police and civil protection costs, lower the credibility of financial markets due to political instability, and so forth.

Illustrative evidence from Spain and Germany shows that fiscal equalization rules are indeed subject to political conflict. In Spain, reranking has led to the discontent of the relatively richer regions and, especially of Catalonia, which has been the leader of the decentralization process. The Catalan government then demanded a full revision of the financing system (including the equalization scheme) in the framework of the new Catalan Constitutional Law drafted in 2006. However, the Catalan Law was blocked by the Constitutional Court. After four years of waiting, the Constitutional Court's ruling on the Catalan Law did not solve the political conflict and set off a huge protest march in Barcelona in July 2010[4]. Recently, the economic crisis has escalated the political confrontation, with demands for a greater fiscal autonomy and a lower contribution to the fiscal equalization system. The lack of agreement between the Catalan and the Central governments provoked in September 2012 the largest ever mass rally in Barcelona, a gathering with 1.5 million people calling for secession[5]. In Germany, the equalization law (Finanzausgleichsgesetz) of 1993 was impugned before the Federal Constitutional Court (FCC) by the Länder of Baden-Württemberg, Bavaria, and Hesse. As a result the equalization was reduced to a degree, shifted to a partial equalization scheme (Fenge and Weizsäcker 2001).

In this chapter political conflict is analyzed through a game where two regions seek to maximize their share of resources devoted to fiscal equalization. The population of each region is modeled as a group of players with identical preferences. These two players are forced to make some contribution to the conflict. The level of political conflict is measured by the total amount of confrontation resources (time, money, etc.).

In this game the central government (CG) is due to implement a vertical equalization grant (Q) between two regions indexed by 1 and

2. The benchmark is defined as in the case where the *CG* distributes *Q* to achieve full equalization of *standard*[6] per capita revenues. This is a reasonable assumption since in most equalization systems full equalization is used as the reference distributional criterion[7]. Thus full equalization will be referred to as the peace solution. However, regions can decide to invest in conflict in order to modify that distributional rule for their best interest. This is the conflict solution. Under conflict the equalization system will depart from full equalization, and the share obtained by each region from the common pool of (equalization) resources will depend on their effort and effectiveness. As a result of conflict, different distributional criteria may emerge, including some involving ranking reversals.

The timing of the game is as follows. In the first stage, each region decides whether to toe the line or whether to reject full equalization. If they decide not to agree, the policy makers of each region will mobilize their citizens and steer their individual contributions to conflict. The total amount of resources spent in each region determines its share of the pool *Q*. Thus, if either region disagrees, each side receives conflict payoffs. Otherwise, they receive peace payoffs defined by full equalization. As will become evident, the emergence of political conflict depends on the degree of publicness of the regional budget. When regional budgets are used to provide pure (regional) public goods, full equalization is politically stable. However, full equalization is not immune to political conflict when budgets are used to provide private goods, or a linear combination of public and private goods, which is a more realistic scenario. The likelihood of political conflict decreases as the regions become similar in size.

The main result derived from the analysis is that full equalization is not immune to conflict when regional budgets are not purely public in nature. Moreover the model provides a rationale for the definition of partial equalization rules as the result of political conflict.

The present work contributes to the literature on social conflict. My analysis is directly inspired by the general model of conflict developed in Esteban and Ray (1999) where social groups expend resources to compete for their preferred outcome. Other works by Esteban and Ray extend this framework, as in Esteban and Ray (2008, 2011). The closest studies to the model of this chapter are Esteban and Ray (2001a, b). In the former work, Esteban and Ray address the issue of the Olson paradox in a model with nonlinear lobbying costs and collective prizes with a varying mix of public and private characteristics. The model of this chapter builds on that framework, but my focus is not on the Olson paradox but on the feasibility of the proportional equalization rule as a function of the publicness of the prize. Thus I analyze the viability of the proportional equalization rule as a peaceful solution to avoid the waste of resources due to confrontation. And in the latter work, Esteban and Ray analyze the immunity to conflict of social decision rules when the social planner has incomplete information and the prize is purely private. I extend their framework on the immunity of the proportional equalization rule to the case of complete information where the prize mixes public and private characteristics.

This chapter is also similar in spirit to Wärneryd's (1998) study of the endogenous formation of jurisdictions under political conflict over resources. From a technical point of view, this chapter belongs to the literature on group contests (e.g., Baik 2008). It also relates to the secession literature as secession can be considered a proxy for conflict when the desire for secession is resisted (Spalaore 2008; Haimanko et al. 2005; Le Breton and Weber 2003,2005; Buchanan and Faith 1987).

The chapter is organized in four sections. Following this introduction, a standard model of conflict is presented. Section 2.3 focuses on analyzing the immunity of fiscal equalization for different budget compositions. Finally, section 2.4 concludes offering some reflections about the political implications of the results obtained.

2.2   A Model of Political Conflict

To begin, suppose that two regions, labeled 1 and 2, compete over resources. Each region is inhabited by N_i identical individuals, such that $N_1 + N_2 = N$ is the total population.

Consider now that the CG is due to implement a vertical equalization grant of Q euros using population as the indicator of regional needs. A frequent indicator of regional needs is population, since it is very simple and easy to compute. See, for example, the regional equalization systems of Canada and Germany (Boadway and Shah 2007; Werner 2008).[8] Let us use full equalization as our benchmark, which is the *peace* solution. Later on we will define more precisely the payoffs under peace.

When regions do not agree with full equalization, they may decide to provoke a conflict in order to increase their share of resource Q. The obtained share by each region depends on its collective effort, namely on the resources invested in the confrontation. The share for region i is defined as,[9]

$$p_i = \frac{R_i}{R},$$ (2.1)

where $R_i = n_i r_i$ is the power of region i, with n_i being the proportion of population engaged in the conflict and r_i the individual contributions (of money and time). We will assume that there is no free-riding so that the r_i individual contributions to the conflict are enforced by the political leader in each region.[10] Social conflict is defined as the total amount of resources spent on a confrontation, $R = n_1 r_1 + n_2 r_2$. In our case we could interpret p_1 and $(1 - p_1)$ as the share of Q obtained by region 1 and 2 in the conflict.[11]

The cost of conflict for each individual is expressed by the isoelastic function

$$c(r_i) = \frac{1}{\alpha} r_i^\alpha, \qquad \alpha > 1,$$ (2.2)

where $c'(r_i) > 0$, $c''(r_i) > 0$, and α is the cost elasticity. Convex costs are suitable when the contributions to conflict are not exclusively monetary such as time.

Formally, once a region has initiated conflict, the objective of its political leader is to maximize the regional per capita payoff:

$$u_i = p_i \Phi_i - c(r_i)$$ (2.3)

where Φ_i is the benefit of region i from conflict, and $c(r_i)$ is the per capita cost of conflict defined in (2.2). Later on we will provide specific definitions for the benefit, Φ_i.

The FOC corresponding to regions 1 and 2 are defined respectively by expressions (2.4) and (2.5) as

$$\Phi_1 n_1 n_2 = R^2 \left(\frac{r_1^{\alpha-1}}{r_2} \right),$$ (2.4)

$$\Phi_2 n_2 n_1 = R^2 \left(\frac{r_2^{\alpha-1}}{r_1} \right).$$ (2.5)

Dividing (2.4) by (2.5) and rearranging terms obtains the relative efficacy of conflict by region 1 as

$$\phi = \frac{r_1}{r_2} = \left(\frac{\Phi_1}{\Phi_2}\right)^{1/\alpha}. \tag{2.6}$$

To fully define the conflict equilibrium solution, we need to find the associated regional payoffs. Then, taking for example region 1, from expression (2.4), we define

$$r_1^\alpha = \Phi_1 p_1 p_2. \tag{2.7}$$

Now, using (2.7), we can express the per capita payoff of region 1 as

$$u_1 = p_1 \Phi_1 - \frac{1}{\alpha} r_1^\alpha = \Phi_1\left(p_1 - \frac{1}{\alpha} p_1 p_2\right). \tag{2.8}$$

Taking into account that $p_2 = (1 - p_1)$ and rewriting (2.8) obtains

$$u_1 = \Phi_1\left(kp_1 + (1-k)p_1^2\right), \tag{2.9}$$

where $k \in (0, 1)$ since $k = (\alpha-1)/\alpha$, $(1-k) = 1/\alpha$, and $\alpha > 1$.

Finally, combining equations (2.1) and (2.6), we can express the budget share under conflict of region 1 as

$$p_1 = \frac{n_1 \phi}{n_1 \phi + (1 - n_1)}. \tag{2.10}$$

Thus equations (2.6), (2.9), and (2.10) define the equilibrium solution under conflict corresponding to region 1. The equilibrium condition for region 2 is defined in a similar way.

2.3 Equalization Rules Immune to Conflict

Regions will initiate conflict when, in doing so, they can profit from the *peace* agreement (full equalization). Under the peace initiative, every region receives $q = Q/N$ per inhabitant, so region i will initiate conflict if and only if

$$p_i \Phi_i - c(r_i) > q. \tag{2.11}$$

Condition (2.11) depends on the nature of Φ_i. We want to consider the extreme cases of private and public regional budgets and the general case where regional budgets are used to provide a linear combination of pure public and private goods. In concrete terms, we will analyze the following scenarios:

• **Private regional budgets** The regional budgets are spent on providing rival public goods; in the extreme case these may be monetary transfers. Since public goods are rival, the utility derived from them depends on population size.

• **Public regional budgets** There is no congestion or rivalry in the provision of public goods, and therefore the derived utility is independent of population size. Externalities among regions in the provision of public goods are not considered; this means that *publicness* is a local property.

• **Private and public regional budgets** The regional budgets are expressed as a linear convex combination of pure public goods and private goods. This is the case where public goods are not purely public and they suffer from some degree of congestion.

2.3.1   Private Regional Budgets
When regional budgets are used to provide private goods or rival public goods, the per capita value for members of region i under conflict is defined by $\Phi_i = q/n_i$, with $q = Q/N$, for $i = 1, 2$. Thus, using (2.9) and (2.11), we can write the condition for region i initiating conflict as

$$\frac{q}{n_i}\left(kp_i + (1-k)p_i^2\right) > q, \tag{2.12}$$

where

$$p_i = \frac{n_i^k}{n_i^k + (1-n_i)^k}, \tag{2.13}$$

and $k \in (0,1)$ since $k = (\alpha-1)/\alpha$, $(1-k) = 1/\alpha$, and $\alpha > 1$. Now, since

$$\frac{\partial p_i}{\partial n_i} = k\frac{\left[n_i(1-n_i)\right]^{k-1}}{\left[(1-n_i)^k + n_i^k\right]^2} > 0,$$

more populated regions have a higher probability of winning.

Proposition 1 *Assume that regional budgets are used to provide private goods. Thus there exists a certain $n_i^* \in (0, 1/2)$ such that regions with a population share $n_i \leq n^*$ will be likely to instigate political conflict. Furthermore this threshold decreases in the cost elasticity α.*

Proof 1 After simplifying, condition (2.12) reduces to $\left(kp_i + (1-k)p_i^2\right) - n_i > 0$. This condition is positive for small values of n_i and negative for large values of n_i. In concrete terms, for $n_i = 1/2$, $p_i = 1/2$, and (2.12) reduces to $k > 1$. However, this condition never holds since $k \in (0, 1)$. Consequently $(kp_i + (1-k)p_i^2) - n_i < 0$ for $n_i \geq 1/2$. Then, since $(kp_i + (1-k)p_i^2) - n_i$ crosses the axis only once and from above, we conclude that condition $(kp_i + (1-k)p_i^2) - n_i > 0$ can only hold for $n_i \leq n_i^*$, where $n_i^* \in (0, 1/2)$. The particular value n_i^* depends on k. For example, for the particular case of $\alpha = 2$, $n_i^* = 1/4$, and for $\alpha = 6$, n_i^* is nearly zero.

In fact the intersection point n_i^* decreases with k converging to zero as k increases; that is,

$$\frac{\partial}{\partial \alpha}\left(k\left(\frac{n_i^k}{n_i^k + (1-n_i)^k} \right) + (1-k)\left(\frac{n_i^k}{n_i^k + (1-n_i)^k} \right)^2 - n \right) \gtreqless 0 \qquad \text{for } n_i \gtreqless \frac{1}{2}.$$

To show that there is a unique intersection point, check that

$$\frac{\partial}{\partial n_i}\left(k\left(\frac{n_i^k}{n_i^k + (1-n_i)^k} \right) + (1-k)\left(\frac{n_i^k}{n_i^k + (1-n_i)^k} \right)^2 - n \right) < 0.$$

The proof is complete. ∎

This result implies that with private regional budgets, full equalization leads to a peaceful solution if and only if regions do not differ too much in terms of population size. There are two forces driving this result: the size of the region and the size of the regional budget. On the one hand, a large region has an advantage in a conflict because the same individual effort has a bigger impact $(\partial p_i/\partial n_i > 0)$. On the other hand, a small region has a bigger incentive to instigate conflict because the value of the contested prize (Q) is private in nature. In the model, the second effect dominates the first, and the payoff from conflict is indeed larger for the small region. This is why only the small region may decide to instigate a conflict when the prize is private. This is an example of the "group size paradox" (Olson 1965).[12]

Notice that the critical value n_i^* depends also on α. Thus, caeteris paribus, n_i^* decreases as α increases, and the probability of political conflict also falls. Figure 2.1 shows the difference between the payoffs under conflict and under peace, represented by C on the y-axis, for different values of $\alpha = (2, 4, 10, 100)$. Any region is willing to initiate political conflict if the payoff of doing so is higher than the payoff under peace. This corresponds to positive values of C in figure 2.1. Thus figure 2.1 shows that only small regions will be likely to initiate political conflict. Below $n_i = 0.5$, the higher curves correspond to lower values

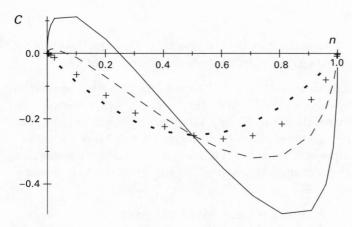

Figure 2.1
Conflict equilibrium condition for different values of α

of α, implying that the intersection point with the x-axis (n_i^*) decreases as α increases, tending rapidly to zero.

Thus far we have argued that when regional budgets are used to provide private goods (in the extreme case, monetary transfers), small regions are more inclined to initiate political conflict, if we define the *peaceful* agreement as full equalization. Next we analyze the other polar case when the budget is used to provide pure public goods.

2.3.2 Public Regional Budgets

Let us suppose that regional budgets are used exclusively to provide pure public goods. To simplify, consider that to produce one unit of any public good, one unit of the budget is required. We define the per capita utility derived from the public good as Ω. Thus the per capita payoff of conflict is defined as $\Phi_i = \Omega$. The payoff corresponding to the *peaceful* agreement (full equalization) is defined as Ωn_i. This definition implies that region i does not take into account the positive externalities derived from the provision of pure public goods in region j. This is equivalent to considering that the benefits obtained from pure public goods are regionally delimited.

Then, using (2.9) and (2.11) and simplifying, we obtain the condition for region i initiating conflict as

$$\Omega\left(kp_i + (1-k)p_i^2\right) > \Omega n_i, \tag{2.14}$$

where

$$p_i = n_i. \tag{2.15}$$

Proposition 2 *Assume that regional budgets are used to provide pure public goods. Then no region has an incentive to initiate political conflict.*

Proof 2 From (2.6) we know that $r_1 = r_2$. Now, using (2.1), we can rewrite $p_i = sn_i (i = 1,2)$, where $s = r_1/R = r_2/R$. Then, since $p_1 + p_2 = 1$, we obtain $s = 1$ and consequently $p_i = n_i$. Finally, substituting p_i by n_i in (2.14) and simplifying, the equilibrium condition for conflict (2.14) reduces to $n_i > 1$, which is impossible since, by definition, $n_i \in (0,1)$. This implies that conflict will never occur and therefore the proportional rule is immune to political conflict. ■

This result shows that with regional public goods full equalization (proportional sharing rule) always leads to a peaceful solution. Therefore full equalization will be immune to political conflict, given that the maximum share of Q that each region obtains under conflict will equal its population share. This is in stark contrast with the previous case where the smaller region had a relative advantage in a conflict because it had a larger incentive to win. Here, on the contrary, since the prize is purely public, this is not the case.

2.3.3 Private and Public Regional Budgets

Let us consider now the general case where regional budgets are used to provide a linear convex combination of both rival and pure public goods. Thus the per capita payoff of region i under conflict is defined as

$$\Phi_i = \left[\lambda \frac{q}{n_i} + (1-\lambda)\Omega \right],$$

where $\lambda \in [0,1]$ refers to the proportion of the budget assigned to provide rival public goods. Thus $(1 - \lambda)$ refers to the proportion of the budget attached to pure public goods provision or, in other words, the degree of publicness of the budget. This proportion λ is exogenous. We discuss the possibility of endogenizing λ in the conclusion section. Likewise the payoff corresponding to the *peaceful* agreement (full equalization) is defined as $\lambda q + (1 - \lambda)\Omega\, n_i$. Thus, using (2.9) and (2.11), we obtain the condition for region i initiating conflict as

$$\left(\lambda \frac{q}{n_i} + (1-\lambda)\Omega \right)\left(kp_i + (1-k)p_i^2 \right) > \lambda q + (1-\lambda)\Omega n_i, \tag{2.16}$$

where

$$p = \frac{n_i \left(\dfrac{\lambda \dfrac{q}{n_i} + (1-\lambda)\Omega}{\lambda \dfrac{q}{1-n_i} + (1-\lambda)\Omega} \right)^k}{n_i \left(\dfrac{\lambda \dfrac{q}{n_i} + (1-\lambda)\Omega}{\lambda \dfrac{q}{1-n_i} + (1-\lambda)\Omega} \right)^k + (1-n_i)}. \tag{2.17}$$

To simplify, let us assume $\alpha = 2$ and $q = \Omega$. Then (2.17) becomes

$$p_i = \frac{n_i \left(\dfrac{\dfrac{\lambda}{n_i} + (1-\lambda)}{\dfrac{\lambda}{1-n_i} + (1-\lambda)} \right)^{1/2}}{n_i \left(\dfrac{\dfrac{\lambda}{n_i} + (1-\lambda)}{\dfrac{\lambda}{1-n_i} + (1-\lambda)} \right)^{1/2} + (1-n_i)}. \tag{2.18}$$

Taking partial derivatives we obtain that $\partial p_i / \partial n_i > 0$. This implies, caeteris paribus, that more populated regions have higher share of resources. However, $\partial p_i / \partial \lambda > 0$ for $n_i \in (0, 1/2)$, and $\partial p_i / \partial \lambda < 0$ for $n_i \in (1/2, 1)$. Thus the share of resources achieved by the small region increases when the proportion of private goods in the budget also increases. In contrast, the share of resources obtained by the large region increases when the proportion of pure public goods increases. This is because the small region is more effective when the budget is private, since its value of the budget is higher. This is not the case for the large region, since being large decreases the value of the budget when it is private in nature. Moreover increasing the publicness of the prize benefits the large region because its comparative disadvantage with respect to the small region diminishes.

Proposition 3 *Assume that regional budgets are used to provide a linear convex combination of private goods and pure public goods. Thus for $\alpha = 2$ and $q = \Omega$, there exists a certain $n^* \in (0, 1/2)$ such that regions with a population share $n_i \leq n^*$ will launch into political conflict*

Proof 3 First, see that condition (2.16) simplifies to $(kp_i + (1-k)p_i^2) - n_i > 0$, where p_i is defined by (2.18). This condition is positive for small values of n_i and negative for large values of n_i, crossing only once the interval $n_i \in (0, 1)$. For $n_i = 1/2$, $p_i(1/2) = 1/2$, and the equilibrium conflict condition, $(kp_i + (1-k)p_i^2) - n_i > 0$, becomes $k > 1$. Since by definition $k \in (0, 1)$ this condition never holds and therefore it should be the case that $(kp_i + (1-k)p_i^2) - n_i < 0$. Thus regions with a population share $n_i \geq 1/2$ will not wish to engage in conflict. Finally, we conclude that there must be a value $n_i^* \in (0, 1/2)$ for which $(kp_i + (1-k)p_i^2) - n_i = 0$, and that $(kp_i + (1-k)p_i^2) - n_i < 0$ for $n_i < n_i^*$. Consequently regions with $n_i < n_i^*$ will have an incentive to initiate conflict. ∎

This result implies that when regional budgets are not purely public, full equalization would be accepted only if regions have similar population sizes. Otherwise, the small region will obtain a higher payoff investing on conflict to depart from such a distributional criterion.

This result is the consequence of two driving forces: the size of the region and the degree of publicness. On the one hand, the large region has an advantage on fighting since the same individual effort has a bigger impact. On the other hand, the small region has a larger incentive to win as the degree of privateness increases. But, when the level of publicness is high, then the relative advantage of the smaller region does not hold and that region avoids conflict. This can be seen in figure 2.2, by the relationship between the population conflict threshold n^* and the degree of privateness λ for $\alpha = 2$. As the level of

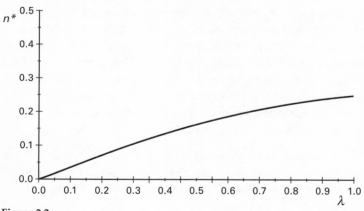

Figure 2.2
Population thresholds and degree of privateness

privateness increases the population interval for which conflict takes place increases.

2.4 Conclusions

In this chapter I analyzed the political viability of fiscal equalization using a standard model of conflict inspired by Esteban and Ray (1999, 2001a, b). I showed that the initiation of political conflict depends on the degree of publicness of the regional budget. When regional budgets are used to provide pure public goods, proportional equalization is immune to political conflict. This implies that full equalization would be politically feasible in this case. However, fiscal equalization is not immune to political conflict when regional budgets are used to provide private goods or a linear convex combination of pure public goods and private goods. In both settings there exists a population share $n_i^* < 1/2$ such that a region with $n_i < n_i^*$ will be inclined to spend resources on conflict in order to achieve a higher share of resources. Consequently partial equalization and ranking reversals can be explained as the result of political conflict. In this regard we should further explore the use of political conflict as a bargaining mechanism to establish new sharing rules as in Powell (2004) and Wagner (2000).

From the analysis, it is clear that small regions are more likely to instigate political conflict when budgets are private. This is because they are more effective relative to their size; that is, the per capita payoffs from conflict are higher, the smaller the group. In contrast, when budgets are public, the size of the group does not affect the prize and the effectiveness advantage of being small disappears. This is why there is less risk of political conflict when the publicness of regional budgets increases.

Throughout the analysis I have assumed that the parameter of privateness λ is exogenous. However, intuitively, if regions could decide the budget composition (i.e., the publicness of the prize), the small region would prefer a higher level of privateness following the logic above. The case of the large region is not so straightforward. On the one hand, the value of the budget increases with the level of privateness ($\partial \Phi_i / \partial \lambda > 0$ since by assumption $q = \Omega$). On the other hand, the relative advantage of the small region also increases with λ. Therefore the large region would prefer a higher level of publicness than the small one.

I also assumed the no existence of externalities across regions. Externalities could be taken into account by considering that public goods are not locally delimited. In addition spillovers could be introduced by considering that regions are altruistic or envious as in Konrad (2004). I plan to explore this issue in future research. A possible extension would be to consider the individual efforts, instead of being substitutes, as complements. Then the large region would be the region prone to conflict, although, by proposition 1, it would still be robust. As Münster (2009) points out, there is in fact no restriction about the sort of relationship between efforts (complementarity or substitutability) in the standard axioms of the contest success functions. Thus one could explore further how different definitions of the contest success function would affect this chapter's results.[13] I leave this for further research.

Furthermore the results obtained relate to the literature on majority voting (e.g., see Tullock 1959) and provide an intuitive argument for decentralizing the provision of public services. The argument would go as follows: When the degree of publicness of regional budgets is high, it is more efficient to centralize the provision of public goods in order to take advantage of the economies of scale. However, when rivalry (congestion) is high, the risk of political conflict increases in inverse proportion to regional size. Therefore the decentralization of pure public goods is recommended since they offer a lower risk of political conflict. This chapter has thus outlined two operating forces in opposite directions that may define the optimal size of a jurisdiction in a similar fashion to the generalized version of the Oates theorem of decentralization (1972).[14] One could explore further this argument using a more complex framework as in Lockwood (2008).

Additional insights might emerge from the introduction of risk aversion in the maximization problem of regional political leaders. This could be done using the concept of political bias as in Jackson and Morelli (2007). Thus the probability of engaging in political conflict would also depend on the private benefit (or cost) that the political party in power would obtain from conflict.

Acknowledgments

I wish to thank Santiago Sánchez-Pagés, Johannes Münster, Joan Esteban, Karl Wärneryd, Daniel Montolio, Wallace Oates, Andrew Street, Cristina de Gispert, and the participants at the New Directions in Welfare (Oxford, 2009), ASSET (Istambul, 2009), EEP (Múrcia, 2010), and the Workshop for Income Distribution and Poverty in Spain

(Madrid, 2010), IEB seminar (Barcelona, 2010), CESifo Venice Summer Institute (Venice, 2011) for their useful comments and discussions.

Notes

1. See, for example, Persson and Tabellini (1996).

2. See Boadway and Shah (2007), Boothe and Vaillancourt F (2007), Vaillancourt (1998), and Werner (2008).

3. See Lambert (2001) for more on this.

4. Battle lines drawn in Catalonia, *The New York Times*, November 23, 2010.

5. Catalonia separatism comes under attack, *Financial Times*, September 12, 2012.

6. I use the term *standard* revenues to refer to those revenues obtained by regional governments when exerting a *standard* fiscal effort. The use of a *standard* fiscal effort is a common feature of equalization grants, since it reduces the strategic decisions by regional governments. Usually the *standard* fiscal effort is exogenously determined by the central government, or is calculated as the average tax rate. For instance, in the Canadian equalization system the average tax rate of the thirteen provinces is used as indicator of *standard* fiscal effort.

7. See Boadway and Shah (2007) and Shah (2007).

8. However, there exist more complex ways to estimate regional needs by taking into account population age, poverty, and so forth. See, for example, Boothe and Vaillancourt (2007) and Shah (2007) for a thorough analysis and examples.

9. See Skaperdas, (1996) and Münster (2009).

10. To include group free-riding, one should introduce in the model the notion of *effective* relative size of the group and allow for rescaling. See Esteban and Ray (2001a) and Kolmar and Rommeswinkel (2011).

11. One could also think of Q as the prize of a lottery where with probability p_1 region 1 wins and with probability $(1 - p_1)$ is region 2 that obtains the prize Q.

12. I thank Johannes Münster for pointing this out.

13. I specially thank Johannes Münster for this comment.

14. Oates (1972), however, does not consider lobbying costs. Instead, he argues that the cost of belonging to the same group increases with the size of the group (n). Thus he defines the optimal population size of the group (jurisdiction) as the one that maximizes the net effect derived from the economies of scale plus the cost of belonging to the group.

References

Baik, K. H. 2008. Contests with group-specific public-good prizes. *Social Choice and Welfare* 30 (1): 103–117.

Boadway, R., and A. Shah, eds. 2007. *Theory and Practice of Intergovernmental Transfers*. Cambridge: MIT Press.

Boothe, P., and F. Vaillancourt. 2007. *A Fine Canadian Compromise. Perspectives on the Report of the Expert Panel on Equalization and Territorial Funding Financing*. Edmonton/Montréal: Institute for Public Econonics/CIRANO.

Buchanan, J. M., and R. L. Faith. 1987. Secession and the limits of taxation: Toward a theory of internal exit. *American Economic Review* 77 (5): 1023–31.

Dalton, H. 1920. The measurement of the inequality of incomes. *Economic Journal* 30 (119): 348–61.

Esteban, J., and D. Ray. 2011. Linking conflict to inequality and polarization. *American Economic Review* 101 (4): 1345–74.

Esteban, J., and D. Ray. 2008. Polarization, fractionalization and conflict. *Journal of Peace Research* 45 (2): 163–82.

Esteban, J., and D. Ray. 2001a. Collective action and the group size paradox. *American Political Science Review* 95 (3): 663–72.

Esteban, J., and D. Ray. 2001b. Social decision rules are not immune to conflict. *Economics of Governance* 2: 59–67.

Esteban, J., and D. Ray. 1999. Conflict and distribution. *Journal of Economic Theory* 87: 370–415.

Fenge, R., and J. V. Weizsäcker. 2001. How much equalization? A constitutional approach. *Journal of Institutional and Theoretical Economics* 157: 623–33.

Haimanko, O., M. Le Breton, and S. Weber. 2005. Transfers in a polarized country: bridging the gap between efficiency and stability. *Journal of Public Economics* 89: 1277–1303.

Jackson, M. O., and M. Morelli. 2007. War, transfers, and political bias. *American Economic Review* 97 (4): 1353–73.

Kolmar, M., and H. Rommeswinkel. 2011. Technological determinants of the group-size paradox. Working paper 3362. CESifo, Munich.

Konrad, K. 2004. Altruism and envy in contests: an evolutionary stable symbiosis. *Social Choice and Welfare* 22 (3): 479–90.

Lambert, P. J. 2001. *The Distribution and Redistribution of Income*. Manchester, UK: Manchester University Press.

Le Breton, M., and S. Weber. 2003. The art of making everybody happy: How to prevent a secession. *IMF Staff Papers* 50 (3): 403–35.

Le Breton, M., and S. Weber. 2005. Secession-proof cost allocations and stable group structures in models of horizontal differentiation. Mimeo.

Lockwood, B. 2008. Voting, lobbying and the decentralization theorem. *Economics and Politics* 20: 416–61.

Münster, J. 2009. Group contest success functions. *Economic Theory* 41 (2): 345–57.

Oates, W. E. 1972. *Fiscal Federalism*. New York: Harcourt Brace Jovanovich.

Olson, M. 1965.. *The Logic of Collective Action: Public Goods and the Theory of Groups*. Harvard University Press.

Persson, T., and G. Tabellini. 1996. Federal fiscal constitutions: risk sharing and moral hazard. *Econometrica* 64: 623–46.

Pigou, A. C. 1912. *Wealth and Welfare*. London: Macmillan.

Powell, R. 2004. Bargaining and learning while fighting. *American Journal of Political Science* 48 (2): 344–61.

Skaperdas, S. 1996. Contest success functions. *Economic Theory* 7: 283–90.

Shah, A., ed. 2007. *The Practice of Fiscal Federalism: Comparative Perspectives*. Montréal: Forum of Federations/McGill-Queen's University Press.

Spalaore, E. 2008. Civil conflict and secessions. *Economics of Governance* 9: 45–63.

Tullock, G. 1959. Problems of Majority Voting. *Journal of Political Economy* 67: 571–79.

Vaillancourt, F. 1998. Equalization in Canada: A critical view. In R. Boadway and P. A. Hobson, eds., *Equalization: Its Contribution to Canada's Economic and Fiscal Progress*. Kingston: John Deutsch Institute for the Study of Economic Policy, 243–47.

Wagner, R. H. 2000. Bargaining and war. *American Journal of Political Science* 44 (3): 469–84.

Wärneryd, K. 1998. Distributional conflict and jurisdictional organization. *Journal of Public Economics* 69: 435–50.

Werner, J. 2008. Fiscal equalization among the states in Germany. Working paper 02–2008. Institute of Local Public Finance, Langen.

3 Natural Resources, Social Conflict, and Poverty Trap

Davide Fiaschi

I would rather be vaguely right than precisely wrong.
—John Maynard Keynes

3.1 Introduction

Many countries whose output is concentrated in primary sectors show low growth rates (see Auty 2001; Sachs and Warner 2001; Mehlum et al. 2006; Humphreys et al. 2007a). The literature has proposed many complementary explanations of the phenomenon, denoted as the *curse of natural resources*, among which are (1) strong exports of natural resources change terms of trade and crowding out of traded-manufacturing activities (Sachs and Warner 2001), (2) rents from natural resources distort the allocation of investments (e.g., less incentive to invest in education; see Gylfason 2001), and (3) rents from natural resources encourage strong rent-seeking activities and/or social conflict in countries with weak institutions (see Mehlum et al. 2006; Collier 2007; Olsson 2007).

This chapter identifies the cause of stagnation of these economies where a high level of social conflict due to the (relative) abundance of natural resources occurs in the presence of an initially low level of per capita GDP, a high social fractionalization, weak institutions, low investment rates, high population growth, high depletion of natural resources, and low life expectancy. The theoretical model presented here provide a rationale for the high persistence of negative shocks in poor economies, as well as for the observed long-run impact of natural disasters.

The theoretical model builds on Olsson (2007) and Mehlum et al. (2003). It attempts to identify conditions under which countries can be trapped into a permanent underdevelopment regime. In the economy there are two sectors: in the natural resources sector, output depends only on natural resources, while in the productive sector, output depends on labor and capital. The economy is populated by two groups of individuals (i.e., society is polarized into two homogeneous ethnic/religious groups). Formally, government owns property rights on natural resources but can only partially appropriate rents from them (i.e., institutions are weak). The two groups compete for appropriation of residual rents. Following Grossman and Kim (1996), who argue that social conflict ("predation" is their term) is particularly fierce when the level of rents does not crucially depend on social conflict, rents from natural resources are assumed to be independent of social conflict, and output in the industrial sector cannot be preyed upon. The source of capital accumulation is therefore the nonconsumed output of the productive sector.

Competition for the residual rent appropriation between the two groups is first modeled as a one-shot game, where both groups simultaneously choose how to allocate their time between the productive sector and the fighting for rent appropriation from natural resources. Technology in the productive sector is linear in capital; therefore, given a sufficiently high level of investment rate, the economy without conflict would grow in the long run. But the waste of resources caused by social conflict can generate a poverty trap, meaning countries with a low initial level of capital can be trapped in a low-income equilibrium. The long-run behavior of economy depends crucially on the quality of institutions: fewer appropriable rents means less incentive to compete for rents, as in Olsson (2007) and Mehlum et al. (2003). But the level of actual stock of per capita capital could be also a crucial factor; capital may in fact determine the *outside option* of competition for rents (Collier et al. 2005 raise a similar point). The *curse of natural resources* is therefore the result of the joint effect of weak institutions and of a low level of per capita income (capital). A counterintuitive example explains the importance of jointly considering institutions and level of per capita income: an increase in resources harvested by government, which are then entirely consumed by that government, thereby reducing the rents to be shared between the two groups that could release the country from the poverty trap. However, in the empirical analysis this could also signal weak institutions.

If, however, the two groups realize that they will always be interacting, in equilibrium an agreement for sharing rents without any social conflict (i.e., a social contract) becomes feasible; the *self-enforcing* agreement between the two groups could be supported by the threat of future social conflict. The expected future gains from accumulation of capital play a key role; these gains positively depend on the investment rate and the productive sector, and negatively on the population's growth rate. The impact of the size of the minority on the intensity of social conflict would be ambiguous: a larger minority may still widen the range of incomes initially, leading to low-income equilibrium, but a large minority also favors the emergence of a social contract by decreasing the gain of any individual thinking of deviating from the agreement.

Finally, two additional explanatory factors could be considered as causes of social conflict: the speed of exploitation of natural resources, and the population's life expectancy. Indeed, both a high-speed exploitation, reducing future rents, and low life expectancy, reduce the time horizon of individuals and raise the incentive to fight for current rents. Collier (2007) discusses anecdotal evidence on these two findings.

From an empirical point of view Auty (2001) provides many historical examples of economy collapses caused by social conflict over natural resource rent appropriations. Many scholars focus on the determinants of civil war to study the wider phenomenon of social conflict within a country, given that a general consensus on the definition of civil war exists, while other types of social conflict, such as riots and military coups, are harder to measure. Among these, the most relevant empirical analyses of the onset of civil war and its long-run effects, by Collier and Hoeffler (2004), Collier et al. (2009), van der Ploeg (2011), and Ross (2012), support the model's main theoretical results. The relationship between the abundance of natural resources and onset of civil war is moreover discussed in Sambanis (2003) through several case studies. Collier et al. (2009) finding that sub-Saharan countries have the highest probability of civil war is further empirical support to the present argument, given the particular characteristics of these countries. Montalvo and Reynal-Querol (2005) find a role of ethnic fractionalization in the onset of civil wars, which correlates with the findings of the model of this chapter. Hegre and Sambanis (2006) presents a sensitivity analysis of the determinants of civil wars, concluding that a large population with low income levels, low rates of economic growth, and bad institutions are potential factors. However, they find only partial support for the role of ethnic dominance. Olsson (2006) and Olsson (2007) document how diamond production has directly triggered civil war in many sub-Saharan countries. However, a strand of literature questions the casual relationship between the prevalence of primary commodities in national output and civil war; see, in particular, the special issue of the *Journal of Conflict Resolution* in 2005 (Ron 2005). Finally, Blattman and Miguel (2010) survey extensive theoretical and empirical literature on civil wars; they highlight the mixed results of empirical research on the causes of civil wars, mostly due to strong collinearity between the potential explanatory variables and, more important, the presence of endogeneity.

Fiaschi (2008) uses a one-shot game in a first analysis of sub-Saharan countries' dynamics over the last thirty years. In spirit the model follows the game-theoretic approach to social conflict in Hirshleifer (2001) and McBride and Skaperdas (2007). The approach adopted by Dixit (2004) is similar; in the limiting case of no existence of government, the issue analyzed is equivalent to the definition of natural resources property rights in an economy without a legal system. On the emergence and characteristics of social contract, Binmore (2005) presents a point of view close to that of the present chapter. Esteban and Ray (2008) analyze the determinants of the onset of class or ethnic conflicts and argue that ethnic conflicts are more likely in countries with high inequality. Besley and Persson (2009) analyze a model with social conflict (civil wars) but without capital accumulation; another crucial difference with respect to the present analysis is the assumption that groups are playing a one-shot Stackelberg game. Tangeras and Lagerlof (2009) find the same result of a nonlinear relationship between the risk of a civil war and the polarization of society. Gonzales (2007) analyzes a growth model with social conflict, but in equilibrium, where the economy is not growing and therefore the opportunity cost of social conflict is constant; moreover his focus is on the welfare implication of social conflict. Benhabib and Rustichini (1996) deal with determinants of social conflict but with a focus on the choice investment/consumption. Ross (2012) discuss a theoretical framework to explain the onset of violent conflicts in oil producers very close to that of the present chapter, where two groups of individuals differ in their geographical locations (rebels are in the region with oil, citizens in the rest of country). Finally, models with occupational choice by Acemoglu (1995), Murphy et al. (1993), and Mehlum et al. (2003) are close to the present model in their focus on the incentives for individuals to become producers or predators and how their choice affects the development of an economy.

3.2 A Brief Review of Empirical Evidence on Economic Growth, Natural Resources, and Social Conflict

This section discusses the empirical evidence linking natural resources to long-run growth of countries via civil wars to make the motivations of the theoretical model proposed below clearer.

Table 3.1 gives some descriptive statistics for a cross section of 109 countries for the period 1970 to 2000 of a set of variables used in the theoretical model.[1]

Countries with at least one civil war in the period 1970 to 2000 show a lower average growth rate of per capita income (AV, GR.GDP, source PWT 7.0), higher growth rate volatility (SD.GR.GDP, my calculations), a lower initial level of per capita GDP (GDP.1970, source PWT 7.0), a lower investment rate (AV.INV.RATE, source PWT 7.0), a higher growth rate of population (AV.GR.POP, source PWT 7.0), and a lower literacy rate (AV.LIT.RATE, source WDI 2011). Countries with civil wars were therefore both very poor in 1970 and doomed to remain poor in 2000; in the theoretical model I show how low (expected) growth (derived by low investment rates, high population growth, etc.) can favor social

Table 3.1
Descriptives statistics of the sample

	With civil wars	Without civil wars
Number of countries	39	70
AV.GR.GDP	1.13%	2.20%
SD.GR.GDP	6.35	5.21
GDP.1970 (international PPP$)	1,859	7,192
AV.INV.RATE	19.5	24.5
AV.GR.POP	2.4%	1.8%
AV.LIT.RATE	57%	71%
LIFE.EXP.1970	51	60
ADULT.MALE.MORT.RATE.1970 (on 1000)	397	312
ETH.LING.DIVERSITY (max 100)	52	38
ETH.DOMINANCE (max 100)	51	40
CONSTRAINTS.ON.EXECUTIVES.1970 (max 10)	3.15	4.05
AV.NAT.RES.ON.GDP	7.17%	5%
AV.SHARE.NO.MANU.EXP (max 100)	67.8	61.5
AV.DEN.POP	0.10	0.08

conflict. The poverty trap is therefore the result of a vicious circle of low income and civil war.[2]

Populations in countries with civil wars also had lower life expectancies (LIFE.EXP.1970, source WDI 2011), and higher adult male mortality rates in 1970 (ADULT.MALE.MORT.RATE.1970, source WDI 2011). In the theoretical model the lower is expected length of life, the higher is the incentive of individuals to be engaged in social conflict.[3]

The measure of ethnolinguistic diversity (ETH.LING.DIVERSITY, source Collier and Hoeffler 2004) and ethnic dominance (ETH.DOMINANCE, source Collier and Hoeffler 2004) shows that countries with civil wars indeed have populations with more ethnic diversity and polarization. The polarization of society, as due to the size of minorities, is included in the theoretical model, even though its relationship with social conflict is expected to be nonlinear.[4]

The quality of the institutions, as measured by constraints on executives in 1970 (*CONSTRAINTS.ON.EXECUTIVES.1970*, source Polity IV), is low in countries with civil wars; this is another feature that the theoretical model takes into account.[5]

Finally, countries with civil wars are more dependent on natural resources, both in sharing of rents from natural resources on total GDP (AV.NAT.RES.ON.GDP, source WDI 2011), and in sharing of non-manufactures on total exports (AV.SHARE.NO.MANU.EXP, source WDI 2011). The high density of population per square kilometer (AV.DEN.POP, source WDI 2011) also signals high pressure on natural resources. This relationship is the main point raised by the theoretical model: the competition for natural resources is a potential trigger for the poverty trap.[6]

It is not this chapter's aims to conduct a rigorous statistical analysis of the causes of civil wars and the effect on the growth of countries. In particular, the analysis does not attempt to identify the causal relationships between the variables reported in table 3.1 and the onset of civil wars. Even though the expression "curse of natural resources" is to be found in Auty (2001), Collier and Hoeffler (2004) represents the pioneering contribution in literature on the economic causes of civil war. Their statistical analysis shows how the rents from natural resources (measured by the share of non-manufactured exports in total exports) have significant explanatory power in predicting civil war and therefore the development of a country (e.g., see Collier and Hoeffler 2012). Their results are, however, widely criticized in the literature (see Blattman and Miguel 2010; Easterly 2009; van der Ploeg 2011).

In particular, Blattman and Miguel (2010) provide an exhaustive review on the empirical analysis of civil war. They argue that inferences about civil wars can be severely biased by the presence of high collinearity among variables, and, overall, of endogeneity; the latter argument is indeed controversial if one accepts that the onset of civil war is caused by low-level income, and vice versa (also known as the greed versus grievance controversy; see Collier and Hoeffler 2007).[7]

Finally, Ross (2012) provides an insightful analysis of the rents from oil and the development of oil producers. Ross convincingly shows how oil production can lead to violent conflicts, in particular, in poor countries with some ethnic divisions, and after the 1970 increase of oil rents (see Ross 2012, fig. 2.5). The strong evidence that supports his claim is the high presence of onshore locations of oil and gas wells at the onset of civil wars compared to off-shore locations elsewhere (as reported in Ross 2012, fig. 5.6).

To complete the picture on the relationship between natural resources and conflict, it is important to remember the existence of many case studies. Sambanis (2003) reviews 22 case studies of civil wars, finding evidence in favor of a role of rents from natural resources in several cases. Olsson (2006) discusses how in some sub-Saharian countries large diamond production fuels endemic social conflict. Minter (1994) shows how before civil war, Angola's economy had high growth rates and the primary sector was not dominant in the output; after 1975, the primary sector become the main source of income, thanks to the increase in the oil price after the first oil shock. A similar analysis is made by Ross (2012); in particular, Ross analyzes the path leading to civil war in Aceh (Indonesia) and in South Sudan, where the separatist movement was inspired by hydrocarbon wealth, and rebellions in the Niger Delta (Nigeria), Colombia, Congo-Brazzaville, and the planned rebellion in Equatorial Guinea, which were instead financed by their local oil facilities.

3.3   The Model

Suppose that economy is composed by two groups of individuals, *citizens* and *rebels*. The existence of these two groups is taken as given, and they will differ only for their cardinality (*citizens* will be assumed more numerous than *rebels*).[8] At period t the cardinality of the groups of *citizens* (C) and *rebels* (R) are equal to N^C and N^R, and $N = N^C + N^R$ is the total population (in the following, time index is omitted if this is not source of confusion). In the economy there exists a flow of income (rents) from natural resources F.[9] A share equal to $1 - \gamma \geq 0$ is appropriate by government and the remaining part γ is appropriate by the two groups.

Parameter γ should measure the quality of institutions, namely a higher γ means less efficient institutions. Given this chapter's purpose, the potential role of government expenditure in preventing/alleviating social conflict and/or the incentives of groups of individuals to capture the government in order to appropriate rents from natural resources will not be developed (e.g., see Esteban and Ray 2008; Besley and Persson 2009). In particular, the possibility that government-collected resources are consumed by the same government and/or used to provide public goods and/or redistributed by lump-sum transfers to all individuals does not change the results discussed below because such policies do not affect incentives of social conflict for the two groups (see equations 3.1 and 3.2).[10] The analysis would not change if citizens, by majority voting, could assume formal control of government, under the assumption that the latter by itself has not got any power of coercion on individuals.

In each period every rebel has to decide how to allocate her time between the productive sector, $l^R \geq 0$, and fighting for the appropriation of income from natural resources, $p \geq 0$. Total endowment of time is normalized to 1, that is, $l^R + p = 1$. The time employed in the productive sector has a reward proportional to the per capita capital of economy $k_t = K_t/N_t$; in particular, a rebel gets $Al^R k_t$ from productive sector (i.e., there is no difference in time reward between citizens and rebels in the productive sector). By the same token, every citizen has to decide how to employ her time between the productive sector, $l^C \geq 0$, and fighting for the appropriation of income from natural resources, $d \geq 0$, with the total endowment of time again normalized to 1, that is, $l^C + d = 1$. Symmetrically, a citizen gets $Al^C k_t$ from the productive sector.

The intensity of *social conflict* is measured by the share of population engaged in the fight for the appropriation of income from natural resources, that is, $\beta^R p + \beta^C d$, where $\beta^R = N^R/N$ is the share of *rebels* on total population and $\beta^C = N^C/N$ is the share of *citizens* on total population ($\beta^R + \beta^C = 1$). We assume that β^R and β^C are constant over time.

Within each group appropriate income is equally shared among the members of the group, so that each member of the same group adopts the same decision on personal time allocation.[11] Given p and d, assume the simplest formulation of the *technology of conflict* discussed in

Hirshleifer (2001), that is, $N^R p/(N^R p + N^C d)$ and $N^C d/(N^R p + N^C d)$ are the shares of γF respectively accruing to *rebels* and *citizens*. The technology of conflict is therefore assumed to be linear in the number of individuals of the two groups engaged in the conflict.[12] With this technology of conflict the model also includes the "the-winner-takes-all" case: the shares $N^R p/(N^R p + N^C d)$ and $N^C d/(N^R p + N^C d))$ being the probabilities of the two groups getting the total amount of income from natural resources. Finally, for the sake of simplicity, fighting does not change the total amount of income from natural resources accruing to the two groups (see Grossman and Kim 1996).

The utility of the representative rebel is linear in its income:

$$U^R = A(1-p_t)k_t + \left(\frac{N^R p_t}{N^R p_t + N^C d_t} \right) \frac{\gamma F}{N^R} = A(1-p_t)k_t + \left(\frac{p_t}{\beta^R p_t + \beta^C d_t} \right) \gamma f,$$

(3.1)

where $f = F/N$ are the per capita rents from natural resources, assumed constant over time, while the utility of the representative citizen is given by

$$U^R = A(1-d_t)k_t + \left(\frac{d_t}{\beta^R p_t + \beta^C d_t} \right) \gamma f.$$

(3.2)

The accumulation of the aggregate stock of capital in the economy depends on the output of productive sector Y^P; in particular,

$$K_{t+1} = (1-\delta)K_t + sY^P = (1-\delta)K_t + s\left[A(1-p_t)k_t N^R + A(1-d_t)k_t N^C \right],$$

(3.3)

where $\delta > 0$ is the depreciation rate of capital, $s \geq 0$ is the constant investment rate from the output of productive sector. Income from natural resources does not contribute to the accumulation of capital. This corresponds to the assumption that income from natural resources is entirely consumed or that income from natural resources cannot be used to increase capital in the productive sector; for example, if capital accumulation is indeed knowledge accumulation and the latter is the result of externalities and/or a by-product of the production activity.[13] Investment rate is assumed to be constant in order to focus only on the effects of the individuals' choices between predation and production (e.g., see Benhabib and Rustichini (1996) for an analysis of the effects of social conflict on the choice investment/consumption).[14]

Equation (3.3) can be expressed in terms of per capita capital as

$$k_{t+1} = \frac{(1-\delta)k_t + s\left[A(1-p_t)k_t\beta^R + A(1-d_t)k_t\beta^C\right]}{1+n}, \tag{3.4}$$

where $n = N_{t+1}/N_t \geq 0$ is the constant growth rate of the population. Income from the productive sector cannot be predated; that is, it cannot be a source of dispute between the two groups (see Grossman and Kim 1996).

The framework can be extended to L different groups. The extension would not provide any additional insight with respect to the issue analyzed here, but as L increases, the time devoted to fighting would tend to decrease as its marginal effect on the share of appropriate rents from natural resources tends to decrease.[15]

3.4   Optimal Strategies of the One-Shot Game

In every period *citizens* and β^R *rebels* choose their time allocation by playing a *one-shot* game. Proposition 1 states the Nash equilibrium of game.

Proposition 1 Assume $\beta^R \leq 1/2$; then in the Nash equilibrium of the one-shot game between *citizens* and *rebels,*

$$p^* = d^* = 1 \quad \text{when } k_t \in \left[0, \bar{k}^d\right],$$

$$p^* = 1 \quad \text{and} \quad d^* = \left(\frac{1}{1-\beta^R}\right)\sqrt{\frac{\beta^R \gamma f}{Ak_t}} \quad \text{when} \quad k_t \in \left[\bar{k}^d, \bar{k}^p\right], \quad \text{and}$$

$$p^* = \frac{\gamma f}{4\beta^R Ak_t} \quad \text{and} \quad d^* = \frac{\gamma f}{4(1-\beta^R)Ak_t} \quad \text{when} \quad k_t \in \left[\bar{k}^p, \infty\right),$$

where $\bar{k}^d = \gamma f \beta^R / A$ and $\bar{k}^p = \gamma f / (4\beta^R A)$ with $\bar{k}^d \leq \bar{k}^p$.

Proof See appendix B. ∎

Proposition 1 shows that the intensity of social conflict depends on the ratio of f to k_t: for low-level k_t ($k_t \leq \bar{k}^d$), all the population is engaged in the fight for the appropriation of natural resources, meaning there is a fierce *civil war*; for a higher but always low-level k_t $\left(k_t \in \left[\bar{k}^d, \bar{k}^p\right]\right)$, only *rebels* are fully engaged in the fight, while most *citizens* are employed in the productive sector; finally for a sufficiently high level of capital ($k_t > \bar{k}^p$), some *rebels* also stop fighting and shift to the productive sector. Therefore, ceteris paribus, social conflict, measured by the share of population engaged in predation $\beta^R p_t^* + \beta^C d_t^*$, monotonically decreases with the level of per capita capital k_t. The result is expected, given that the *opportunity cost of fighting* is proportional to k_t. If $\beta^R > 1/2$ in the intermediate range of capital all *citizens* would be engaged in fight while some *rebels* would be in the productive sector.

It is straightforward to prove that if $k_t > \bar{k}^d$, social conflict decreases with A (the opportunity cost of fighting) and increases with γf (the reward of fighting). Finally, if $k_t \in \left[\bar{k}^d, \bar{k}^p \right]$ social conflict increases with β^R (the size of minority in the country); in fact, when the minority is entirely engaged in fighting, the linear technology of conflict induces the majority to fight more as its relative size $1 - \beta^R$ decreases. Moreover, given a certain level of per capita capital, an increase in A decreases the probability of social conflict with high intensity—in the sense of decreasing both capital thresholds $\bar{k}^d$ and $\bar{k}^p$—while the opposite holds true for γf. From the same point of view, an increase in β^R increases the probability of civil war ($\bar{k}^d$ increases), but decreases the probability of social conflict in which the minority is entirely engaged in fighting ($\bar{k}^p$ decreases). All these findings broadly agree with the empirical evidence on the causes and intensity of civil wars discussed in Collier and Hoeffler (2004) and in Collier et al. (2009).

The social optimal allocation of time $p^* = d^* = 0$ cannot be reached because there is no *self-enforcing agreement* on the sharing of rents from natural resources in the one-shot game. On the contrary, in the repeated-game where individuals' time horizon is indefinite, the simple application of *Folk Theorems* suggests that social optimal allocation could be reached. The issue will be discussed in section 3.6.

3.5 Long-Run Equilibrium with One-Period Time Horizon

Equation (3.4) and proposition 1 give the dynamics of per capita capital when individuals have a time horizon of one period:

$$k_{t+1} = \begin{cases} \left(\dfrac{1}{1+n}\right)(1-\delta)k_t & \text{when} \quad k_t \in \left[0, \bar{k}^d\right], \\[2ex] \left(\dfrac{1}{1+n}\right)\left[(1-\delta+sA)k_t - s\sqrt{\beta^R \gamma f A k_t}\right] & \text{when} \quad k_t \in \left[\bar{k}^d, \bar{k}^p\right], \quad (3.5) \\[2ex] \left(\dfrac{1}{1+n}\right)\left[(1-\delta+sA)k_t - s\gamma f/2\right] & \text{when} \quad k_t \in \left[\bar{k}^p, \infty\right). \end{cases}$$

Proposition 2 states under which configuration of parameters economy displays multiple (two) equilibria.

Proposition 2 Assume $\beta^R \leq 1/2$ and

$$sA > \delta + n. \tag{3.6}$$

Then two equilibria $k^{Es} = 0$ and $k^{Eu} > 0$ exist, the first stable and the second unstable. Moreover, if

$$sA \in \left(\delta + n, \frac{\delta + n}{1 - 2\beta^R}\right), \tag{3.7}$$

then

$$k^{Eu} = \frac{s\gamma f}{2(sA - \delta - n)}, \tag{3.8}$$

where $k^{Eu} > \bar{k}^p$; otherwise, if

$$sA \in \left(\frac{\delta + n}{1 - 2\beta^R}, +\infty\right), \tag{3.9}$$

then

$$k^{Eu} = \frac{\beta^R s^2 A \gamma f}{(sA - \delta - n)^2}, \tag{3.10}$$

where $0 < k^{Eu} < \bar{k}^p$.

Proof See appendix C. ∎

The graph in figure 3.1 illustrates proposition 2 when $k^{Eu} > \bar{k}^p$ (i.e., condition 3.7 holds). Note in the figure that an economy displays two different dynamics according to its initial level of capital; an economy with a low initial level of per capita capital, $k_0 < k^{Eu}$, will be converging toward equilibrium E_S with zero capital, whereas an economy with a sufficiently high initial level of per capita capital, $k_0 > k^{Eu}$, will grow forever. The model therefore exhibits an (absolute) *poverty trap*.

Proposition 3 characterizes the long-run dynamics of economy.

Proposition 3 Assume $\beta^R \leq 1/2$ and that condition (3.6) holds. If $k_0 < k^{Eu}$, then the per capita capital of economy will be converging toward k^{Es}, whereas, if $k_0 > k^{Eu} = 0$, then $\lim_{t \to \infty} k_{t+1}/kt = sA - \delta - n$.

Proof See appendix D. ∎

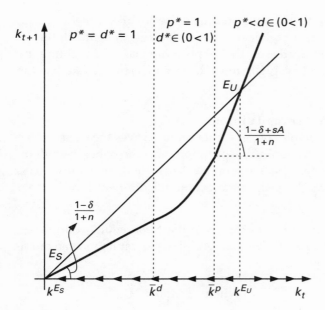

Figure 3.1
Dynamics of an economy with two equilibria

The level of k^{Eu} is therefore the threshold of per capita capital which determines the long-run dynamics of economy. Remark 1 shows the relationship between k^{Eu} and the most relevant parameters of the economy.

Remark 1 The threshold level of per capita capital k^{Eu} increases with f, n, γ, and decreases with A and s. If condition (3.7) holds, then k^{Eu} increases with β^{R}.

Proof Derivatives of k^{Eu} reported in proposition 2 with respect to f, n, γ, A and s directly prove the results. If condition (3.7) holds, then k^{Eu} is defined by equation (3.8) and the first derivative of k^{Eu} directly proves the result. ■

Remark 1 says that given a certain level of initial per capita capital k_0, the probability of a country being trapped in an equilibrium with low income and strong social conflict increases with rents from natural resources (f), population growth rate (n), weakness of institutions (γ), and size of minority (β^{R}); that probability decreases with investment rate (s) and productivity of productive sector (A). Higher rents from natural resources, higher weakness of institutions, larger size of minority, lower productivity of productive sector mean higher social conflict and therefore a higher waste of resources; in contrast, higher population growth decreases the opportunity cost of fighting by diluting the per capita capital, and a higher investment rate has the opposite effect.

3.5.1 Dynamics of Per capita Income

In the model the dynamics of per capita capital drives the dynamics of economy. However, the country's per capita income depends both on the level of per capita capital and on the rents from natural resources. Proposition 4 shows the per capita income for different levels of per capita capital.

Proposition 4 Assume $\beta^R \leq 1/2$; then in the Nash equilibrium of the one-shot game between *citizens* and *rebels* the per capita income of the economy is given by

$$y_t = f \qquad\qquad\qquad\text{when}\quad k_t \in \left[0, \bar{k}^d\right],$$

$$y_t = \left(1 + \beta^R\right) A k_t - \sqrt{\gamma f \beta^R A k_t} + f \quad \text{when}\quad k_t \in \left[\bar{k}^d, \bar{k}^p\right],$$

$$y_t = A k_t + f\left(1 - \frac{\gamma}{2}\right) \qquad\quad \text{when}\quad k_t \in \left[\bar{k}^p, \infty\right),$$

where $\bar{k}^d = \gamma f \beta^R / A$ and $\bar{k}^p = \gamma f / (4\beta^R A)$ with $\bar{k}^d \leq \bar{k}^p$.

Proof At period t per capita income is given by

$$y_t = \left(1 - d_t^*\right) A k_t \beta^C + \left(1 - p_t^*\right) A k_t \beta^R + f. \tag{3.11}$$

Proposition 1 and equation (3.11) prove the results. ∎

Proposition 5 describes the dynamics of per capita income with poverty trap.

Proposition 5 Assume $\beta^R \leq 1/2$ and $sA > \delta + n$. If $y_0 < y^{Eu}$, then the per capita income will be converging toward $y^{Es} = f$; otherwise, if $y_0 > y^{Eu}$, then in the long run the per capita capital will be growing at rate $sA - \delta - n$, where

$$\text{if } sA \in \left(\delta + n, \frac{\delta + n}{1 - 2\beta^R}\right), \quad \text{then}\quad y^{Eu} = f\left[1 + \frac{\gamma(\delta + n)}{2(sA - \delta - n)}\right]; \tag{3.12}$$

$$\text{if } sA \in \left(\frac{\delta + n}{1 - 2\beta^R}, +\infty\right), \quad \text{then}\quad y^{Eu} = f\left[1 + \frac{\gamma \beta^R sA\left(sA\beta^R + \delta + n\right)}{(sA - \delta - n)^2}\right]. \tag{3.13}$$

Proof See appendix E. ∎

Propositions 2 and 5 show that in the poverty trap equilibrium capital is zero but per capita income is positive and is entirely derived from natural resources. Positive shocks to income from natural resources (e.g., an increase in the real price of raw materials) increase the level of per capita output but make less probable an escape from the poverty trap, also increasing the threshold level of per capita income (note that the difference $y^{Eu} - y^{Es}$ is proportional to f).

It is straightforward to show that y^{Eu} (like k^{Eu}) increases with f, n, γ, and decreases with s and A; moreover, if condition (3.7) holds, then y^{Eu} increases with β^R.

Finally, from equation (3.5) and proposition 4 the overall investment rate of economy (total investment over aggregate income) is increasing in k_t, being equal to 0 for $k_t \in \left[0, \overline{k}^d\right]$ and converging to s for $k_t \rightarrow +\infty$. The positive relationship between the growth rate of per capita income and investment rate is a by-product of the different output compositions of the economy as per capita capital increases (a direct result of the assumption that rents from natural resources cannot affect the accumulation of capital).

3.5.2 Government Consumption

In the model, government consumption could have a positive impact on the development of a country if it dissipates rents from natural resources. For the sake of simplicity, assume that government consumes all income it collects from natural resources, and consider the share of government consumption on total income c_t^G to be near but below the threshold of the poverty trap y^{Eu} in equation (3.12), that is,

$$c_t^G = \frac{(1-\gamma)f}{y_t} = \frac{(1-\gamma)f}{Ak_t + f(1-\gamma/2)},$$

given some level of per capita capital. A decrease in γ (i.e., a higher capacity of government to appropriate rents from natural resources) causes an increase in c_t^G and in y_t but also a decrease in y^{Eu} (see equation 3.12). An increase in government consumption therefore increases the country's probability of escaping a poverty trap (i.e., $y_t - y^{Eu}$ decreases). The intuition behind this result is straightforward: in this economy, government consumption wastes resources. However, because such a waste derives from a decrease in γ, it lowers the incentive to fight; more resources will consequently be allocated to the

productive sector. The latter positive effect outweighs the former negative effect (at least in the long run).

3.6 Indefinite Time Horizon

So far in this analysis, groups could make their decisions with a time
horizon of one period. This excluded the possibility that the two groups
could find a *self-enforcing* agreement on the share of rents from natural
resources, meaning a social contract. The *Theory of Repeated Games*,
however, suggests that when the individuals' horizon is indefinite (or
infinite) a self-enforcing agreement on the sharing of rents without
social conflict can be reached. The following analysis is indeed closed
to the issue of the emergence of property rights and, consequently, of
a social contract in the primitive economy discussed in Muthoo (2004).
Also McBride and Skaperdas (2007) highlight the importance of the
agents' horizon in the explanation of conflict (but in their model,
income is constant over time).

Heuristically, the payoff of deviation from an agreement becomes
smaller as the per capita capital of economy increases; consider therefore the worst situation for reaching a self-enforcing agreement, namely
$k_t \in \left[0, \overline{k}^d \right]$, where social conflict is at its maximum in the one-shot
game, $p^* = d^* = 1$. From equations (3.1) and (3.2) the utilities of the
representative *citizen* and *rebel*, U_{SC}^C and U_{SC}^R, are, respectively, equal to

$$\left(U_{SC}^C, U_{SC}^R \right) = \left(\gamma f, \gamma f \right). \tag{3.14}$$

Suppose that at beginning of every period the two groups can
bargain to decide how to share rents from natural resources. If such
bargaining fails then they play their optimal strategies reported in
proposition 1. Otherwise, if they reach an agreement, there is not any
social conflict in the period, $p^* = d^* = 0$, even if such agreement is not
automatically enforceable. As in Muthoo (2004) assume that the bargaining process is such that the equilibrium is characterized by a *Nash
bargaining solution* (*NBS*) with disagreement point $\left(U_{SC}^C, U_{SC}^R \right)$. Muthoo
(2004) shows that this NBS is the outcome of a third stage where agents
bargain on side-payments. The NBS is characterized by the *Split-the-
difference* rule, that is, each individual receives her disagreement payoff
plus a share of surplus deriving from the agreement and allocates all
its time to productive activity. The surplus deriving from agreement is
given by

$$\Delta_t = \underbrace{NAk_t + \gamma F}_{\text{Total output of economy with agreement}} - \underbrace{\gamma F}_{\text{Total output of economy without agreement}} = NAk_t.$$

(3.15)

Assume that such output is equally shared among all the individuals of economy. This means that the bargaining power of the two groups is proportional to their population size β^C and β^R. Therefore the utilities of representative *citizen* and *rebel* in the NBS, U^C_{NBS} and U^R_{NBS}, are, respectively, equal to

$$(U^C_{NBS}, U^R_{NBS}) = (Ak_t + \gamma f, Ak_t + \gamma f).$$

(3.16)

A comparison between the payoffs in equations (3.14) and (3.16) confirms the intuition that the incentive to deviate from the agreement decreases with per capita capital.

In order to evaluate under which conditions the NBS can effectively be played by both groups, consider the *trigger-strategy* approach. In this strategy each group respects the agreement of the NBS until the other group breaks the agreement and starts the fight, which continues *forever* as specified by the optimal strategy of one-shot game.

Proposition 6 describes the conditions under which a *trigger strategy equilibrium (TSE)* would exist where both groups respect the agreement of the NBS.

Proposition 6 Assume $\beta^R \le 1/2$ and $sA > \delta + n$. Suppose that the initial per capita capital $k_0 \in \left[0, \overline{k}^f\right]$, where

$$\overline{k}^f = \frac{\beta^R(1+n)\gamma f}{A(1+sA-\delta)} < \overline{k}^d.$$

(3.17)

Let $\rho \in [0,1]$ be the discount factor of individuals; then using the trigger strategies the agreement of the NBS can be sustained as a perfect subgame equilibrium if (1) $\rho \in [\hat{\rho}, 1]$ or (2) $\rho \in [0, \hat{\rho}]$ and $k_0 > \overline{k}^{TSE}$; on the contrary, using trigger strategies the agreement of the NBS cannot be sustained as a perfect subgame equilibrium if $\rho \in [0, \hat{\rho}]$ and $k_0 \in \left[0, \overline{k}^{TSE}\right]$, where

$$\overline{k}^{TSE} = \frac{(1-\beta^R)}{A\beta^R}\left[\frac{1+n}{\rho(1+sA-\delta)} - 1\right]\gamma f$$

(3.18)

and

$$\hat{\rho} = \frac{1+n}{1-\delta+sA} \tag{3.19}$$

Proof See appendix F. ∎

Proposition 6 says that if $\rho \in [0, \hat{\rho}]$, a range of low per capita capital always exists where, using the trigger strategies, a self-enforcing agreement is not attainable. In the limiting case of $\rho = 0$, when the time horizon of individuals is one period, $\bar{k}^{TSE} \to +\infty$: for all levels of per capita capital in the range $\left[0, \bar{k}^f\right]$ fighting is the only equilibrium strategy for both groups (as in the one-shot game). Otherwise, proposition 6 says that a *social contract* between the two groups will emerge; such a social contract declares rents from natural resources to be equally shared by all individuals in the economy (see equation 3.16) without any social conflict. Of course, many other different equilibria are possible (e.g., not using the trigger strategies), namely many different social contracts can represent an equilibrium of the repeated game just analyzed. However, Binmore (2005) suggests that the *fairness* of this social contract, even though based on the NBS, makes it a *natural* solution in the long run.

3.6.1 The Long-Run Equilibrium with Indefinite Time Horizon
Proposition 7 characterizes the long-run dynamics of economy.

Proposition 7 Assume $\beta^R \leq 1/2$, $sA > \delta + n$, and the initial per capita capital $k_0 \in \left[0, \bar{k}^f\right]$. In the long run per capita capital of economy will grow at rate $g_k = sA - \delta - n$ when (1) $\rho \in [\hat{\rho}, 1]$ or (2) $\rho \in [0, \hat{\rho}]$ and $k_0 > \bar{k}^{TSE}$, while $\lim_{t \to +\infty} k_t = k^{Es} = 0$ (poverty trap equilibrium) when $\rho \in [0, \hat{\rho}]$ and $k_0 \in \left[0, \bar{k}^{TSE}\right]$.

Proof See appendix G. ∎

The results in propositions 6 and 7 are summarized in figure 3.2, which shows the loci in the space (ρ, k_0) where a self-enforcing agreement is sustainable, namely where an economy with social contract is growing in the long run (area *CDGH*), and where it is unsustainable, namely where an economy with social conflict is a poverty trap (area *OBCD*). The frontier of these two areas is defined by $\bar{k}^{TSE}$ in equation (3.1) and

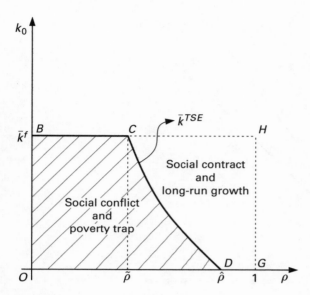

Figure 3.2
Long-run behavior of economy as a function of initial per capita capital k_0 and discount rate ρ.

$$\tilde{\rho} = \left[\frac{1 + sA - \delta}{1 + n} + \frac{(\beta^R)^2}{1 - \beta^R} \right]^{-1} \tag{3.20}$$

is the level of ρ such that $\bar{k}^f = \bar{k}^{TSE}$.

Figure 3.3 shows the dynamics of an economy with a long run of fierce social conflict (i.e., $\rho \in [0, \hat{\rho}]$). In particular, note that if $k_0 < \bar{k}^{TSE} < \bar{k}^f$— the combination (ρ, k_0) that belongs to area $OBCD$ in figure 3.2—then the economy will converge toward $k^{E_S} = 0$, where social conflict is *permanent* and the economy is trapped in the low-income equilibrium E_S. In contrast, if $k_0 > \bar{k}^{TSE}$—the combination (ρ, k_0) that belongs to area $CDGH$ in figure 3.2—with the trigger strategies of the NBS agreement being self-enforcing, the social contract enables the economy to grow forever.

3.6.2 Comparative Statics

Remark 2 shows the relationships between $\bar{k}^{TSE}$ and $\hat{\rho}$ in proposition 6 and the most relevant parameters of the economy.

Remark 2 $\bar{k}^{TSE}$ *increases with* γ, n, δ, *and f and decreases with* β^R, s, A, *and* ρ, *while* $\hat{\rho}$ *increases with n and* δ *and decreases with s and A.*

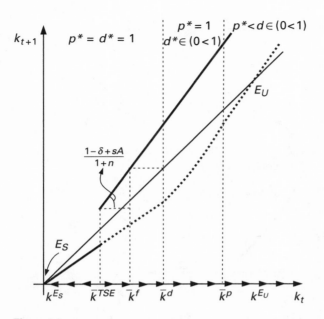

Figure 3.3
Dynamics of an economy with poverty trap (bold line) when the time horizon of individuals is indefinite (infinite)

Proof Taking simple derivatives of $\bar{k}^{TSE}$ and $\hat{\rho}$ with respect to parameters γ, n, δ, f, β^R, s, and A prove the results. ∎

A comparison of remark 1 with remark 2 shows how changes in γ, n, f, s, and A has qualitatively the same impact on the dynamics of economy when the time horizon of individuals is one or indefinite (infinite) with the additional feature for n, s, and A to change the threshold also for ρ. As figure 3.4 shows, a rise in f and/or γ increases the combinations of (ρ, k_0), leading to social conflict and a poverty trap at *OBCD* (i.e., $\bar{k}^f$ shifts upward while $\hat{\rho}$ is constant; see equations 3.1 and 3.20). This is a result of the higher gains, which are proportional to γf, deviating from the NBS.

Figure 3.5 shows that an increase in n or δ and/or a decrease in s and A has the same effect of widening the area leading to social conflict and poverty trap at *OBCD* (i.e., $\bar{k}^f$, $\tilde{\rho}$, and $\hat{\rho}$ rise). This result is caused by the lower value placed on evading the poverty trap, since the growth rate of capital with the social contract is a negative function of n and δ and a positive function of s and A. In other words, if the expected gains from the accumulation of capital are low (i.e., the expected growth rate

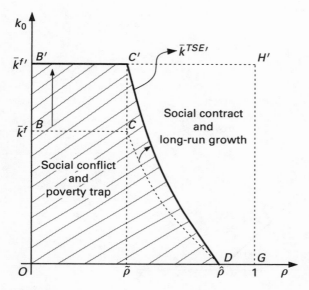

Figure 3.4
Effect on the long-run behavior of an economy with an increase in f and/or in γ.

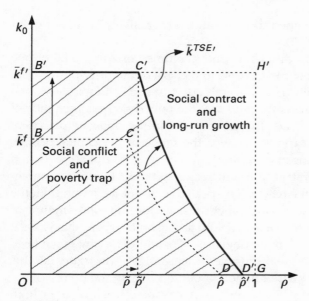

Figure 3.5
Effect on the long-run behavior of an economy with an increase in n or δ and/or a decrease in s or A

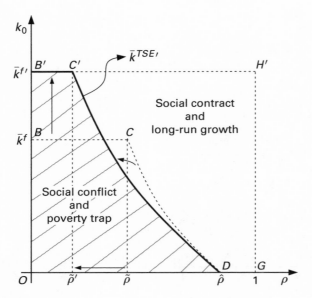

Figure 3.6
Effect on the long-run behavior of an economy of an increase in the size of a minority β^R.

of income decreases), then social conflict is more likely (a similar point
is made in Collier 2007).

Another important difference from the time-horizon model of one
period is the impact of the increase in the size of minority β^R on social
conflict. Figure 3.6 shows the overall effect of such an increase on the
area leading to social conflict and that the poverty trap is then indeed
indeterminate (at *OBCD*). Two effects pull in the opposite direction:
a direct effect of the conflict widens the range of per capita income,
and hence the low-income equilibrium (i.e., $\bar{k}^f$ .goes up; see equation
3.1). In contrast, a strategic effect increases incentive to reach an agreement by decreasing the rebel's (one-period) gains of deviating from the
NBS agreement. In fact, each rebel must divide the total amount of
income from natural resources γF with all the other rebels; that is, each
rebel gains $\gamma F / N^R = \gamma f / \beta^R$ by deviating. Therefore, for any given level
of ρ, an increase of β^R will cause a decrease in $\bar{k}^{TSE}$ (in figure 3.6 this
means a counterclockwise rotation of curve *CD* with the pivot at *D*).

Finally, the existence of a poverty trap may justify regarding the high
persistence of negative shocks in poor countries as natural disasters. A
country's recovery from a negative shock that causes considerable
decline in the level of capital can be blocked by social conflict.

Sections 3.6.3 and 3.6.4 propose two other explanatory variables concerning the threshold of capital $\overline{k}^{TSE}$: the depletion rate of natural resources and individuals' life expectancies.

3.6.3 Natural Resources as an Asset

Individuals with an indefinite time horizon should consider natural resources not only for their current flow of rents. In particular, Humphreys et al. (2007b) argue that natural resources should be considered as nonrenewable assets (e.g., oil) as their rates of regeneration are very low compared to their rates of depletion (e.g., wood from virgin forests). This means that the flows of rents from natural resources F cannot be considered constant over time.

For the sake of simplicity, suppose that the stock of natural resources follows

$$W_t^F = W_0^F \left(1 - \pi^D\right)^t, \tag{3.21}$$

where W_0^F is the initial stock of natural resources and $\pi^D > 0$ is the constant rate of depletion (the rate of regeneration is therefore assumed to be equal to zero). Since $\pi^D > 0$, then $\lim_{t \to +\infty} W_t^F = 0$. Given that population follows $N_t = N_0(1 + n)^t$, then from equation (3.2),

$$w_t^F = w_0^F \left(\frac{1 - \pi^D}{1 + n}\right)^t, \tag{3.22}$$

where w_t^F is the per capita stock of natural resources at period t. The flow of per capita rents from natural resources at period t, f_t, is therefore equal to:

$$f_t = \pi^D w_t^F = \pi^D w_0^F \left(\frac{1 - \pi^D}{1 + n}\right)^t. \tag{3.23}$$

An increase in π^D changes the time path of f, increasing the flow of income in the first $\hat{t} = (1 - \pi^D)/\pi^D$ periods and decreasing the flow in all the remaining periods.[16] Equation (3.2) therefore suggests that an increase in the rate of depletion π^D makes it more difficult to reach a self-enforcing agreement by decreasing the future gains from the agreement. Proposition 9 confirms the intuition.

Proposition 9 Assume $\beta^R \leq 1/2$, $sA > \delta + n$, and the initial per capita capital to be $k_0 \in \left[0, \overline{k}_0^f\right]$, where

$$\bar{k}_0^f = \frac{\beta^R (1+n)\gamma \pi^D w_0^F}{A(1+sA-\delta)}.$$

When using the trigger strategies, the NBS agreement can be sustained as a subgame perfect equilibrium if (1) $\rho \in [\hat{\rho},1]$ or (2) $\rho \in [0,\hat{\rho}]$ and $k_0 > \bar{k}_W^{TSE}$; in contrast, using the trigger strategies the NBS agreement cannot be sustained as a subgame perfect equilibrium if $\rho \in [0,\hat{\rho}]$ and $k_0 < \bar{k}_W^{TSE}$, where

$$\bar{k}_W^{TSE} = \frac{(1-\beta^R)}{A\beta^R}\left[\frac{1+n}{\rho(1+sA-\delta)}-1\right]\gamma \pi^D w_0^F. \tag{3.24}$$

Proof The proof of the proposition follows the steps in appendix F, but with $f = f_t$, where f_t is defined as in equation (3.23). ∎

An increase in $\bar{k}_W^{TSE}$, that is, in π^D and/or in w_0^F, has the same effect of an increase of γ and/or f reported in figure 3.4, which is to widen the area of social conflict in the space (ρ, k_0). Indeed proposition 9 shows that an increase in the rate of depletion π^D increases both $\bar{k}_0^f$ and $\bar{k}_W^{TSE}$ for any given ρ. This finding suggests that not only the amount of rents from natural resources but also the rate of depletion should be considered as a potential explanation of social conflicts. In the empirical analysis, however, to disentangle the two possible determinants of an increase in rents from natural resources, that is, an increase in the stock of natural resources w_0^F or in its rate of depletion π^D, appears very difficult. Only anecdotal evidence exists that a "supposed" increase in the rate of depletion of natural resources can trigger strong social conflict (e.g., of wood from virgin forests in Brazil and of oil in the Niger Delta).[17]

Finally, the level of π^D could be the result of bargaining between the two groups; heuristically, with linear utilities in income, the optimal level of π^D would be 1, which is no incentive to smoothing utilities over time. Otherwise, if utilities were concave in income, π^D would negatively depend on the discount rate of individuals ρ: more patient individuals (i.e., with high ρ) would prefer higher smoothing of income from natural resources (i.e., low π^D). This means that when ρ is low, the emergence of a social contract would be further contrasted by a high level of π^D.

3.6.4 Life Expectancy

The discount factor reflects the intertemporal preferences of individuals. However, it should also reflect the expected "lengths" of their lives, namely their life expectancies. For the sake of simplicity, suppose that S_t, the probability calculated at period 0 that an individual is still alive at period t, is given by

$$S_t = \left(1 - \pi^M\right)^t,$$

where $\pi^M > 0$ is the constant probability to die in every period (therefore $\lim_{t \to \infty} S_t = 0$). The life expectancy of an individual with an indefinite (infinite) time horizon, LE, is therefore equal to[18]

$$LE = \sum_{t=0}^{\infty} t\left(1 - \pi^M\right)^t = \frac{1 - \pi^M}{\left(\pi^M\right)^2}. \tag{3.25}$$

LE is therefore decreasing with π^M. Thus, if an individual has a positive probability to die in each period equal to π^M, then the discount factor ρ should reflect such a probability. But the change of the discount factor also affects the conditions under which a social contract between the two groups can emerge. Proposition 10 confirms such intuition.

Proposition 10 Assume $\beta^R \leq 1/2$ and $sA > \delta + n$. Further assume that the initial per capita capital $k_0 \in \left[0, \bar{k}^f\right]$, where

$$\bar{k}^f = \frac{\beta^R (1+n)\gamma f}{A(1-\delta+sA)}.$$

When we use the trigger strategies, the agreement of the NBS can be sustained as a subgame perfect equilibrium if (1) $\rho \in [\hat{\rho}/(1-\pi^M),1]$ or (2) $\rho \in [0,\hat{\rho}/(1-\pi^M)]$ and $k_0 > \bar{k}_{LE}^{TSE}$; in contrast, when we use the trigger strategies the agreement of the NBS cannot be sustained as a subgame perfect equilibrium if $\rho \in [0,\hat{\rho}/(1-\pi^M)]$ and $k_0 < \bar{k}_{LE}^{TSE}$, where

$$\bar{k}_{LE}^{TSE} = \frac{(1-\beta^R)}{A\beta^R}\left[\frac{1+n}{\rho(1-\pi^M)(1+sA-\delta)} - 1\right]\gamma f. \tag{3.26}$$

Proof The proof follows the same steps as the proof reported in appendix F, but the discount factor net of the probability to survive is equal to $\rho(1 - \pi^M)$.

Figure 3.7 shows that an increase from π^M to $\pi^{M'}$, that is, a decrease in life individual expectancy LE (see equation 3.2), widens the area in the space (ρ, k_0), leading to social conflict and poverty trap.

Indeed proposition 10 shows that an increase in π^M causes an increase in $\bar{k}_{LE}^{TSE}$ (see equation 3.26) for any given ρ (in figure 3.7 this means a

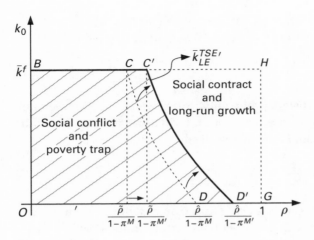

Figure 3.7
Effect on the long-run behavior of an economy with an increase in π^M

shift from CD to $C'D'$). All sub-Saharan countries could suffer from their inhabitants' very short life expectancies. Moreover the strong negative shock on life expectancy represented by the HIV plague could have contributed to a higher social conflict in those regions.

Finally, social conflict could in turn negatively affect life expectancy; the resulting increase in π^M would further lower the possibility of a country to escape the poverty trap. Note, however, that if the decrease in life expectancy caused by social conflict were expected, individuals could have a higher incentive to reach an agreement-and recognize that social conflict would hurt future incomes and, additionally, lower life expectancy. This would mean a lower threshold in capital to cooperate.[19]

3.7   Concluding Remarks

The analysis has shown how social conflict can lead to a poverty trap in line with Collier and Hoeffler (2004), who find that the stagnant growth regime caused by civil war is persistent over time. The explanatory factors of the onset of social conflict identified in the analysis—as low level of per capita income, high level of population growth rate, and high rents from natural resources—find an empirical corroboration (e.g., see Auty 2001; Collier and Hoeffler 2004; Collier et al. 2009; Ross

2012). The minority's size has instead an ambiguous effect on social conflict by increasing, on one hand, the range of per capita income leading to the poverty trap and, on the other, the incentive to reach an agreement without fighting, namely a social contract. This could explain why many empirical analysis do not find any statistically significant relationship between ethnic/religious/linguistic fractionalization and social conflict (e.g., Collier and Hoeffler 2004). In addition the model suggests that high rates of natural resource depletion and low life expectancy could be two further explanatory variables of social conflict and persistence in a low-income equilibrium. Growth patterns and anecdotal evidence of sub-Saharan countries provides some empirical support. The possible endogeneity of institutions should support these conclusions, given the vicious cycle of poor institutions, risk of civil war, and low accumulation of capital.

The next steps in the analysis should aim at (1) endogenizing the strength of each group by allowing different fertility rates between the two groups (e.g., in de la Croix and Dottori 2008), (2) deepening the factors causing the emergence/disruption of a social contract following the insights by Binmore (2005), and (3) endogenizing group formation following Weinstein's (2005) suggestions. Last, (4) the theoretical model could be extended to analyze the impact of foreign aid on the risk of civil war (see de Ree and Nillesen 2009).

Appendix

A Country List

Algeria, Argentina, Bangladesh, Benin, Bolivia, Botswana, Brazil, Burkina Faso, Burundi, Cameroon, Central African Republic, Chad, Chile, China, Colombia, Congo, Dem. Rep., Congo, Rep., Costa Rica, Cote d'Ivoire, Cyprus, Dominican Republic, Ecuador, Egypt, El Salvador, Fiji, Gambia, Ghana, Greece, Guatemala, Guyana, Honduras Hungary, India, Indonesia, Iran, Islamic Rep., Israel, Italy, Jamaica, Jordan, Kenya, Latvia, Madagascar, Malawi, Malaysia, Mali, Malta, Mauritania, Mexico, Morocco, Nepal, Nicaragua, Niger, Nigeria, Pakistan, Panama, Papua New Guinea, Paraguay, Peru, Philippines, Rwanda, Saudi Arabia, Senegal, Seychelles, Sierra Leone, Singapore, South Africa, Sri Lanka, Sudan, Swaziland, Switzerland, Syrian Arab Republic, Thailand, Togo, Trinidad and Tobago, Tunisia, Turkey, Uruguay, Venezuela, RB, Zambia, Zimbabwe.

B Proof of Proposition 1

Suppose first that in the Nash equilibrium $p^*, d^* \in (0, 1)$. Then the first-order conditions of the maximization of U^R and U^C are given by

$$\frac{\partial U^R}{\partial p_t} = -Ak_t + \frac{\gamma f \beta^C d_t}{\left(\beta^R p_t + \beta^C d_t\right)^2} = 0 \quad \text{and}$$

$$\frac{\partial U^C}{\partial d_t} = -Ak_t + \frac{\gamma f \beta^R p_t}{\left(\beta^R p_t + \beta^C d_t\right)^2} = 0$$

from which:

$$p^* = \frac{\gamma f}{4\beta^R A k_t} \quad \text{and} \quad p^* = \frac{\gamma f}{4\beta^C A k_t}. \tag{3.27}$$

Since $\beta^R \le 1/2$, then $p^* \ge d^*$. From equation (3.2) the constraint on p^* (i.e., $P^* \in (0,1)$) becomes binding for $k_t \le \overline{k}^p = \gamma f/(4\beta^R A)$, meaning $p^* < 1$ for $k_t \ge \overline{k}^p$ and $p^* = 1$ for $k_t \le \overline{k}^p$. If we take $p^* = 1$, the first-order condition for the maximization of U^C becomes

$$\frac{\partial U^C}{\partial d_t} = -Ak_t + \frac{\gamma f \beta^R}{\left(\beta^R + \beta^C d_t\right)^2} = 0$$

from which

$$d_t^* = \left(\frac{1}{1-\beta^R}\right)\sqrt{\frac{\beta^R \gamma f}{Ak_t}} - \frac{\beta^R}{1-\beta^R} \quad \text{for } k_t > \overline{k}^d \quad \text{and}$$

$$d_t^* = 1 \quad \text{for } k_t \le \overline{k}^d,$$

where $\overline{k}^d = \gamma f \beta^R / A$ and $\beta^C = 1 - \beta^R$. Finally since $\beta^R \le 1/2$, then $\overline{k}^d \le \overline{k}^p$. ■

C Proof of Proposition 2

First note that if $sA > \delta + n$, then

$$\frac{\partial k_{t+1}}{\partial k_t} = \begin{cases} \dfrac{1-\delta}{1+n} < 1 & \text{when } k_t \in \left[0, \overline{k}^d\right], \\[2ex] \left(\dfrac{1}{1+n}\right)\left[1-\delta+sA-s\sqrt{\dfrac{\beta^R \gamma fA}{2k_t}}\right] > 0 & \text{when } k_t \in \left[\overline{k}^d, \overline{k}^p\right], \\[2ex] \dfrac{1-\delta+sA}{1+n} > 1 & \text{when } k_t \in \left[\overline{k}^p, \infty\right), \end{cases} \tag{3.28}$$

and

$$\frac{\partial^2 k_{t+1}}{\partial k_t^2} = \begin{cases} 0 & \text{when } k_t \in \left[0, \overline{k}^d\right], \\ \left[\frac{s\sqrt{\beta^R \gamma f A}}{4(1+n)}\right] k^{-3/2}{}_t > 0 & \text{when } k_t \in \left[\overline{k}^d, \overline{k}^p\right], \\ 0 & \text{when } k_t \in \left[\overline{k}^p, \infty\right). \end{cases} \tag{3.29}$$

Suppose that there exists an equilibrium in the range $k_t \in \left[\overline{k}^p, \infty\right)$; then in this equilibrium per capita capital is given by

$$k^{Eu} = \frac{s\gamma f}{2(sA - \delta - n)}.$$

The condition for the existence of this equilibrium is that $\overline{k}^p < k^{Eu}$ (for the sake of simplicity, in the proof of stability of k^{Eu} the frontier of the range is excluded), that is,

$$sA < \frac{\delta + n}{1 - 2\beta^R}. \tag{3.30}$$

This equilibrium is locally unstable since $sA > \delta + n$ (see equation 3.28). If condition (3.30) holds, then $k_{t+1} < k_t$ in $k_t = \overline{k}^p$, while $k_{t+1} = 0$ in $k_t = 0$: at least an equilibrium in the range $\left[0, \overline{k}^d\right]$ therefore exists. The monotonicity and convexity of k_{t+1} with respect to k_t in the range $\left[0, \overline{k}^d\right]$ (see equations 3.28 and 3.29) ensures that there exists only the stable equilibrium $k^{Es} = 0$ in the range, that is, $\partial k_{t+1}/\partial k_t < 1$ in $k^{Es} = 0$. Indeed, in a possible second equilibrium, it should be that $\partial k_{t+1}/\partial k_t > 1$, that is, k_{t+1} should cross from below the bisector; in such a case, equation (3.29) implies that $\partial k_{t+1}/\partial k_t > 1$ for all levels of capital higher than the capital of equilibrium. But this contrasts with the fact that k_{t+1} must be below the bisector in $k_t = \overline{k}^p$.

If $sA < (\delta + n)/(1 - 2\beta^R)$, then $k_{t+1} > k_t$ in $k_t = \overline{k}^p$, and therefore $\overline{k}^p > k^{Eu} > \overline{k}^d$. In fact, because k_{t+1} is monotone, and convex in k_t (see equations 3.28 and 3.29), there is no other equilibrium in $k_t \in \left(\overline{k}^p, \infty\right)$ $\left(k_{t+1} > k_t \text{ in } k_t = \overline{k}^p \text{ and } \partial k_{t+1}/\partial k_t > 1 \text{ in } k_t \in \left(\overline{k}^p, \infty\right)\right)$ and in $k_t \in \left(0, \overline{k}^d\right)$ $\left(k_{t+1} = 0 \text{ in } k_t = 0 \text{ and } \partial k_{t+1}/\partial k_t < 1 \text{ for } k_t \in \left(0, \overline{k}^d\right)\right)$; hence $k_{t+1} < k_t$ in $k_t \in \left(0, \overline{k}^d\right)\right)$. The monotonicity, convexity, and continuity of k_{t+1} with respect to k_t in the range $\left(\overline{k}^d, \overline{k}^p\right)$ ensures that $k^{Eu} \in \left(\overline{k}^d, \overline{k}^p\right)$ is unique and is given by

$$k^{Eu} = \frac{\beta^R s^2 A \gamma f}{(sA - \delta - n)^2}. \quad \blacksquare$$

D Proof of Proposition 3

Given conditions (3.6), proposition 2 states the existence of two equilibria, $k^{Es} = 0$ and $k^{Eu} > 0$, the first locally stable and the second locally unstable, and that growth path is continuous. A simple graphical inspection of figure 3.1 reveals that if $k_0 < k^{Eu}$, then economy will be converging toward $k^{Es} = 0$ while, if $k_0 > k^{Eu}$, then economy will be growing forever. In the latter case $\lim_{t \to +\infty} k_{t+1}/k_t - 1 = sA - \delta - n$. $\blacksquare$

E Proof of Proposition 5

Proposition 4 shows that the dynamics of per capita income is driven by the dynamics of per capita capital. If $sA > \delta + n$, proposition 2 states that there exists a threshold in per capita capital k^{Eu}; the corresponding value in terms of per capita income (denote it y^{Eu}) is such that all the countries with a per capita income under y^{Eu} will see their income converge to f ($k^{Es} = 0$). In contrast, all the countries with a per capita income over y^{Eu} will see their income to grow at the same rate of per capita capital, $sA - \delta + n$, in the long run. In fact, as k_t increases, y_t/k_t tends to constant A (the term $f(1 - \gamma/2)k_t$ tends to zero as $k_t \to +\infty$). The threshold of per capita income y^{Eu} is calculated from the threshold of per capita capital k^{Eu} reported in proposition 2, namely y^{Eu} depends on which range of capital to which the threshold of per capita capital k^{Eu} belongs.

F Proof of Proposition 6

The use of trigger strategies means that the group of *rebels* will respect the agreement of the NBS when the group of *citizens* will make the same action; otherwise, the group of *citizens* deviates from the agreement. That is to say, it takes all the rents from natural resources by allocating a small but positive ϵ of its time to predate the rents; then in the next period the group of *rebels* will play its optimal strategy given in proposition 1. The same rule symmetrically applies for the group of *citizens*. Suppose that the level of capital k_0 is sufficiently low (such a level will be calculated below), that if the group of *rebels* does not respect the agreement of NBS, the next period the optimal strategy of the group of *citizens* will be $d^* = 1$ and therefore also the group of *rebels* will play $p^* = 1$. Then the representative rebel will respect the agreement of the NBS if

$$\underbrace{\sum_{t=0}^{\infty}(\gamma f + Ak_t^{NBS})\rho^t}_{\text{Total payoff from }NBS} \geq \underbrace{Ak_0 + \frac{\gamma f}{\beta^R}}_{\text{Payoff at period 0 from not respecting the }NBS}$$

$$+ \underbrace{\sum_{t=0}^{\infty}\gamma f\rho^t}_{\text{Total payoff from fighting from period 1 to }\infty}, \quad (3.31)$$

where $\rho \in [0,1]$ is the discount factor. The left-hand side of equation (3.31) is the sum of discounted payoffs in the NBS, where k_t^{NBS} is the per capita capital at period t in the NBS. The payoff at period 0 to deviate from the NBS for the representative rebel is equal to $Ak_0 + \gamma f/\beta^R$ (total rents from natural resources is appropriate by *rebels* and equally shared among all rebels). From period 1 to ∞ both groups will allocate all their time to the social conflict. From equation (3.31) this yields

$$A\sum_{t=0}^{\infty} Ak_t^{NBS}\rho^t \geq Ak_0 + \gamma f\left(\frac{1-\beta^R}{\beta^R}\right). \quad (3.32)$$

Since $\beta^R \leq \beta^C$, equation (3.32) shows that if the representative rebel has no incentive to deviate, then also the representative citizens will have no incentive to deviate. From equation (3.4) in the NBS the per capita capital follows:

$$k_{t+1}^{NBS} = \frac{(1-\delta+sA)k_t^{NBS}}{1+n}$$

from which

$$k_t^{NBS} = \left(\frac{1-\delta+sA}{1+n}\right)^t k_0.$$

Therefore

$$A\sum_{t=0}^{\infty} Ak_t^{NBS}\rho^t = A\sum_{t=0}^{\infty}\left[\frac{(1-\delta+sA)\rho}{1+n}\right]^t k_0$$

from which if $\rho \in [(1+n)/(1-\delta+sA),1]$, then $A\sum_{t=0}^{\infty} Ak_t^{NBS}\rho^t \to 0$, and therefore condition (3.32) will be always satisfied.

If $\rho \in [0,(1 + n)/(1 - \delta + sA)]$, then

$$A\sum_{t=0}^{\infty} Ak_t^{NBS}\rho^t = \frac{A(1+n)k_0}{1+n-(1-\delta+sA)\rho}$$

and condition (3.32) becomes

$$\frac{A(1+n)k_0}{1+n-(1-\delta+sA)\rho} \geq Ak_0 + \gamma f\left(\frac{1-\beta^R}{\beta^R}\right),$$

that is,

$$k_0 \geq \left(\frac{1-\beta^R}{A\beta^R}\right)\left[\frac{1+n}{(1-\delta+sA)\rho} - 1\right]\gamma f = \bar{k}^{TSE} \tag{3.33}$$

Equation (3.3) shows that if $\rho \in [(1 + n)/(1 - \delta + sA),1]$, then $\bar{k}^{TSE} > 0$.

Summarizing, for $\rho \in [(1 + n)/(1 - \delta + sA),1]$, the NBS is always sustained as a subgame perfect equilibrium (independent of k_0, while for $\rho \in [0,(1 + n)/(1 - \delta + sA)]$. The k_0 must be not lower than $\bar{k}^{TSE}$; otherwise, for $k_0 < \bar{k}^{TSE}$, social conflict is the outcome.

Given condition (3.6), proposition 3 states that if $k_t \in \left[0, \bar{k}^d\right]$, then $\forall t > 0$ k_t will be in $\left[0, \bar{k}^d\right]$ when $d^* = p^* = 1$. However, condition (3.31) is more binding, and it requires that also *after one period* with $d^* = p^* = 0$ the economy must not reach a level of per capita capital higher than $\bar{k}^d$. This is guaranteed by the condition $0 < k_0 < \bar{k}^f < \bar{k}^d$, where

$$\bar{k}^f = \frac{\beta^R(1+n)\gamma f}{A(1-\delta+sA)} < \bar{k}^d. \blacksquare$$

G Proof of Proposition 7

Under assumptions $\beta^R \leq 1/2$, $sA > \delta + n$, and $k_0 \in \left[0,\bar{k}^f\right]$, proposition 8 states that if $\rho \in [(1 + n)/(1 - \delta + sA),1]$, then there is no social conflict in the economy, meaning $d^* = p^* = 0$. Therefore from equation (3.4),

$$k_{t+1} = \frac{(1-\delta+sA)k_t}{1+n} \tag{3.34}$$

from which $\lim_{t\to\infty} k_{t+1}/k_t - 1 = sA - \delta - n$.

Likewise, if $\rho \in [0, (1 + n)/(1 - \delta + sA)]$ and $k_0 > \bar{k}^{TSE}$, there is no social conflict, meaning $d^* = p^* = 0$, and k_{t+1} is given by equation (3.3): the increase in the per capita capital implies that in the future periods using the trigger strategies the agreement of the NBS will be always self-enforcing. Therefore, again, $\lim_{t \to \infty} k_{t+1}/k_t - 1 = sA - \delta - n$. Otherwise, if $\rho \in [0, (1 + n)/(1 - \delta + sA)]$ and $k_0 \leq \bar{k}^{TSE}$, then $d^* = p^* = 1$, and $\Delta k_{t+1} < 0 \ \forall k_t \in \left(0, \bar{k}^f\right]$ in all periods (see figure 3.3). Hence $\lim_{t \to +\infty} k_t = k^{Es} = 0$. ∎

Acknowledgments

I thank Luciano Boggio, Neri Salvadori, seminar participants in Bologna, Lucca, Milano, Modena, and Pavia, and an anonymous referee for very useful comments on an early draft of the paper. All remaining errors are, of course, mine.

Notes

1. Variables are drawn from the World Economic Indicators 2011 (hereinafter denoted by WDI 2011), Penn World Tables 7.0 (hereinafter denoted by PWT 7.0), Politi VI, Collier and Hoeffler (2004), and Hegre and Sambanis (2006). The country list is provided in appendix A.

2. Collier (2007) discusses how civil wars, one of the main explanations for the very low and stagnant level of income per capita of most sub-Saharan countries, (negatively) depend on the expected growth rate of income. However, Easterly (2009, p. 434) considers Collier's (2007) analysis to be severely biased by the presence of endogeneity (both income growth and civil wars are endogenous in the theoretical model). Miguel et al. (2004) takes into account the issue of endogeneity and shows how negative shocks increase the probability of civil war. All in all, how to control the presence of endogeneity in cross-country regression on civil war is still an open question in the literature due to the lack of a good "instrument" (see Easterly 2009; Blattman and Miguel 2010).

3. The relationship between life expectancy (time horizon of individuals) and civil wars has not been explored in empirical literature; needless to say, a potential reversal causation effect could be at work in the empirical evidence.

4. The common feature of several civil wars is the ethnic difference of parties to the conflict, but the precise role of ethnic factors at the onset of conflicts is not clear (see Blattman and Miguel 2010).

5. Much of the literature points to bad institutions as the key instigator of civil war (see Blattman and Miguel 2010). Again, the main difficulty in testing this hypothesis is the likely presence of endogeneity.

6. Collier (2007) has contributed a large body of works that explains civil war as a result of conflicting claims to rents from natural resources. This literature is extensively surveyed in Blattman and Miguel (2010) and van der Ploeg (2011).

7. Another controversy is the proxy used to measure the abundance of natural resources of countries used by Collier and Hoeffler. In particular, Brunnschweiler and Bulte (2009) argue that the share of nonmanufactures' exports on total exports is a measure of dependence on primary resources and endogenous to civil wars. They shows that the

relationship between natural resource abundance of a country, measured by the sum of future rents from natural resources, and civil war disappears, and the abundance of natural resources of a country explains its level of income per capita once endogneity is taken into account in the analysis. Van de Ploeg (2011), however, argues that also their measure of abundance of natural resources is potentially endogenous.

8. See Esteban and Ray (2008) for a discussion of why ethnicity, and not the levels of individuals' wealth, are generally at the basis of the group formations.

9. In section 6.3, I analyze the case where the stock of natural resources is fixed and not (or partially) renewable; F is therefore the result of an exploitation whose length is limited over time (see Humphreys et al. 2007b).

10. However, in Fiaschi (2008), I analyzed an economy where government uses collected resources to increase capital accumulation of economy.

11. The implicit assumption is that the individual allocation of time is perfectly observable; however, the equal-sharing rule of appropriate income within a group would incentive free-riding behavior.

12. Hirshleifer (2001) discusses in detail alternative technologies of conflict and their implications for the individuals' equilibrium strategies.

13. The dynamics of capital accumulation would be qualitatively the same (i.e., rents from natural resources do not affect capital accumulation at low level of incomes) under the plausible assumption that total rents were decreasing with the intensity of social conflict; but the analysis would be much more involved.

14. It is worth noting that under these assumptions, by an appropriate redefinition of parameter A, individual utility becomes a function of consumption (and not of income).

15. In a more general setting the number of groups should be endogenously determined by the trade-off between the advantage to coordinate actions within a group (due to technology of conflict) and the free-riding behavior within the same group (the benefit of fighting equally shared among all the members of the group). This extension should help explain the empirical evidence that groups are generally composed of members who share some cultural, economic, and/or social characteristics and their number derives from how such factors are distributed among the population (see Weinstein 2005).

16. The first derivative of f_t with respect to π^D easily proves the statement.

17. See, for example, http://en.wikipedia.org/wiki/Movement_for_the_Emancipation_of_the_Niger_Delta.

18. In the calculation the following property of geometric series is used:

$$\sum_{i=0}^{T} iq^i = \frac{1}{1-q}\left[\frac{q(1-q^T)}{1-q} - Tq^{T+1}\right].$$

19. I thank Nicola Meccheri for pointing out this possibility.

References

Acemoglu, D. 1995. Reward structures and the allocation of talent. *European Economic Review* 39: 17–33.

Auty, R., ed. 2001. *Resources Abundance and Economic Development*. New York: Oxford University Press.

Benhabib, J., and A. Rustichini. 1996. Social conflict and growth. *Journal of Economic Growth* 1: 125–42.

Besley, T., and T. Persson. 2009. The incidence of civil war: Theory and evidence. Discussion paper 5. Economic Organisation and Public Policy. STICER, London.

Blattman, C., and E. Miguel. 2010. Civil wars. *Journal of Economic Literature* 48 (1): 3–57.

Binmore, K. 2005. *Natural Justice*. New York: Oxford University Press.

Brunnschweiler, C., and E. Bulte. 2009. Natural resources and violent conflict: Resource abundance, dependence, and the onset of civil wars. *Oxford Economic Papers* 61: 651–74.

Collier, P. 2007. *The Bottom Billion*. Oxford: Oxford Economic Press.

Collier, P., and A. Hoeffler. 2004. Greed and grievance in civil war. *Oxford Economic Papers* 56: 563–95.

Collier, P., A. Hoeffler, and N. Sambanis. 2005. The Collier-Hoeffler model of civil war onset and the case study project research design. In P. Collier, and N. Sambanis, eds., *Understanding Civil War: Evidence and Analysis*, vol. 1. Washington, DC: World Bank, 1–34.

Collier, P., A. Hoeffler, and D. Rohner. 2009. Beyond greed and grievance: Feasibility and civil war. *Oxford Economic Papers* 61: 1–27.

Collier, P., and A. Hoeffler. 2007. Civil war. In T. Sandler and K. Hartley, eds., *Handbook of Defense Economics*, vol. 2. Amsterdam: North Holland.

Collier, P., and A. Hoeffler. 2012. High-value Natural Resources, Development, and Conflict: Channels of Causation. In *High-Value Natural Resources and Peacebuilding*, ed. P. Lujala and S. A. Rustad. London: Earthscan.

de la Croix, D., and D. Dottori. 2008. Easter Island's Collapse: a Tale of a Population Race. *Journal of Economic Growth* 13:27–55.

Dixit, A. 2004. *Lawlessness and Economics*. Princeton: Princeton University Press.

Easterly, W. 2009. Can the West save Africa? *Journal of Economic Literature* 47: 373–447.

Esteban, J., and D. Ray. 2008. On the Salience of Ethnic Conflict. *American Economic Review* 98:2185–2202.

Fiaschi, D. 2008. Natural Resources and Social Conflict: an Explanation of sub-Saharan Countries Stagnation. In *Geography, Structural Change and Economic Development*, ed. P. Commendatori, N. Salvadori, and M. Tamberi. Cheltenham: Elgar.

Gonzales, F. 2007. Effective property rights, conflict and growth. *Journal of Economic Theory* 137 (1): 127–39.

Grossman, H., and M. Kim. 1996. Predation and accumulation. *Journal of Economic Growth* 1 (3): 333–50.

Gylfason, T. 2001. Natural resources, education, and economic development. *European Economic Review* 45: 847–59.

Hegre, H., and N. Sambanis. 2006. Sensitivity analysis of empirical results on civil war onset. *Journal of Conflict Resolution* 50 (4): 508–35.

Hirshleifer, J. 2001. *The Dark Side of the Force: Economic Foundations of Conflict Theory.* Cambridge, UK: Cambridge University Press.

Humphreys, M., J. Sachs, and J. Stiglitz. 2007a. *Escaping the Resource Curse.* New York: Columbia University Press.

Humphreys, M., J. Sachs, and J. Stiglitz. 2007b. What is the problem with natural resource wealth. In M. Humphreys, J. Sachs, and J. Stiglitz, eds., *Escaping the Resource Curse.* New York: Columbia University, 1–20. Press.

McBride, M., and S. Skaperdas. 2007. Explaining conflict in low-income countries: Incomplete contracting in the shadow of the future. In M. Gradstein and K. A. Konrad, eds., *Institutions and Norms in Economic Development.* Cambridge: MIT Press, 141–62.

Mehlum, H., K. Moene, and R. Torvik. 2003. Predator or prey? Parasitic enterprises in economic development. *European Economic Review* 47: 275–94.

Mehlum, H., K. Moene, and R. Torvik. 2006. Institutions and the resources curse. *Economic Journal* 116: 1–20.

Miguel, E., S. Satyanath, and E. Sergenti. 2004. Economic shocks and civil conflict: An instrumental variables approach. *Journal of Political Economy* 112: 725–53.

Minter, A. 1994. *Apartheid's Contras: An Inquiry into the Roots of War in Angola and Mozambique.* London: Zed.

Montalvo, J. G., and M. Reynal-Querol. 2005. Ethnic polarization, potential conflict and civil war. *American Economic Review* 95: 796–816.

Murphy, K., A. Shleifer, and R. Vishny. 1993. The allocation of talent: Implication for growth. *Quarterly Journal of Economics* 106: 503–30.

Muthoo, A. 2004. A model of the origins of basic property rights. *Games and Economic Behavior* 49: 288–312.

Olsson, O. 2006. Diamonds are a rebel's best friend. *World Economy* 29: 1133–49.

Olsson, O. 2007. Conflict diamonds. *Journal of Development Economics* 82: 267–86.

Penn World Table Version 7.0. 2011. Philadelphia: A. Heston, R. Summers and Bettina Aten, Center for International Comparisons of Production, Income and Prices at the University of Pennsylvania.

Polity IV Project. 2010. M. Marshall and K. Jaggers, Political Instability Task Force, Societal-Systems Research, and Center for Systemic Peace.

de Ree, J., and E. Nillesen. 2009. Aiding violence of peace? The Impact of Foreign Aid on the Risk of Civil Conflict in Sub-Saharan Africa. *Journal of Development Economics* 88: 301–13.

Ron, J. 2005. Paradigm in distress? Primary commodities and civil war. *Journal of Conflict Resolution* 49: 443–50.

Ross, M. 2012. *The Oil Curse: How Petroleum Wealth Shapes the Development of Nations.* Princeton: Princeton University Press.

Sachs, J., and A. M. Warner. 2001. The curse of natural resources. *European Economic Review* 45: 827–38.

Sambanis, N. 2003. Using case studies to expand the theory of civil war. CPR Working Paper Series 5. Syracuse University.

Tangeras, T., and N. P. Lagerlof. 2009. Ethnic diversity, civil war and redistribution. *Scandinavian Journal of Economics* 45: 827–38.

Weinstein, J. 2005. Resources and the information problem in rebel recruitment. *Journal of Conflict Resolution* 49: 598–624.

World Development Indicators. 2011. Washington, DC: World Bank.

van der Ploeg, F. 2011. Natural resources: Curse or blessing? *Journal of Economic Literature* 49: 366–420.

4 A Game of Thrones: Power Structure and the Stability of Regimes

Ruixue Jia and Pinghan Liang

4.1 Introduction

It's a long intellectual history that the power structure might affect the stability of regime. In chapter 4 of *The Prince*, Niccolo Machiavelli famously investigated "Why the Kingdom of Darius, Conquered by Alexander, Did Not Rebel against the Successors of Alexander at His Death." He compared the contemporary Ottoman regime and French regime. In terms of power structure, the Ottoman domain was more centralized, and "once it is conquered, great ease in holding it. . . ." French domains were decentralized, and "one can easily enter there by gaining over some baron of the kingdom . . . but if you wish to hold it afterwards, you meet with infinite difficulties." Scholars in the Eastern world held similar views. Ch'ien Mu, one of the greatest historians and philosophers in twentieth-century China, also connected the power structure with the different fortunes of the Tang and Song dynasties, whose capitals were lost in similar sudden disastrous military failures (Ch'ien 1982). While the decentralized Tang dynasty succeeded in gathering local strength to recover the capital from the conspirator generals, the highly centralized Song regime lost half of the country to the northern Tungusic invaders.

In the modern world, even though no large threat from foreign invaders exists, corrupt schemes of public officials remain a worry of governments in many developing countries. The traditional wisdom of protecting a regime through centralization from the machinations of elites outside of government still has merit. In this chapter we formally incorporate the insights of Machiavelli and a government's conceivable concerns for plots against its regime in a game-theoretic model to study the relationship between the power structure and the occurrence and outcome of plots, in particular, *coups d'état*.

We set up a sequential game between a plotter, or group of plotters in the case of a coup, and the existing government. But mostly we will focus on the power structure of the government, namely by the extent of decentralization into local jurisdictions. We introduce, in a multiple-rounds contest, the possibility of bargaining. A plotter decides whether to carry out a covert activity against the incumbent two-layer government, and the central government optimally invests to defend itself. If the plotter succeeds, he will take over the resources held by the central incumbent, form a new government, and bargain with the local government over a peaceful resolution. The novel part of our model is that the resistance decision is made by a strategic player—the local government in our model. We show that even though each player has limited commitment in that it cannot commit not to stage a civil conflict after the negotiation, honoring a peace agreement always dominates in times of war. Conditional on the power structure within the original government, the consolidation of a post–military coup government as a restoration of the deposed government is possible. As a result our model predicts a negative relationship between decentralization and the duration of new regime conditional on a successful outcome.

Consequently the power structure affects the incentives of plotters in attempting an attack. A plotter might consider whether he can win the conflict against the central government, and if winning, how long he can hold the office. In a more centralized country, it may be difficult for a plotter to defeat a strong central government, but it may be easy for him to hold the office after winning. So centralization entails both high opportunity costs and high available rents for plotters.

The key intuition underlying our main results is the double effects of limited commitment. First, in the game of thrones the central government and the local government move sequentially. But resistance against the post–military-coup government is a strategic decision made by the last mover, the local government. The local governor cannot ex ante commit to fight against a successful plotter, thus equal shares of power might not suffice to incentivize the local government to deter a plotter. Second, neither the new regime nor the local government can commit not to resort to violent conflicts after negotiation, thus any peaceful agreements have to be ex post optimal for any player, with the weak player guaranteed with some minimal payoff. In effect the expected payoff of a plotter is bounded and weakly increasing with the strength of the incumbent central government. While the first effect encourages a plotter, the second one reduces the expected payoff to a plotter. Therefore we obtain the region of decentralization that rent-seeking concerns dominate opportunity cost concerns, and establish an inverse-U relationship between decentralization and threats.

We apply our model to analyze an important kind of threat to regimes in the modern world: coups d'état. Coups d'état are sudden and short-term actions with long-term impacts. There is a large body of research on an important type of civil conflict: civil war. However, the key difference between a civil war and a coup d'état is that the former is more grassroots-based whereas the techniques of executing a coup are available only to a small group of elites, usually military forces (Calvert 1979). Moreover the coup plotter needs to consolidate his position and seek legitimacy by getting support from other bodies of power, usually regional rulers, courts, and the supporters of former government. Therefore political power structure plays a role in forming the post–coup government, and a rational plotter will take this into account when plotting a coup. Using cross-sectional data from non–OECD countries since 1975, we find that our theoretical predictions to a large extent are supported

Generally, in contrast with the most studies on decentralization, which focus on a coup's effects on the accountability of local governments such as the provision of public goods,[1] our model argues that conditional on the initial power structure, decentralization might increase incentives for the plotter and jeopardize political stability. This negative consequence should be taken into account when implementing any reform of government structure.

The rest of this chapter is organized as follows: section 4.2 reviews the related works, section 4.3 lays out the model and presents the analysis and the main results, and section 4.4 applies our model to study coups d'état. Within the latter section, section 4.4.1 presents three country cases of military coups, in which the power structure hadnegative consequences for the coups, and section 4.4.2 empirically tests our model with the cross-country data on coups. Section 4.5 concludes.

4.2 Related Literature

On the role of the power structure in defending a regime, Machiavelli's famous view about the relationship between government structure and regime vulnerability receives surprisingly little attention. Most literature treats the regime as an integral part when facing external threats, and ignores the internal organization of government.[2] Few works in the defense literature consider the economy as a network, and investigate the robustness of economy against external shocks. For instance, Frey and Luechinger (2004) and Dreher and Fischer (2010) show that decentralization of an economy can diversify the risk of terrorist attacks and consequently reduce the incentives of terrorists. While in this line of research the player (node) has a passive role, we take that notion a step further by considering the strategic incentives of the players within a government in that the local government cannot ex ante commit to fight against the plotter.

The scholarship on military coups connects socioeconomic and political variables with the incidence of coups to look for the underlying structural factors, just to name a few, Fossum (1967) and Hoadley (1973) on coups d'état in Latin America, and then Wells (1974), Jackman (1978), Johnson et al. (1984), Jenkins and Kposowa (1990), and Lunde (1991) on African coups. These results contribute to our understanding about the incidence and role of military coups, but have been subject to many controversies about validity and interpretation (Jackman et al., 1986) due to the lack of a formal strategic foundation. However, the researchers in development studies mainly focus on the impact of coups on long-term economic development (Londdregan and Poole, 1990; Alesina, Olzer, Boubini, and Swagel, 1996; Fosu, 2002). To the best of our knowledge, there has been no game-theoretical analysis studying the effects of centralization/decentralization on the stability of regimes against coups d'état.

Some political scientists stress interactions between the military side and the civilian government (e.g., Huntington 1957; Luttwak 1969; and Hettne 1980)[3] and recognize the uncertainty in staging coups (O'Kane 1993). An emerging body of literature in political economy formulizes the civilian–military relationship. Leon (2009a) studies the relationship between the likelihood of war and the coups, Collier and Hoeffler (2007) and Leon (2009b) establish the empirically nonmonotonic relationship between military spending and the incidence of coups, Acemoglu et al. (2010) and Besley and Robinson (2010) analyze the government's trade-off in building up a strong army when taking into account the risk of coups d'état, Bhave and Kingston (2010) examine the role of army in elite-popular relationship, and Bueno de Mesquita et al. (2003) and Gandhi and Przeworski (2007) explore the role of winning coalition in the survival of political leaderships. We follow the tradition of political scientists in looking at a structural factor that may *facilitate* military coups, the power structure.

Noteworthy, as clarified by previous literature, there are many factors underlying coups d'état. We do not claim that government structure is the only cause or the most important cause of any particular coup. Instead, we attempt to explore regularities between the power structure and the incidence and outcome of plots against regimes.

4.3 The Model

4.3.1 Environment

There are three players in our game of thrones: central government (C), local government (L), and the plotter (P). A two-layer government consisting of C and L^4 controls the exogenously given fiscal resources, which flow in two periods: the current revenue y and the future revenue y', realized in the second period (e.g., the discoveries of oil fields whose revenues mostly are realized in the future). Let s and $1 - s$ denote the share of fiscal revenues controlled by C and L, respectively. Each player is risk neutral and attempts to maximize his own payoff. The strength of P (x_P) is assumed to be exogenously given. In the first period, given x_P, P decides whether to carry out a conspiracy against the central government. To defend himself, C can invest in defense, including policemen, civil guards, mobilizing the core supporters by target unproductive social spending, and so forth.[5] In the second period, if P succeeds, he might meet resistance from L. Thus he will bargain with L over the peaceful resolution, and a civil war will occur if either P or L wants to engage into it. In effect, L could be understood as the deposed government that still controls some resources. The key point here is that this player cannot commit to fight contest the new government after a successful plot. To be more concrete, we state the time structure as follows:

Timing There are two periods in our sequential game, and each period is divided into two stages.

Period I In stage 1, P moves first by choosing between conspiracy and subordination. Under subordination, P retains the status payoff x_P. If P undertakes a conspiracy, he wins with probability $x_P/(x_P + x_C)$, where x_C is the defense effort later made by C.

In stage 2, if P makes the challenge, C allocates $x_C < sy$ to internal security to fight against P. C retains power and enjoys the sum of payoff $\pi_C = s[y + E(y')]$ whenever P chooses subordination or the plot fails. If

C fails, P grabs power and gets π_C.[6] The payoff to the loser is normalized to zero. The game ends if the coup is defeated by C. Otherwise,
the successful P establishes a new government, and period II (stage 3)
commences.

Period II   In stage 3, the future rent y' is realized, L and P bargain over
the terms of peaceful resolution, namely they simultaneously propose
an offer to the counterpart. The plotter returns the power to the deposed
government (*compromise*) if the terms are in accordance with L's offer.
The plotter consolidates his position if the terms are in accordance with
his offer. In other words, L *surrenders* to the plotter. If no one accepts
the other's offer, the *status quo* resources distribution maintains. After
the bargaining procedure L and P can decide whether to stage a violent
conflict. If at least one side decides to engage into conflict, we enter
stage 4, the onset of war.

In stage 4, both sides simultaneously invest resources x_L and x'_P in
the war, respectively. The payoff to the winner of the war is the total
resources minus the investments in the war. L wins the war and restores
the overthrown government with probability $x_L/(x'_P + x_L)$, while P
unifies the country with the complementary probability.

All the information about the strengths and revenues is public.
Therefore we can derive a subgame perfect Nash equilibrium in our
complete information sequential game. We can get the results regarding the duration of power by solving stages 4 and 3, and the results for
the risk of plots by solving stages 2 and 1.

4.3.2   Length of Power

Stage 4 War   If the war occurs in stage 4, the prize to the winner is
the total fiscal revenue $y + y'$ minus the unproductive war investment
$x'_P + x_L$. A would choose x'_P to maximize

$$\frac{x'_P}{x'_P + x_L}[y + y' - x'_P - x_L]. \tag{4.1}$$

Similarly L selects x_L to maximize

$$\frac{x_L}{x'_P + x_L}[y + y' - x'_P - x_L]. \tag{4.2}$$

The first-order conditions for both sides are as follows:

$$x_i = \sqrt{x_{-i}(y + y')} - x_{-i}, \qquad i = L, P. \tag{4.3}$$

First we look at the interior solutions, namely both players have sufficient resources to invest in the war. In equilibrium both players will invest the same amount in the confrontation. Hence we get the investment in the civil war for either player as

$$x'_P = x_L = \frac{y + y'}{4}.$$

Both players have an equal probability to win the war, and the expected payoff to each player is

$$E\pi_i = \frac{(y + y')}{4}.$$

To make this solution feasible, the optimal investment in the war cannot exceed the resources in the hand of each party at that stage. Thus we need:

$$\frac{y + y'}{4} \le \min\{(1 - s)(y + y'), s(y + y')\},$$

which is equivalent to

$$s \in \left[\frac{1}{4}, \frac{3}{4} \right].$$

If $s \le 1/4$, which indicates that the country is very decentralized, then the plotter will be resource constrained. In equilibrium we have

$$x'_P = s(y + y') \quad \text{and} \quad x_L = \left(-s + \sqrt{s} \right)(y + y'),$$

$$E\pi_P = \sqrt{s} \left(1 - \sqrt{s} \right)(y + y') \quad \text{and} \quad E\pi_L = \left(1 - \sqrt{s} \right)^2 (y + y').$$

Since $E\pi_P > s(y + y')$, the expected prize from a war exceeds the current resources at hands, thus the resource-constrained P has the incentive to fight against the local government.

Then again, if $s > 3/4$, that is, is a highly centralized country, the local government will be resource constrained. In equilibrium we have

$$x'_P = \left[\sqrt{1 - s} - (1 - s) \right](y + y') \quad \text{and} \quad x_L = (1 - s)(y + y'),$$

$$E\pi_P = \left(1 - \sqrt{1 - s} \right)^2 (y + y') \quad \text{and} \quad E\pi_L = \sqrt{1 - s} \left(1 - \sqrt{1 - s} \right)(y + y').$$

Similarly, since $E\pi_L > (1-s)(y+y')$, for the local government conflicts dominate status quo payoffs, thus the local governor prefers to challenge the plotter's new government. In general, the resource-constrained player always has the incentive to challenge the strong counterpart and to invest all resources in the war.

Stage 3 Bargaining   Now we turn to stage 3 in which P and L negotiate over the allocation of the available resource. The outcome of war in stage 4 actually is the outside option for each party. A usual problem in bargaining over peaceful settlement is that the player cannot commit not to resort to violent confrontation after receiving transfers from the other side. From stage 4 it is clear that under an extreme imbalance of power, the weak player always has the incentive to challenge the strong player since the expected prize from the conflict overrides the status quo payoff. Therefore any successful transfer scheme t is self-enforcing if it guarantees each side with at least one-quarter of the total resource. Thus a sufficient condition for a peace resolution is that the resources' distribution between the two players after the enforcement of the peace agreement not be too skewed. In particular, the weak player may use the threat of war to grab some resources from the strong party and secure a minimal payoff level.

The intuition is that for a giventotal resource, any gain for one player implies a loss for the other. On the one hand, a transfer will increase the receiver's opportunity cost of conflict; on the other hand, it will reduce the prize if the receiver starts a war. Ultimately, even if the initial power structure is severely skewed to one player, the receiver will not stage a violent conflict if his after-transfer payoff exceeds the expected value of winning a war.

Then we can specify the bargaining process. The bargaining structure is simple: Both players propose a counterpart offer. If offer t_L (resp., t_P) from L (resp., P) is accepted by the other side, then P (resp., L) *compromises* (resp., *surrenders*) in exchange of the offer promised. If no offer is accepted, then both sides keep their own resources and decide whether to stage the war.[7]

P will propose offer t_P if the payoff from compromise is higher than that from war:

$$\frac{y+y'}{4} \le s(y+y') - t_P. \tag{4.4}$$

And the local government will accept if

$$t_P \geq \frac{y+y'}{4}. \tag{4.5}$$

Thus peace is feasible if L can be guaranteed that the transfer exceeds the expected payoff from the war. It is also straightforward to see that the compromise is possible if $s \leq 1/2$. Similarly surrender is feasible as long as $s \geq 1/2$ is satisfied. Moreover, if we take into account each player's status quo payoff, then it is straightforward to see that whenever $1/4 \leq s \leq 3/4$, both L and P prefer status quo to accepting the offer from the other side. In this range, L has neither the incentive to challenge P nor the willingness to offer P enough to get compromise. Thus the status quo maintains, the plotter consolidates his position and gets $V = s(y + y')$.

If $s < 1/4$, meaning that buying L's surrender is not feasible and P has the incentive to start a war if no transfer is offered, then L can offer P the t_L that is similar to (4.5), and A will accept it. The outcome is a compromise, whereby the plotter returns the power to the civilian government, and keeps $V = (y + y')/4$. If instead $s > 3/4$, due to the sharp imbalance of power, L has the incentive to start a war against the plotter. P can consolidate his position by promising $t_P = (y + y')/4$. The payoff to P is thus $V = 3(y + y')/4$.

We summarize the results in the proposition below and figure 4.1.

Proposition 1 If $s < 1/4$, then the only outcome of peace agreement is a compromise where the plotter hands over power to the local government. If $s \in [1/4, 3/4]$, then the status quo persists and the plotter retains power. If $s > 3/4$, the only negotiation outcome is that the local government surrenders and the plotter consolidates. Moreover the value to the plotter (i.e., payoff to P) is

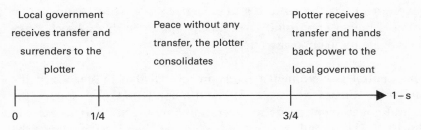

Figure 4.1
Bargaining solution

$$
V = \begin{cases} \dfrac{1}{4}(y+y') & \text{if } s < \dfrac{1}{4}, \\[2mm] s(y+y') & \text{if } \dfrac{1}{4} \leq s \leq \dfrac{3}{4}, \\[2mm] \dfrac{3}{4}(y+y') & \text{if } s > \dfrac{3}{4}. \end{cases} \tag{4.6}
$$

This proposition shows that the payoff to the plotter is weakly increasing as the share of the central government in fiscal revenues raises. This is straightforward since once the plotter succeeds, he takes over the resource of the overthrown central government, so s measures his strength provided that the plot succeeds. Because of the threat of wasteful violent conflict, the payoff to the plotter (local government) in an even very centralized (decentralized) country is still bounded from above. Since $1 - s$ measures the degree of decentralization of a state, we can establish the relationship between the government structure and the length of the plotter's power, conditional on a successful plot.

Prediction 1 *The length of power after a successful plot is longer (shorter) in more centralized (decentralized) countries.*

This proposition may shed light on the survival of new regimes once the plotter wins. It implies that in more centralized countries, a violent governmental transformation has persistent effects.

4.3.3 The Threats to the Regime

In the analysis above we showed that the length of power is longer in more centralized countries because the plotter has the advantages of entering in peace negotiations with the local governments. Hence centralization provides ambitious plotters with big prizes and encourages conspiracies. However, it is also intuitively true that a powerful central government has the resources to defeat plotters. Thus centralization entails a higher opportunity cost for the plotter. In this subsection we investigate these opposing effects.

The Central Government's Decision   Recall that in stage 2, if the plotter has already decided to follow through with the conspiracy, the central government needs to determine how much effort to exert to thwart P. The central government's objective then is to maximize the expected payoff:

$$\max \frac{x_C}{x_C + x_P} \{s[y + E(y')] - x_C\} \tag{4.7}$$

subject to $\quad x_C \leq sy.$ $\qquad\qquad\qquad\qquad\qquad\qquad\qquad$ (4.8)

Equation (4.7) shows that the benefits to C will be deducted by an investment in defense. Moreover C can only use current resources to combat the conspirators. It is straightforward to derive the best-response function of C from the first-order condition as follows:

$$x_C = \begin{cases} \sqrt{x_P[s(y + E(y')) + x_P]} - x_P & \text{if } E(y') \leq \overline{E(y')}, \\ sy & \text{otherwise.} \end{cases} \tag{4.9}$$

Here $\overline{E(y')}$ is the threshold level defined by

$$\overline{E(y')} = y + s\frac{y^2}{x_P}. \tag{4.10}$$

The investment decision of C not only depends on the expected future revenues $E(y')$ but also is constrained by the current available resources y. When the current resources are high ($E(y) \leq \overline{E(y')}$)—namely both the benefits of future control and the current resources are high/ low—the budget constraint (4.8) is slack and we have first equation of (4.9). In this situation, C optimally invests in defense as the best response to conspiracies, so x_C is a function with respect to x_P. Otherwise, when the current revenues are low—the benefits for future control are high, but the current resources are low—the budget constraint (4.8) is binding. Although C would like to invest more to ensure his control, his hands are tied by the available resources, thus we have the second equation of (4.9).

This threshold level (4.10) is determined by the current revenues y. The larger the y, the more resources C has to carry out his ambition, the higher the benefits for future control of the government. Moreover this threshold level is increasing with respect to s. So the larger the share of the central government in fiscal revenues, the more C can use to defend himself.

The Plotter's Decision   We categorized the plotter's decision as stage 1. Recall that P will carry out a conspiracy if and only if the expected payoff from the plots exceeds his current resources, that is,

$$\frac{x_P}{x_C + x_P} E[V] \geq x_P, \tag{4.11}$$

where $E[V]$ is the expected value to the attacker, the continuation value defined in (4.6) in expectation term. Since the RHS of (4.11) is given, the LHS of (4.11) represents the incentive of a plotter, which also measures the threats. Thus we name (4.11) the *plot condition*.

Incidences of Plots   We substitute (4.6) into (4.11) and get the following conditions of the incidence of plots.

1. In the centralized regime $(s > 3/4)$, $E[V] = 3[y + E(y')]/4$, the plot condition (4.11) becomes

$$\frac{x_P}{x_C + x_P}\left[\frac{3}{4}(y + E[y'])\right] \geq x_P. \tag{4.12}$$

2. In the intermediately centralized regime $(3/4 \geq s > 1/4)$, $E[V] = s[y + E(y')]$. The plot condition is

$$\frac{x_P}{x_C + x_P}[s(y + E[y'])] \geq x_P. \tag{4.13}$$

3. In the decentralized regime $(s \leq 1/4)$, $E[V] = [y + E(y')]/4$. The plot condition becomes

$$\frac{x_P}{x_C + x_P}\left[\frac{1}{4}(y + E[y'])\right] \geq x_P, \tag{4.14}$$

where x_C is defined by (4.9), the optimal response of C. It is straightforward to see that the probability of successful coups $(x_P/(x_P + x_C))$ is decreasing in s because the defense investment x_C is strictly increasing in s. This implies that other things being equal, the probability of a successful plot is higher in more decentralized countries.

For cases 1 and 3, the prize for a successful plot, that is, V, is invariant with respect to s. For the plotter, decentralization only raises the probability of winning. Thus the return to a plot increases and conspiracies become likely.

However, when the extent of decentralization is in the intermediate range $(3/4 \geq s > 1/4)$, on the one hand, C can invest more to defeat conspiracies, so the opportunity cost of coup plotters increases; on the other hand, the available rents to a successful conspiracy also raise. The following proposition shows that in this range the latter effect dominates, regardless of the specification of x_C in (4.9).

Proposition 2 In an intermediately centralized country $(3/4 \geq s > 1/4)$, the incentive of a plotter increases with respect to s.

Proof The threat to regimes can be measured by the incentive of a plotter, which is the LHS of (4.13). Differentiating this formula, we have

$$\frac{d}{ds}\left\{\frac{x_P}{x_P + x_C}[s(y + E(y'))]\right\} = \frac{y + E(y')}{(x_P + x_C)^2} x_P \left[x_P + x_C - s\frac{dx_C}{ds}\right].$$

The sign of the formula above is determined by the terms in the bracket: $x_P + x_C - s(dx_C/ds)$. If the current revenues are low, $x_C = sy$, then this term becomes $x_P > 0$. Otherwise, we substitute $x_C = \sqrt{x_P s[y + E(y')] + x_P^2} - x_P$ from (4.9) into the differentiation above and get

$$\frac{s x_P\left[(y + E[y']) + x_P^2\right]/2}{\sqrt{x_P[s(y + E[y']) + x_P]}} > 0.$$

We see that in both specifications the differentiation results are positive. Thus the incentive of a plotter is monotonically increasing in s.

Therefore, when a country is intermediately centralized, the temptation from high rents outweighs the disincentive effect from a strong government. The plotter would be less likely to take risks as the state becomes even more decentralized. We are led to the following prediction:

Prediction 2 *In either highly centralized or highly decentralized countries the threats to a regime are higher as countries become more decentralized. For intermediate centralized countries, however, the threats increase (decrease) as the country becomes further centralized (decentralized).*

This nonlinear relationship is illustrated in figure 4.2, which describes the incentive to a potential plotter in different regimes. The nonmonotonic relationship between the extent of decentralization and the risk of conspiracies suggests that the effects of decentralization on political stability vary with the initial condition. If a country is already highly centralized, the implementation of decentralization reform may make the regime vulnerable and increase the threats. This also works if a decentralized country keeps on decentralizing. However, decentralization might contribute to stabilizing a regime when the allocation of power lies in the intermediate range.

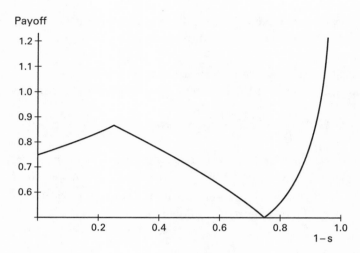

Figure 4.2
Incentive of a plotter ($y + Ey'$ is normalized to 2)

4.4   Coups d'État

We have developed a model of sequential contests among strategic players to study the impacts of power structures on the risk and consequences of conspiracies. In the modern world, domestic challenges to leadership are an increasingly important threat to political survival, and the coups d'état is a salient form of this kind of threats.

Coups d'état are sudden and short-term actions with long-term impacts. Some countries may even be trapped in the "coup trap," a key example being Bolivia, which experienced ten coups from1975 to 2009. Bolivia's experience suggests that there might exist country-specific structural factors underlying the occurrence of coups. There is a large body of research on an important type of civil conflict: civil war.[8] However, the coup d'état is more likely to be about power struggles among political elites. Therefore general economic and institutional factors alone (national income, poverty, inequality, ethnic polarization, weak institutions, etc.)[9] are unlikely to be the explanations of coups d'état. For instance, several countries with weak institutions and high ethnic cleavages rarely experience coups d'état;[10] resources-abundance countries also have quite different histories of coups.[11] Even though a military coup is a sudden unconstitutional attack that aims at deposing the government, the plotter still faces the matter of what type of government to establish. Moreover the plotter needs to consolidate his position and seek legitimacy by getting support from other power brokers, such as regional rulers, courts, and the supporters of the former government. Therefore the political power structure has a role in forming the post–coup government, and a rational plotter will take this into account when planning a coup.

Various cases suggest that the grab of executive power at a national level is rarely the end of a coup d'état. Rather, the interaction between the post–coup government and other power bodies, frequently occurs after a successful coup. This interaction has significant long-term effects, like the occurrence of civil war, the consolidation of junta, and the length of regime.

If we consider the power of coup plotters—for example, the military forces controlled by a conspirator general, as is exogenously determined by the need of national defense or suppressing rebellion—then the occurrences and outcomes of coups d'état provide a suitable dataset to empirically examine our theoretical predictions regarding power structure and political stability. In subsection 4.4.1 we use three cases of military coups to demonstrate the interactions between the successful coup plotters and other power bodies, such as the supporters of the overthrown government, regional governments, and courts. Then we formally test our theory in subsection 4.4.2.

4.4.1 Case Illustrations

Nigeria, 1965 to 1966   When Nigeria gained its independence from United Kingdom in 1960, it was a federal republic consisting of three regions: northern, eastern, and western, dominated by the ethnicities Hausa, Igbo, and Yoruba, respectively. The strong regionalism made the federal government, as well as Nigeria as a unity, especially vulnerable. Corruption, controversy over the past election, and various crises became the main theme of political life in the early years of new independent Nigeria.

The history of military intervention in Nigeria's politics started on January 15, 1966, when a group of young Igbo officers succeeded in murdering most Hausa and Yoruba senior officers and political leaders. Major-General J. T. U. Aguiyi-Ironsi escaped the coup and assumed the reins of power. However, later the dissatisfaction from other ethnicities at regional level, especially that of Yoruba, led to a successful countercoup under the head of northern military officers on July 29, 1966, which killed many Igbo officers and civilians including Major-General Ironsi. The most senior northern officer, Lieutenant Colonel Yakubu Gowon, was chosen as the head of state.

The violence against the Igbo increased their desire for autonomy and protection from the military's wrath. Lt. Col. Odumegwu Ojukwu, military governor of the Igbo dominant eastern region, refused to recognize Gowon. In order to win public acceptance for his regime, Gowon sought a compromise with Ojukwu. However, Ojukwu finally decided to secede from Nigeria and refused to attend the meeting over peaceful settlement. Further attempts at peaceful resolution all failed. On May 30, Ojukwu declared the state of Biafra, and the 30-month civil war started, which would end with the death of more than one million people and the re-conquered southeastern Igbo region.

Congo, 1960 to 1965 Congo (Kinshasa) achieved independence from Belgian on 1960, with Joseph Kasavubu and Patrice Lumumba as elected president and premier minister, respectively. However, soon this new state was trapped into political crisis featured by intense regional conflict and especially the secession of the most resource-rich province, Katanga. The leadership crisis between Kasavubu and Lumumba then occurred only two months after independence. On September 14, 1960, the Chief of Staff of the Army, Joseph Mobutu seized power in a military coup, suspending Parliament and the Constitution. Lumumba later is assassinated in Katanga on January 17, 1961.

Though Mobutu succeeded in staging the coup and gaining the support of Western governments, he still faced the challenges from various local powers and the supporters of Lumumba. In particular, Lumumba's Vice Prime Minister Antoine Gizenga set up a rival government in the eastern city of Stanleyville with the help of pro-Lumumba forces and the recognition of Soviet bloc countries. Later Congo's central government arrived at a compromise with Gizenga's regime (Blum 2003), and Lumumba was proclaimed a national hero and martyr by Mobotu. Only under UN military intervention did the secession of Katanga end.

On November 25, 1965, with the help of the CIA, Mobutu seized power from President Kasa-Vubu by a coup d'état. Mobutu established a one-party state, banning all other political organizations except his own. The former Premier Minister Tshombe fled. Although Mobutu succeeded in taking power, his position was soon threatened by the mutinies by the supporters of Tshombe in Kisangani (formerly Stanleyville), one in 1966 and the other in 1967. After the crush of 1967 mutiny, Congo settled into political stability for the next three decades, over which Mobutu led one of the most enduring dictatorial and corrupt regimes in Africa, until his final depose by a rebellion in 1996.

Pakistan Since the independence of Pakistan in 1947, this country experienced three successful military coups. And for more than thirty years over the past six decades, Pakistan was ruled by a government headed by officers. By the Constitution, the Supreme Court of Pakistan is the final arbiter of legal and constitutional disputes. However, the Supreme Court didn't stand against the coups; instead, it managed to maintain its independence and some authority by cooperating with the army.

Because the Supreme Court gains strong support from the people and the elite, even the leaders of these three coups, General Ayub Khan, Muhammad Zia-ul-Haq, and Pervez Musharraf, respectively, had to rely on it to gain legitimacy in ruling the country. In exchange, the Supreme Court maintained its institutional authority and influence over some political events, and established it as the de facto check on military power. In 1977 and 2000, respectively, the Supreme Court rejected the suits from the overthrown government who challenged the legitimacy of the coups, and legalized the coup on the ground of the Doctrine of State Necessity. In the latter case the Supreme Court asserted that it had the inherent power to examine the validity of Musharraf's orders, and used the principle "that the government should be by the consent of the governed, whether voters or not,"[12] to validate the military coup. Musharraf then publicly submitted to the judgment of the Court, retained executive and legislative authority with the promise to hold election within three years. The Supreme Court further allowed Musharraf to stand for elections in October 2007, in which he succeeded to become the constitutional president.

This compromise between the Supreme Court and Musharraf ended soon after the electoral victory of Musharraf, since he attempted to suspend the Constitution and fire the Chief Justice, Iftikhar Muhammad Chaudhry. The Supreme Court boycotted this move and sparked the protests among lawyers; then the protests spread to the whole country. The protesters and opposition parties took out huge rallies against Musharraf and his tenure as army chief was also challenged in the courts. Musharraf soon lost his popularity. In the following year the opposition parties won the overwhelming victory in the general election. Finally, on August 2008, under the threat from the opposition parties of carrying out impeachment, Musharraf had to announce his resignation. The judges of the Supreme Court who were removed by Musharraf were restored in 2009.

4.4.2 Empirical Analysis

In this subsection we bring the theory in section 4.3 to the data of coups d'état to statistically test the derived predictions 1 and 2. As Luttwak (1968) observes, coups d'état almost all occur in developing countries. Therefore we will highlight non–OECD countries in empirical analysis.

Data   In this subsection we describe the data and measures we used for the econometric analysis. The dataset on decentralization, outcomes of coups, and various control variables available to use covers up to 67 non–OECD countries.[13]

Ideally, we should test the theoretical prediction with panel data analysis. However, the lack of annual fiscal decentralization data among non–OECD countries considerably limits the ability to implement this analysis.[14] Moreover there is very little variation of the extent of political decentralization in most countries within this period. Decentralization of a country is measured by the log of the average subnational government expenditure/revenue share in a country between 1970 and 2000. These data have been collected and used in Enikolopov and Zhuravskaya (2007). We think this might measure the de facto distribution of resources across hierarchies within a government.

The data on coups come primarily from a recent dataset collected by Powell and Thyne (2011). It reports both successful and failed coups since 1950. There are 211 coups taking place in the dataset during the period 1975 to 2009. No coup d'état attempt ever led to civil war within this period.

We calculate the length of a military power after a successful coup based on the information on regime changes in the Database of Political Institutions (Keefer 2005). It provides the detailed information on the change of national leadership in each country from 1975 to 2009. We calculate two measures for the length of power, by ruler and by regime. For instance, Jerry Rawlings ruled Ghana as a military dictator in 1981 to 1992 and then as the elected president in 1992 to 2001. In this case

Table 4.1
Summary statistics

	Mean	Standard deviation	Min	Max
Average coups in a country	1.61	2.28	0	10
Average of length of power	5.56	5.66	0.80	27
Log(subnational exp. share of total gov exp)	2.32	0.99	0.43	4.01
Military spending share (% of GDP)	2.81	2.14	0.26	13.8
Government expenditure share (% of GDP)	20.6	9.96	5.00	69.8
Population sizes (1,000)	6614	8773	621	61704
Political institutions	1.87	2.70	0	10
GDP per capita (in constant 2005 USD)	33452	127957	255	114249
Area (1,000 square kilometers)	757	1935	0.316	17075

the numbers for two measures of power length are 20 years and 11 years, respectively.

Table 4.1 reports some summary statistics. On average, the countries in our sample experienced 1.61 coup within this period, and one country even experienced 10 coups (Bolivia). The average length of power after a successful coup is 5.56 years, with the maximal 27 years (Tunisia). The average decentralization extent in terms of log is 2.32, which is about 10 percent. The control variables include the averages of military spending share per GDP, government spending per GDP, GDP per capital, and population sizes from 1975 to 2009. The political institutions are measured by the average value of the democracy index in Polity-IV dataset during 1970 to 2000. We define two discrete measures: autocracy for the index below 2 and democracy for the index above 7. The military spending data are from the US Arms Control and Disarmament Agency, and all the variables are from the Penn World Table 6.2 version.

Empirical Evidence Because the dependent variables are counting data and their distribution is right skewed, we employ a Poisson regression as our empirical strategy. Because the non–OECD countries in our sample are generally not highly decentralized, we can reasonable preclude this case from our empirical test.

As prediction 1 demonstrates, our model predicts that there exists negative linear relationship between the length of power and decentralization. Thus the Poisson regression is specified as follows:

$$\log y_i = \alpha D_i + \beta X_i + \varepsilon_i,$$

where y_i is the average length of power after successful coups in country i in this period, D_i is the average decentralization measure in country i, and X_i are the average of the control variables.

Based on prediction 2, there should exists nonlinear relationship between the coup risk and decentralization. Hence the empirical specification is as follows:

$$\log n_i = \alpha_1 D_i + \alpha_2 D_i^2 + \beta X_i + \varepsilon_i,$$

where n_i is the total number of coups in country i, D_i again is the average decentralization measure in country i, and X_i are the average of the control variables.

The results are shown in table 4.2. Column 1 shows the results for the average length of rulers. We observe a negative and significant

Table 4.2
Regression results

Dependent variable	(1) Average length by ruler	(2) Average length by regimes	(3) Average number of coups
Log (subnational revenue share)	−0.584***	−0.286*	1.125*
	(0.169)	(0.159)	(0.593)
Log (subnational revenue share)_square			−0.267*
			(0.139)
Democracy	−0.429	−1.467**	−1.005**
	(0.514)	(0.734)	(0.488)
Autocracy	0.460	0.754**	−0.649***
	(0.293)	(0.294)	(0.223)
Area	−0.058	−0.099	0.086
	(0.221)	(0.210)	(0.092)
Population	−1.014	−1.287	−0.146
	(0.700)	(0.787)	(0.254)
GDP per capita	−0.039	−0.022	−0.226***
	(0.076)	(0.078)	(0.069)
Military expenditure share	0.366***	0.414***	−0.034
	(0.136)	(0.155)	(0.073)
Observations	33	33	79

Note: Standard errors are in the brackets; ***$p < 0.01$, **$p < 0.05$, *$p < 0.1$.

correlation between decentralization and the duration. Among the control variables, only military spending is significantly correlated with the duration of the post-military-coup government. This may suggest that the new rulers would spend more on military forces to purchase loyalty, or that the countries with a strong military will be ruled under the military government longer. This question of endogeneity, though interesting, is not the primary focus of our chapter.

Column 2 presents the regression results for the average length of regimes. The coefficients are still negative, though less significant than those for rulers. To understand the magnitude of the impact of decentralization, the estimated coefficient suggests that a point decrease in the log of decentralization measure (i.e., while the subnational government expenditure share increases by about 2.7 percent) will increase the expected length of power by $\exp(0.29) = 1.34$ years, which is about one-fourth of the average length in the dataset.

By comparing columns 1 and 2, it can be shown that the impact of decentralization on the duration of power is even greater if we look at the lengths of power of the individual rulers. Besides the positive correlation between military spending and length of power, political institutions affect the fate of post–coup-governments, and democracy reduces the lengths of military governments, while autocracy increases lengths.

Column 3 presents the regression results for the average number of coups. Consistent with prediction 2, we can observe an inverse-U relationship between the number of coups and decentralization. The coefficients of the log of subnational revenue share and its square are around 1.12 and −0.26, respectively. A stronger military force is not correlated with a coup risk, but richer countries do have a lower likelihood of a coup d'état. Both autocratic and democratic countries will have a lower coup risk, which may suggest a nonmonotonic relationship between institutions and the risk of coups. Therefore the empirical results support the predictions that there is a nonmonotonic relationship between decentralization and the risk of a coup.

4.5 Conclusion

This chapter formulizes the insights of Machiavelli on the role of power structure in the stability of regimes and develops a sequential contest model with imperfect commitment in order to study decentralization and the inceptions and consequences of conspiracies, an important kind of threat to political survival. We show that while decentralization can reduce the length of power, its impacts on the risk of plots are ambiguous. We apply our model to study coups d'état, and the empirical results to a large extent support our theoretical predictions. An important implication of our chapter is that in contrast with the literature on the role of decentralization in delivering growth and equality, our theory suggests that decentralization can affect power structure, and consequently regime stability. Thus the dark side of decentralization should be taken into account when implementing a reform of government structure.

Even though our empirical part concentrates on coups d'état, it is noteworthy that our model has the potential to be generalized to explore incentives underlying other conspiracies in order to challenge the incumbent, such as foreign invaders, revolutionaries, and coup plotters. Moreover players' limited commitment prevails in the arena of political competition, for example, in alliances formation. The two-tier government in our model essentially could be considered a military alliance of two players, so our model could be extended to study the role of power distribution in the survival of alliances. These interesting directions are left to further research.

Acknowledgments

We would like to thank Joan Esteban, Nicola Gennaioli, Dan Kovenock, Gabriel Leon, Torsten Persson, James Robinson, Petros Sekeris, Jan-Egbert Sturm, and the attendants at the Jan Tinbergen Peace Science Conference (2010), the European Political Economy Workshop at Silvaplana (2010), the ICCMPP in Beijing (2010), the CESifo summer meeting (2011), and the seminar in SWUFE, Zhejiang University, for their helpful comments.

Notes

1. Qian and Weingast (1997) and Bardham (2002) provide excellent surveys on research in this field.

2. Reynal-Querol (2002) and Fjelde (2010) are among the few exceptions.

3. For a thorough review of existing studies, see Belkin and Schofer (2003).

4. This assumption of two layers is for simplicity; our main results hold for more layers. Additionally we ignore the coordination problem among different governments within the same layer, and we don't allow for the violent conflict within the government. In

other words, we don't consider the formation of alliances between the local government and the plotter.

5. It also could be interpreted as buying loyalty from a fraction of military force.

6. This implies that the new government will take over the defense power of the overthrown government.

7. Alternatively, we can use Nash bargaining to study this "deadlock" situation by introducing bargaining power on each side. As long as the bargaining power is increasing with the players' strength, the basic results would not change.

8. See Blattman and Miguel (2010) for an excellent survey on this topic.

9. Collier and Hoeffler (1998), Miguel et al. (2004), and Montalvo and Reynal-Querol (2005) identify different causes of civil war.

10. Bhutan, Kazahstan, Russia, China, and Vietnam have low scores on democracy and high ethnic fractionalization, but no recent history of coups d'état.

11. Since World War II, Iran experienced only one coup, while its neighboring Iraq has had a record thirteen military coups.

12. The court took note of the fact that the takeover was widely welcomed, and little protested, and hence that the regime had the implied consent of the governed.

13. As Huntington (1957) demonstrates, coups d'état could be classified into different categories, such as breakthrough coup d'état, guardian coup d'état, and veto coup d'état. In our empirical study we chose not to identify the coup types, and to ignore whether a coup was externally instigated. Moreover, because our data only cover coups after 1975, the limit from ignoring foreign intervention becomes less a problem.

14. We interpolated the decentralization measure using information from the nearest year. The results are qualitatively similar to the analysis reported here.

References

Acemoglu, Daron., Davide Ticchi. and Andrea Vindigni. 2010. Persistence of civil wars. *Journal of the European Economic Association* 8: 664–76.

Alesina, Alberta, Sule Olzer, Nouriel Boubini, and Phillip Swagel. 1996. Political instability and economic growth. *Journal of Economic Growth* 1: 189–211.

Bardham, Pranab. 2002. Decentralization of governance and development. *Journal of Economic Perspectives* 16: 185–205.

Belkin, Aaron, and Evan Schofer. 2003. Toward a structural understanding of coup risk. *Journal of Conflict Resolution* 47: 594–620.

Besley, Tim, and James A. Robinson. 2010. Quis custodiet ipsos custodes? Civilian control over the military. *Journal of the European Economic Association* 8: 655–63.

Bhave, Aditya, and Christopher Kingston. 2010. Military coups and the consequences of durable de facto powers: The case of Pakistan. *Economics of Governance* 11: 51–76.

Blattman, Chris, and Edward Miguel. 2010. Civil war. *Journal of Economic Literature* 48: 3–57.

Blum, William. 2003. *Killing Hope: US Military and CIA Interventions since World War II*. London: Zed Books.

de Mesquita, Bueno Bruce, Alastair Smith, Randolph M. Siverson, and James D. Morrow. 2003. *The Logic of Political Survival*. Cambridge: MIT Press.

Calvert, P. 1979. The coup: A critical restatement. *Third World Quarterly* 1: 89–96.

Ch'ien, Mu. 1982. *Traditional Government in Imperial China: A Critical Analysis*. London: Palgrave Macmillan.

Collier, Paul, and Anke Hoeffler. 1998. Military spending and the risks of coups d'état. Working paper. Oxford University.

Dreher, Axel, and Justina A. V. Fischer. 2010. Government decentralization as a disincentive for transnational terror? An empirical analysis. *International Economic Review* 51: 981–1002.

Enikolopov, Ruben, and Ekaterina Zhuravskaya. 2007. Decentralization and political institutions. *Journal of Public Economics* 91: 2261–90.

Fjelde, Hanne. 2010. Generals, dictators, and kings: Authoritarian regimes and civil conflict, 1973–2004. *Conflict Management and Peace Science* 27: 195–218.

Fossum, Egil. 1967. Factors influencing the occurrence of military coups d'état in Latin America. *Journal of Peace Research* 4: 228–51.

Fosu, Augustin Kwasi. 2002. Political instability and economic growth: Implications of coup events in sub-Saharan Africa. *American Journal of Economics and Sociology* 61: 329–48.

Frey, Bruno S., and Simon Luechinger. 2004. Decentralization as a disincentive for terror. *European Journal of Political Economy* 20: 509–15.

Gandhi, Jennifer, and Adam Przeworski. 2007. Authoritarian institutions and the survival of autocrats. *Comparative Political Studies* 40: 1279–1301.

Hettne, Bjorn. 1980. Soldiers and politics: The case of Ghana. *Journal of Peace Research* 17: 173–93.

Hoadley, J. Stephen. 1973. Social complexity, economic development, and military coups d'état in Latin America and Asia. *Journal of Peace Research* 10: 119–20.

Huntington, Samuel P. 1957. *The Soldier and the State: The Theory and Politics of Civil Military Relations*. Cambridge, MA: Belknap Press.

Jackman, Robert W. 1978. The predictability of coups d'état: A model with African data. *American Political Science Review* 72: 1262–75.

Jackman, Robert W., Rosemary H. T. O'Kane, Thomas H. Johnson, Pat McGowan, and Robert O. Slater. 1986. Explaining African coups d'état. *American Political Science Review* 80: 225–49.

Jenkins, J. Craig, and Augustine J. Kposowa. 1990. Explaining military coups d'état: Black Africa, 1957–1984. *American Sociological Review* 55: 861–75.

Johnson, Thomas H., Robert O. Slater, and Pat McGowan. 1984. Explaining African military coups d'état, 1960–1982. *American Political Science Review* 78: 622–40.

Keefer, P. 2005. *Database of Political Institutions: Changes and Variable Definitions*. Washington, DC: World Bank.

Leon, Gabriel J. 2009a. Soldiers or bureaucrats? Conflict and the military's role in policymaking. Working paper. Cambridge University.

Leon, Gabriel J. 2009b. The economic causes of coups: Loyalty for sale? Working paper. Cambridge University.

Lunde, Tormod K. 1991. Modernization and political instability: Coups d'état in Africa, 1955–85. *Acta Sociologica* 34: 13–32.

Luttwak, Edward. 1968. *Coup d'état: A Practical Handbook*. London: Penguin Press.

Machiavelli, Niccolo. [1532] 2005. *The Prince*. New York: Oxford University Press.

Miquel, Edward, Shanker Satyanath, and Ernest Sergenti. 2004. Economic shocks and civil conflict: An instrumental variables approach. *Journal of Political Economy* 112: 725–53.

Montalvo, Jose G., and Marta Reynal-Querol. 2005. Ethnic polarization, potential conflict, and civil wars. *American Economic Review* 95: 796–816.

O'Kane, Rosemary H. 1993. Coups d'état in Africa: A political economy approach. *Journal of Peace Research* 30: 251–70.

Reynal-Querol, Marta. 2002. Political systems, stability and civil wars. *Defence and Peace Economics* 13: 465–83.

Powell, Jonathan M., and Clayton L. Thyne. 2011. Global instances of coups from 1950–present: A new dataset. *Journal of Peace Research* 48: 249–59.

Qian, Yingyi and Barry R. Weingast. 1997. Federalism as a commitment to preserving market incentives. *Journal of Economic Perspectives* 11: 83–92.

Wells, Alan. 1974. The coup d'état in theory and practice: Independent black Africa in the 1960s. *American Journal of Sociology* 79: 871–87.

5 The Probability of Military Rule in Africa, 1970 to 2007

Raul Caruso, Jacopo Costa, and Roberto Ricciuti

5.1 Introduction

Since the start of the so-called third wave in 1974, and the acceleration after the fall of the Berlin Wall in 1989, democratization has been impressive. According to the Economist Intelligence Unit (2011), one-half of the world's population now lives in a democracy of some sort. More specifically, 12.3 percent lives in full democracies, 37.2 percent in flawed democracies, 14.0 percent in hybrid regimes, and still 36.5 percent in authoritarian regimes. Authoritarian regimes, in which the military plays a direct (when a junta rules the country) and indirect role (when the army guarantees the monopoly of violence for a civilian despotic government), are the second largest regime group. A similar ancillary role can be found in hybrid regimes. A recent literature in political economy (Acemoglu et al. 2010; Besley and Robinson 2010) analyzes the relationship between the civil undemocratic government and the military as an agency problem: the civilian government needs the army to avoid internal violence, but a larger army reduces the opportunity cost for the military to run a coup d'état and seize power. These papers derive three main causes of military coups: income inequality, ethnic fractionalization, and external threat.

The current work is intended to empirically analyze a step forward. We in fact investigate the existence of a military rule on a panel of 48 African countries for the period 1970 to 2007, controlling for a number of economic variables. According to Freedom House (2009), among these countries 10 (21 percent) were rated Free in calendar year 2008, while 23 were rated Partly Free (48 percent) and 15 were rated Not Free (31 percent). In 1980, only 4 were rated Free (9 percent), 15 were ranked Partly Free (32 percent), and 27 were ranked Not Free (59 percent). Therefore we can observe a widespread diffusion of dictatorships in sub-Saharan Africa and also a slow process of democratization, which mainly increased the number of Partly Free countries. For these reasons sub-Saharan Africa is a natural testing ground of economic models of military dictatorships.

We do not analyze the outbreak of military dictatorships, but the economic conditions that make a military rule possible. Of course, actual conflicts do not take shape in *vacuum*. An actual conflict would not take shape in the absence of a continuing and latent conflict. Put differently, the outbreak of an actual conflict (as a civil war or a coup d'état) can be considered as a revelatory event of a permanent continuing conflict. Then we are interested in the existence of a continuing conflict and the institutions that take shape consequently. In a game-theoretic perspective, institutions as the rules of the game are the equilibrium of a game between parties in a society. This idea, in a game-theoretic perspective, has been labeled "the institution as-an-equilibrium approach" (Aoki 2001, p. 15). This approach underpins our empirical study. In sum, the current work is intended to empirical analyze some determinants that make a "military equilibrium" possible at a given point in time.

In other words, when studying the factors associated with the existence of a military rule, we are highlighting the "pillars" of that societal equilibrium. Needless to say, it must be also remarked that results have to be interpreted *cum grano salis*. A military rule can effectively affect at least some of the economic and political variables that we henceforth use as explanatory. In order to draw some additional insights in this respect, we also use one- and five-lags of the economic variables on the presumption that, for example, the GDP per capita of five years ago is not determined by the presence of a military dictatorship today, whereas bad economic conditions at that time can influence the existence of such a dictatorship later on.

The chapter is organized as follows: Section 5.2 reviews the literature on military dictatorships drawing both from economics and political science. Section 5.3 describes the empirical model and the data, whereas results are discussed in section 5.4. Section 5.5 concludes.

5.2   Literature Review

There are several strands of literature that are related to the topic of this work. The complex relationship between the civil power and the military is becoming important in the recent political economy literature. Seminal works on political economy of dictatorships are Wintrobe (1988; 1990), and McGuire and Olson (1996). Recently Besley and Robinson (2010) analyzed the opposition between civil government (democratic or nondemocratic) and military dictatorship, and Acemoglu et al. (2010)[1] analyzed the three categories of nondemocratic civil government, military dictatorship and democratic civil government. Both studies identify the army as agent of the powerful elite, an instrument to guarantee its survival through the repression.[2] The relationship between the uneven income distribution and the relevance of the army becomes stronger, overall, in a contest where the political competition takes shape between polarized groups, which fight to obtain power and rents. These groups originate along different cleavages, as ethnic or regional origins, religion, ownership of the production factors, and so on. The clash between these polarized and fragmented groups determines winners and losers, those who violently fight to gain the control of the state (Hammond and Axelrod 2006; Montalvo and Reynal-Querol 2010; Alesina et al. 2003; Fearon and Laitin, 2004). Therefore a social situation with different groups fighting for power raises the opportunity for civil war and coup d'état.

Sub-Saharan Africa, in particular, is characterized by the turnovers of unconsolidated democracies, hybrid democracies, civil autocracies, and military dictatorships. For example, authoritarian systems are based on a nonexistent political pluralism and the power is shared among some organizations that guarantee support and security to the regime. In military dictatorship the army has the most important role on stage, its power is less checked and may show worrying examples, like kleptocratic regimes (Acemoglu et al. 2003), where the dictator can grab a lot of resources and guarantee his survival through the *divide-et-impera*. In this context it is possible to see a challenge between the elite of different groups to gain the control of the state. In human history, moving from the land and agricultural production to the industry and manufacturing production, the social relations among groups have produced cleavages and violence that characterize the different societies. The emergence of new groups gives rise to new elites that want to handle the rents and revenues (Acemoglu and Robinson 2006). In the context of the developing countries—where productive sectors like manufacturing, productive agriculture, utilities, services, and others are very weak—this process has the goal to obtain central power, with the wealth given by oil, diamond, or others.[3] We can see the groups compete for the control of the three basic aspects regarding the production factors: appropriation, division, and production. In our framework, this drives differences in the opportunity to enjoy the public goods between losers and winners, through different enforcement of the property rights and contracts (Tangerås and Lagerlöf 2009; Gonzalez 2005, 2010; Dal Bò and Powell 2009).

As noted in Bohlken (2010), the risk of a coup d'état could be a strong deterrent to uncontrollable episodes of rent-seeking, corruption, and extra-budget funds than the electoral process in democracies. The combination between the democratic checks and military risk reduces the appropriation of the state wealth. This is the same dynamics that Acemoglu and Robinson (2006) use to explain the transformation of the political system: (1) A situation is without violence because there is redistribution (fairness) between the groups, driving to cooperation. They claim that here income inequality would be very low, so that the elite does not feel threat from the extending of the redistribution. (2) To respond to the violence caused from no fairness in the redistribution, the ruling elite could co-opt the most productive and dangerous groups, sharing with them the wealth and the rents of the country. Here income inequality is higher than before, and this threats the conservative elite. (3) The elite does not want to share the rents with other groups, therefore causing competition and violence. Once again, income inequality is very high. Hence it is possible to say that higher income inequality could raise the probability of a civil war, and consequently request a larger army for the repression. But, at least, this could increase the opportunity for coup d'état. In this contest, Besley and Robinson (2010) and Acemoglu et al. (2010) see the army like a guardian of the elite, as an agent that acts to defend it from the risk of civil war. The central government will choose the size of the army, but it faces an agency problem: the army may not only be the instrument to defend the elite but may seize the power. If the government increases the size of the army to respond to a higher risk from the loser groups, this raises the opportunity for a coup d'état because it diminishes its opportunity cost.[4]

Besley and Robinson (2010) follow the way paved by Besley and Persson (2008, 2009) in which the state capacity, the quality of institution and the problem of violence are analyzed. In particular, state capacity is the quality of the legal and fiscal capability of the central power. The low level of these two aspects raises income inequality, uneven distribution of public goods, and bad use of wealth, creating tensions and grievances in the society. When property rights and contracts are not properly enforced (low legal capacity) and the level of taxation is collected from a source that is not under the complete control of the government—like natural resources (low fiscal capacity), the distribution of the public goods between the different groups is highly uneven, thus raising the risk of civil unrest. To maintain their economic, social, and cultural insulation, the elite have to establish an efficient monopoly of violence. The loser groups that are not protected by right and contract, and that could not check the use of taxation and state rents, presenting unequal and low income, have the opportunity to use the civil war to gain the central power. So the government has to create an army in order to counter this threat. However, the establishment of a bigger army may turn out to be dangerous because the military can actually exploit the use of force. In such a case, a classical principal–agent problem would take shape. As pointed out by Besley and Robinson (2010) and Acemoglu et al. (2010), the military could act no more like agent of the government but in their own interest. In particular, if the military believes that they are not paid a "fair wage," they could behave as more like self-interested agent than agent of the central government. In sum, this increases the probability of a coup d'état.[5]

Acemoglu et al. (2010) identify three different patterns to underline this: (1) The civil government could decide not to use the repression and hence establishes a little army, favoring the cooperation and a smooth transition to democracy. The new democratic government faces a big problem: in order to consolidate democracy it is necessary to reform the army, but they do not want to be reformed. Here it is possible to find a commitment problem, because the government has to promise to the military that it will not reform it—otherwise, they will block the transitional process—but to permit the consolidation of the democracy this reform is necessary. (2) The civil government may want to use repression against social opposition. They create a big army, but they have to pay a right price (wages and public goods) that avoids the recourse to coup d'état. The nondemocratic government remains in office and the coup d'état does not happen. (3) The government uses the army to deter an opposition from taking the power.The government creates a big army but is unable, or does not want, to pay the right price for its services. Eventually, the army takes the power, establishing a military dictatorship. The same dynamics could be extrapolated from Besley and Robinson (2010): the civil government needs the help of the army, through the repression, to block the social opposition and the risk of civil war, but has to pay the right price for this action and protection. If this does not happen, the military seize the power, putting down the government. This vicious cycle characterizes both models, and helps explain the relationship of the redistribution of public goods with civil war and coup d'état.

There is growing evidence that a low level of institutional quality is a fundamental source of waste of wealth (La Porta et al. 1999).In addition it determines an uneven distribution of public goods between different groups. So a low institutional quality stimulates the grievances of the loser groups, boosting their willingness to use the violence and increasing the probability that a civil war takes shapes. This makes more likely that the central elite/government will resort to the repression by the army, creating a larger one, raising the likelihood of a military dictatorship. In general, provision of public goods differs dramatically between democracies and dictatorships: democracies exceed dictatorial provision (Deacon 2009).

Needless to say, there is predictable linkage between the availability of natural resources and such an argument. A large mining sector, for example, increases the size of a contestable "pie" between competing groups. Put differently, the rents emerging from controlling the mining sector increase the likelihood of an actual conflict between the ruling group and the military or another competing group. That is, the existence of natural resources contributes to the insulation of the elite in charge, by reducing the capacity of enforcing property rights and contracts, thus raising the risk that the loser groups use violence and civil war to depose the government. Consequently, natural resources increase the probability in the use of repression through the army, and, eventually the likelihood of a military dictatorship.[6]

External factors can also affect the probability of a coup d'état: if a country has some neighbors experiencing ethnic wars and violence, and inside its borders it reproduces the same cleavages, it could be influenced by this circumstance, reproducing these problems. That is, a contagion effect may exist. However, Besley and Robinson (2010) and Acemoglu et al. (2010) emphasize that if a country perceives a serious threat of a war between two states, this would reduce the risk of a coup d'état because the army is now necessary for the survival of both the government and the state. Therefore the politicians (democratic or nondemocratic) have to pay the right wage to soldiers, solving the commitment problem that we have analyzed before. A credible threat on the borders can reduce the coup's risk. De Groot (2011) emphasizes the role of external influences in determining political freedom in Africa. He finds that the probability of an improvement in political freedoms increases with a history of political freedom, openness, and improvements in ethnolinguistically similar neighboring countries. Weede (1986) argued that external threat may lead the elite to increase military spending, which in turn may have positive effects on growth, for example through to the formation of mass armies that teach discipline and possibly some modern skills to a sizable proportion of young men.

Geddes (2010) analyzes different survival strategies for dictators. Those who draw their support from a professionalized military do not need to distribute substantial resources to civilian supporters and to provide large numbers of jobs in the state sector for party militants as dictators who create parties generally need to do. In contrast, dictators who create parties must devise ways of paying for the support of party leaders and activists by employing them in the state bureaucracy and state enterprise sector. Dictators supported by professionalized militaries have leaned toward more market-oriented policy favored by technocrats, and dictators who have created parties tend to opt for more state intervention. Similarly Gandhi (2008) analyzes legislative and partisan institutions under dictatorships and argues that these institutions are an important component in the operation and survival of authoritarian regimes because they provide a forum in which to organize political concessions to potential opposition in an effort to neutralize threats to their power and to solicit cooperation from groups outside of the ruling elite. This bargaining has also significant effects on policies and outcomes under dictatorship.

Coups d'état in Africa have received some attention in the literature by sociologists and political scientists. Jackman (1978) is the seminal work in this field. He estimates a model of the structural determinants of coups d'état for the new states of sub-Saharan Africa in the years from 1960 through 1975. Results indicate that social mobilization and the presence of a dominant ethnic group are destabilizing; a multiparty system is destabilizing (especially when a dominant ethnic group exists) while electoral turnout in the last election before independence is stabilizing. Johnson et al. (1984) replicate the previous work concentrating on military coups, finding serious weaknesses in the original Jackman model. Their dataset includes 35 sub-Saharan African states from 1960 through 1982. They find that states with relatively dynamic economies[7] whose societies were not very socially mobilized before independence and that have maintained or restored some degree of political participation and political pluralism have experienced fewer military coups, attempted coups, and coup plots than have states with the opposite set of characteristics.

Jenkins and Kposowa (1990), using data on military coups in 33 sub-Saharan African states between 1957 and 1984, find strong support for modernization and competition theories of ethnic antagonisms, military centrality theory, and aspects of dependency theory. Political development theory is not supported. Ethnic diversity and competition, military centrality,[8] debt dependence, and political factionalism are major predictors of coup activity. Ethnic dominance is a stabilizing force creating social integration and weakening opposition. Intractable conflicts rooted in ethnic competition and economic dependence appear to create a structural context for military coups and related instabilities.

O'Kane (1993) argues that the underlying causes of coups are specialization in and dependency on primary goods for export, exacerbated by poverty. A testable hypothesis is deduced from this theory which is examined through the application of discriminant analysis to data for three sets of African countries. The models support the theory. Moreover the chance of a successful coup is negatively related with the absence of a previous coup and the continuing or historic presence of foreign troops since independence. Tusalem (2010) finds that over the 1970 to 1990 period the likelihood of a military coup is reduced by the protection of property rights.

Lunde (1991) studies African coups d'état during the period 1955 to 1985. The starting point is a replication of Jackman (1978) when continuous-time hazard models of event history data are used instead of the panel regression approach. The event history approach focuses on the rate of coup d'état over time rather than some index of coup d'état. The results lend some support to modernization theory. The social contagion hypothesis and the history of political instability are also supported. Finally, the results indicate that the likelihood of a coup strongly depends on time

Collier and Hoeffler (2005b) in a panel of African countries from 1960 to 2001 highlight strong similarity in the causes of coups and civil wars, finding that low income and lack of growth are among the main determinants. Both are also subject to "traps"—once a coup or civil war has occurred, further events are much more likely. Finally, policies that favor the military (high military spending) may increase the risk of a coup.

5.3 Empirical Model and Data

We estimated the following panel data probit model:

$$Military_{it} = \alpha_1 + \alpha_2 \, X_{it} + \alpha_3 \, Z_{it} + \alpha_4 W_{it} + \alpha_5 P_{it} + \alpha_6 \, S_{it} + \alpha_7 \, C_{it} + \varepsilon_{it}.$$

The dependent variable is a dummy equal to 1 if the current ruler is a military junta and 0 otherwise. Data are taken from the Database of Political Institutions 2010 (Beck et al. 2001).[9] The vector X_{it} includes GDP per capita, derived from Penn World Tables 6.3[10] (Heston et al. 2009), and the added value of the agricultural, manufacturing, and mining sector[11] as a percentage of GDP, using the UNCTAD database.[12] The vector Z_{it} includes variables concerned with ethnic fragmentation, distinguishing between polarization and fractionalization, we use the data from Reynal-Querol.[13] W_{it} is a vector that includes variables concerned with the external sector: openness (the sum of imports plus exports over GDP, from the Penn World Tables 6.3) and the intensity of external treat,[14] defined as level of hostilities on a 0 to 5 scale, taken from the database Militarized Interstate Disputes 3.10 (Ghosn et al. 2004).[15] The vector P_{it} includes agricultural produce prices, taken from the Free Market Price Index, and the crude oil price, derived from the Free Market Price Index (calculated as the average of Dubai/Brent/Texas crudes equally weighted in US$/barrel) from UNCTAD. We want to check whether higher levels of the commodity market prices can lead to riots, which in turn could influence an army to take action. Because changes in oil price can have different effects depending on whether the countries are exporters or importers of oil, we include a dummy variable that is equal to 1 if the share of oil export exceeds 10 percent, and 0 otherwise.[16] C_{it} is a vector of dummy variables describing the colonial rule of a country. Finally, ε_{it} is a random error.

All estimates are obtained by using random effect probit panel data. The random effects panel probit model is the best viable option, since it is not possible to estimate a fixed effects probit model consistently with a fixed number of periods (see Verbeek 2000, p. 337). All variables are in logs. Table 5.1 reports the summary statistics.[17] Military dictatorships are widespread in our dataset, and they account for about 41 percent of our observed regimes.

Table 5.1
Summary statistics

	Mean	Standard deviation	Min	Max
Military	0.409	0.492	0	1
GDP per capita (logged)	7.547	0.836	5.031	10.062
Manufacturing share of GDP (logged)	2.097	0.762	−3.432	3.703
Mining share of GDP (logged)	1.351	1.379	−3.971	4.526
Primary share of GDP (logged)	3.199	0.757	0.616	4.591
Polarization	0.537	0.190	0.020	0.840
Fractionalization	0.633	0.262	0.050	0.960
Openness (logged)	4.068	0.655	0.685	5.773
Intensity of external threat	0.823	1.623	0	5
Crude oil price (logged)	4.133	0.794	2.015	5.530
Agricultural produce price (logged)	4.621	0.319	3.683	5.101
Landlocked (dummy)	0.313	0.464	0	1
Oil producer (dummy)	0.163	0.370	0	1
UK colonial origin (dummy)	0.416	0.493	0	1

We should note that manufacturing is, in general, a small percentage of output (mean at 10.20 percent, median at 8.83 percent). The only country with a sizable manufacturing sector is South Africa (mean at 21.250 percent). South Africa also stands out for a much higher average GDP per capita ($8,055.456 vs. $ 2,798.751). For these reasons South Africa is a natural candidate for outlier; therefore we replicate the estimations with and without it as a robustness check.

The results cannot be interpreted as causal, since military rule can affect at least some of the economic and political variables that we treat as independent. Therefore we also use one- and five-lag economic variables on the assumption that the GDP per capita of five years ago, for example, is not determined by the presence of a military dictatorship today, although bad economic conditions at that time could influence the existence of such a dictatorship later on.

5.4   Results

Table 5.2 reports our baseline results. The coefficient of income per capita is significantly negative. Higher income per capita reduces the likelihood of experiencing a military rule. Its marginal effect on average is equal to −0.14. This does suggest the "modernization hypothesis," which claims that the higher income is, the higher is the interest of the

Table 5.2
Existence of military rule, baseline results (panel RE probit)

	1	2	3	4	5	6	7	8	9	10†	11†
GDP per capita	-0.702***	-0.467***	-0.148	-0.457***	-0.343***	-0.599***	-0.240	-0.860***	-0.113	-0.348**	0.060
	(0.105)	(0.129)	(0.143)	(0.129)	(0.127)	(0.157)	(0.149)	(0.182)	(0.162)	(0.190)	(0.167)
Manufacturing share of GDP		0.318***	0.709***	0.311***	0.337***	0.392***	0.490***	0.512***	0.342***	0.469***	0.371***
		(0.098)	(0.113)	(0.101)	(0.101)	(0.110)	(0.117)	(0.115)	(0.112)	(0.114)	(0.116)
Mining share of GDP		-0.042		-0.041		-0.125**		-0.087		-0.068	
		(0.054)		(0.055)		(0.061)		(0.062)		(0.062)	
Primary sector share of GDP			0.920***		0.550***		1.205***		0.844***		0.891***
			(0.197)		(0.159)		(0.207)		(0.216)		(0.215)
Polarization	0.373***	0.431***	0.083	0.386***	0.502***	0.151	0.087	0.846***	0.327***	-0.369***	0.572***
	(0.107)	(0.116)	(0.116)	(0.115)	(0.116)	(0.135)	(0.135)	(0.161)	(0.130)	(0.150)	(0.145)
Fractionalization	-0.556***	-0.484***	-0.064	-0.487***	-0.605***	-0.190	-0.264**	-1.081***	-0.417***	0.049	-0.667***
	(0.111)	(0.115)	(0.114)	(0.116)	(0.116)	(0.136)	(0.130)	(0.191)	(0.128)	(0.153)	(0.140)
Openness		-0.275***	-0.002	-0.204***	-0.117***	0.057	0.194*	-0.238***	0.133	-0.310**	0.143
		(0.083)	(0.101)	(0.084)	(0.094)	(0.107)	(0.119)	(0.104)	(0.130)	(0.101)	(0.128)
Intensity of external threat						-0.031	-0.032	-0.024	-0.011	-0.0144	-0.039
						(0.037)	(0.036)	(0.036)	(0.037)	(0.039)	(0.037)

Table 5.2
(continued)

	1	2	3	4	5	6	7	8	9	10+	11+
Crude oil price				−0.285***	−0.296***	−0.224	−0.188	−0.159	−0.161	−0.164	−0.146
				(0.106)	(0.102)	(0.155)	(0.157)	(0.158)	(0.162)	(0.161)	(0.162)
Agricultural produce price								−0.431	−0.430	−0.414	−0.377
								(0.352)	(0.355)	(0.355)	(0.356)
Oil producer		0.826***	1.556***	0.856***	2.093***	0.891***	1.242***	1.142***	1.916***	0.741***	1.229***
		(0.183)	(0.240)	(0.187)	(0.193)	(0.215)	(0.207)	(0.233)	(0.259)	(0.237)	(0.245)
Landlocked		0.156	0.081	0.064	0.163	0.013	0.064	0.849***	−0.169	−0.152	−0.496***
		(0.126)	(0.123)	(0.121)	(0.135)	(0.138)	(0.134)	(0.171)	(0.149)	(0.134)	(0.171)
UK								−0.597***	−0.738***	−0.629***	−0.884***
								(0.132)	(0.160)	(0.141)	(0.173)
Constant	4.391***	3.376***	−4.369***	4.20***	1.070	3.915***	−4.349***	7.99***	−1.12	4.911**	−2.445
	(0.748)	(0.891)	(1.524)	(1.014)	(1.507)	(1.292)	(1.919)	(2.13)	(2.584)	(2.219)	(2.578)
Observed	1,353	1,352	1,353	1,352	1,353	1,105	1,106	1,105	1,106	1,078	1079
Log likelihood	−534.83	−521.702	−512.163	−517.713	−512.907	−415.747	−405.622	−417.684	−407.757	−409.682	−406.062
Wald χ^2	56.75	72.44	97.30	75.75	165.96	50.02	77.99	127.57	106.98	100.90	110.38

Note: *** significant at 1 percent, ** significant at 5 percent, * significant at 10 percent. In columns with †, South Africa is excluded from the sample.

bourgeoisie to take part in the political arena, and thus to establish democratic institutions. Obviously, it is not possible to establish a clear-cut causal relationship, since even an inverse relationship can hold (i.e., the military affects negatively economic growth). Manufacturing and primary sector are significantly positive, raising the probability of the army taking office. While this may be understandable in agrarian economies where large owners tend to support conservative political parties (and likely the military) against the possibility of land reforms, we expected an opposite result for manufacturing, since this is usually connected with an emerging bourgeoisie that rallies for democratic institutions. Our results suggest instead that entrepreneurs are likely to seek protection from the military. In particular, this appears to be true for foreign direct investments. For example, in sub-Saharan African countries, a large share of the manufacturing sector depends on foreign direct investments.[18] In quantitative terms, the average marginal effect on the probability of a military junta on manufacturing is 0.11, whereas for the mining sector it is −0.02 and ultimately for the primary sector 0.10.

Polarization and fractionalization have opposite effects; the former increases the probability of a military rule whereas the latter decreases it. Marginal effects are 0.12 and −0.14, respectively. These results are similar to those of Montalvo and Reynal-Querol (2005), where these two variables likewise have opposite effects on civil conflict.[19] Larger openness to international trade negatively affects military rule. A country that is more connected with the world, in which democratic countries have a large presence, probably perceives negative effects (both culturally and in economic terms) in its relationship with partners after relinquishing democracy in favor of military rulers. This confirms the liberal idea of closed and authoritarian regimes that precipitate into underdevelopment. Yet, though statistically significant, the marginal effect turns out to be small (i.e., −0.05). The price of oil is remarkably insignificant, and even negative when significant, and the intensity of any external threat and of prices of fresh agricultural produce are always insignificant. In contrast, being an oil producer increases significantly the probability of military rule. Ultimately, being landlocked increases the probability of a military rule as well, thus indirectly confirming that landlockedness affects negatively societal development, fueling civil unrest and military coups. A British colonial legacy, however, decreases the probability of a military junta.

Table 5.3 addresses the issue of dynamic effects in the relationship between military rule and our covariates. We include as regressors

Table 5.3
Existence of military rule (panel RE probit)

	1	2	3	4	5	6†	7†
GDP per capita, 1 year lagged	-0.510*	-0.581**	0.065	-0.479*	-0.262	-0.888***	-0.277
	(0.304)	(0.302)	(0.311)	(0.294)	(0.303)	(0.317)	(0.379)
GDP per capita, 5 years lagged	0.292	-0.015	0.141	0.375	0.198	0.133	-0.016
	(0.292)	(0.323)	(0.322)	(0.334)	(0.326)	(0.342)	(0.326)
Manufacturing share of GDP, 1 year lagged		0.456***	0.607***	0.287	0.440***	0.376**	0.646***
		(0.181)	(0.1800)	(0.186)	(0.188)	(0.187)	(0.223)
Manufacturing share of GDP, 5 years lagged		-0.293*	-0.171	-0.054	-0.161	-0.198	-0.063
		(0.178)	(0.181)	(0.180)	(0.189)	(0.186)	(0.196)
Mining share of GDP, 1 year lagged		0.244***		0.202*		0.376***	
		(0.108)		(0.114)		(0.119)	
Mining share of GDP, 5 years lagged		-0.206**		-0.352***		-0.331***	
		(0.105)		(0.112)		(0.113)	
Primary sector share of GDP, 1 year lagged			0.777**		0.887**		1.016***
			(0.378)		(0.397)		(0.417)
Primary sector share of GDP, 5 years lagged			0.359		0.194		0.185
			(0.383)		(0.397)		(0.409)
Polarization	0.788***	1.247***	0.323***	0.114	0.490***	0.675***	0.766***
	(0.169)	(0.186)	(0.130)	(0.142)	(0.138)	(0.168)	(0.184)
Fractionalization	-0.631***	-1.226***	-0.627***	-0.151	-0.338***	-0.562***	-0.402***
	(0.158)	(0.194)	(0.133)	(0.139)	(0.134)	(0.164)	(0.160)
Openness, 1 year lagged	-0.018***	-0.019***	-0.013***	-0.015***	-0.014***	-0.017***	-0.012***
	(0.004)	(0.004)	(0.004)	(0.004)	(0.004)	(0.004)	(0.004)
Openness, 5 years lagged	0.006	0.011***	0.013***	0.013***	0.019***	0.011***	0.015***
	(0.004)	(0.004)	(0.004)	(0.004)	(0.005)	(0.004)	(0.005)
Intensity of external threat, 1 year lagged	0.004	0.018	-0.015	0.013	0.003	0.060	0.009
	(0.037)	(0.039)	(0.038)	(0.040)	(0.039)	(0.040)	(0.045)

Table 5.3
(continued)

	1	2	3	4	5	6†	7†
Intensity of external threat, 5 years lagged	0.094***	0.091**	0.074*	0.069	0.067	0.132***	0.070
	(0.041)	(0.042)	(0.042)	(0.043)	(0.044)	(0.044)	(0.049)
Crude oil price 1, year lagged				-0.270	-0.308*	-0.257	-0.297
				(0.184)	(0.185)	(0.180)	(0.185)
Crude oil price, 5 years lagged				0.462***	0.465***	0.490***	0.446***
				(0.152)	(0.150)	(0.150)	(0.151)
Agricultural produce price, 1 year lagged				-0.184	-0.046	-0.131	-0.168
				(0.430)	(0.431)	(0.428)	(0.430)
Agricultural produce price, 5 years lagged				-1.400***	-1.319***	-1.589***	-1.29***
				(0.343)	(0.337)	(0.337)	(0.345)
Oil producer	0.974***	-0.245	1.528***	1.167***	1.232***	0.918***	1.249***
	(0.200)	(0.250)	(0.225)	(0.236)	(0.235)	(0.248)	(0.393)
Landlocked	0.583***	-0.559***	0.451***	-0.154	0.131	-0.381**	-0.617***
	(0.182)	(0.149)	(0.148)	(0.162)	(0.160)	(0.169)	(0.232)
United Kingdom				-0.888***	-0.330***	-1.07***	-0.855***
				(0.146)	(0.141)	(0.171)	(0.201)
Constant	1.49	4.993***	-7.728***	6.628***	0.903	12.52***	2.88
	(1.157)	(1.207)	(2.31)	(2.462)	(3.371)	(2.48)	(3.72)
Observed	1,093	1,091	1,093	1,091	1,093	1,063	1065
Log likelihood	-394.700	-390.426	-380.027	-364.184	-371.375	-368.482	-372.980
Wald χ^2	100.80	91.27	113.85	111.03	111.36	151.54	98.17

Note: *** significant at 1 percent, ** significant at 5 percent, * significant at 10 percent. In columns with †, South Africa is excluded from the sample.

one- and five-lags of all variables but fractionalization and polarization, which have very limited variability. Typically five-year lagged variables are more significant than one-year lagged variables. The main results are confirmed in terms of the variables that were significant when treated simultaneously. This is also true in terms of marginal effects. Indeed the two most important variables that turn out to be significant are (1) intensity of external threat, in particular when lagged five years, though with a small marginal effect (0.027), and (2) the mining share of GDP, with both lags showing marginal effects equal to 0.09. When a serious external threat occurs, the military is likely to become more powerful (in terms of resources and political role), and afterward this can lead to a coup. This is in contrast to the predictions of the benchmark theoretical models by Acemoglu et al. (2010).

5.5 Concluding Remarks

In this chapter we analyzed the probability of a country experiencing a military dictatorship. We use a panel of 48 African countries over the period 1970 to 2007. We found a number of results, which are summarized below:

1. Income per capita negatively affects the probability of a military rule. In particular, lower levels of income per capita increase the probability of the military taking office, but as income increases, the probability gets smaller. Richer countries are less likely to experience a military coup. Indirectly this confirms the modernization theory.

2. The size of the manufacturing sector appears to be positively connected with the probability of a military coup. That is, the larger is the share of manufacturing, the higher appears to be the probability of a military rule. To some extent, this result recalls the question on whether a military rule can turn out to be an engine of economic growth and development. In the past, this argument had been proposed for the Chilean economic performance under Pinochet. However, a more plausible interpretation is that both foreign and local entrepreneurs demand security and safety for their business activities. This appears to be more the case in low-income countries of Africa. Further research is needed on this point in particular.

3. The degree of openness is negatively related with the probability of a military coup. That is, larger openness to trade negatively affects

military rule. In other words, open economies are less likely to support military juntas. This may conflict with the previous result so as to affirm that relationship between entrepreneurship and military regimes is complex.

4. Polarization and fractionalization have opposite effects; the former increases the probability of a military rule, and the latter decreases it.

5. The existence of an external threat becomes significantly positive only when lagged. Perhaps societies have "memory" of external threat that has stuck in their set of beliefs. In other words, past threats affect current probabilities because individuals elaborate only beliefs that are persistent over time. On an aggregate basis, this seems to be confirmed by this result.

6. A higher crude oil price may negatively affect military rule, whereas an agricultural produce price is usually not significant.

Future research may address the issue of duration of military regimes and the distinction between civilian and military dictatorships both in terms of the socioeconomic circumstances that may lead to such governments and differences among the policies implemented by these regimes.

Acknowledgments

We thank Arye Hillman, Dan Kovenock, Pierpaolo Pierani, Martin Gassebner, the audiences at the Centre for the Study of African Economies Conference 2011 (University of Oxford), EIB (University of Barcelona), 21st Silvaplana Workshop in Political Economy, the 16th Meeting of the "Society for the Study for the Diffusion of Democracy" (Florence), and The CESifo Venice Summer Institute "The Economic of Conflict: Theory and Policy Lessons" for suggestions. We remain responsible for any mistakes.

Notes

1. They follow Acemoglu and Robinson (2006).

2. Huntington (1957, 1995) characterizes the civil and military relations in industrial democracies as "objective civilian control," which involves (1) meticulous military professionalism and recognition by military officers of their professional responsibilities, (2) the subordination of the military to civilian political leaders in basic decisions on foreign and military policy, (3) recognition by that leadership of the autonomy of the military,

and (4) minimal military intervention in politics and minimal political intervention in the military. These features are lacking in military dictatorships.

3. Caruso (2010) and Ricciuti and Costa (2010).

4. Besides income inequality there is a growing literature on "horizontal inequality" and conflict. Horizontal inequality relates to bigotry in the treatment of groups based on their religion, ethnicity or race in political, economic, and cultural interactions (Stewart 2008; Cederman et al. 2011).

5. Kimenyi and Mbaku (1996) argued that in autocratic regimes the military elite is in a position to extract rents because without the support of the military the government is, in general, not able to sustain itself. They empirically confirmed for developing countries the negative relationship between transfers to the military and the extent of democracy.

6. Aslaksen and Torvik (2006), Collier and Hoeffler (2005a), Collier et al. (2009), Brunnsch-weiler and Bulte (2009) and Bornhorst et al. (2008).

7. Defined as those experiencing growth in industrial jobs, GDP, and urbanization.

8. Military centrality is an index that includes the number of troops and internal security forces and the defense budget as a percentage of GNP.

9. The dataset is available at http://econ.worldbank.org/WBSITE/EXTERNAL/EXTDEC/EXTRESEARCH/0,,contentMDK:20649465~pagePK:64214825~piPK:64214943~theSitePK:469382,00.html.

10. The database is available at https://pwt.sas.upenn.edu//.

11. Original data include "Mining, manufacturing and utilities" from which we subtract the item "Manufacturing." Utilities create some noise in the measurement of the mining sector, but its size is small.

12. The database is available athttp://unctadstat.unctad.org.

13. The dataset is available at http://www.econ.upf.edu/~reynal/data_web.htm.

14. We have also tried a variable for internal conflict, since one can expect a military dictatorship to arise in response to social turmoil. However, this variable turned out never to be significant. Details are available on request.

15. The dataset is available at http://www.correlatesofwar.org/.

16. CIA Factbook.

17. A correlation matrix is available upon request from the authors.

18. The role of FDI in gross capital formation in Africa can be surmised from data available every year in the World Investment Report by UNCTAD. For example, in 1990 to 2010 the annual contribution of FDI inflows to gross capital formation in West Africa rose from 13.8 to 26.8 percent, in central Africa from 0 to 40.8 percent, in east Africa from 1.7 to 12.9 percent, and in southern Africa from 0 to 14.5 percent. On average, in 1990 in sub-Saharan Africa the contribution of FDI to gross capital formation was 3.9 percent in 1990 and 23.75 percent in 2012 (Unctad 2010).

19. Plotted together, there is backward-bending relationship between these variables.

References

Acemoglu, D., D. Ticchi, and A. Vindigni. 2010. A theory of military dictatorships. *American Economic Journal: Macroeconomics* 2: 1–42.

Acemoglu, D., and J. A. Robinson. 2006. *Economic Origins of Dictatorship and Democracy*. New York: Cambridge University Press.

Acemoglu, D., J. A. Robinson, and T. Verdier. 2003. Kleptocracy and divide-and-rule: A model of personal rule. *Journal of the European Economic Association* 2: 162–92.

Alesina, A., A. Devleeschauwer, W. Easterly, S. Kurlat, and R. Wacziarg. 2003. Fractionalization. *Journal of Economic Growth* 2: 155–94.

Aoki, M. 2001. *Toward a Comparative Institutional Analysis*. Cambridge: MIT Press.

Aslaksen, S., and R. Torvik. 2006. A theory of civil conflict and democracy in rentier state. *Scandinavian Journal of Economics* 108: 571–85.

Beck, T., G. Clarke, A. Groff, P. Keefer, and P. Walsh. 2001. New tools in comparative political economy: The database of political institutions. *World Bank Economic Review* 15: 165–76.

Besley, T., and J. A. Robinson. 2010. Quis custodiet ipsos custodes? Civilian control over the military. *Journal of the European Economic Association* 8: 655–63.

Besley, T., and T. Persson. 2008. Wars and state capacity. *Journal of the European Economic Association* 6: 522–30.

Besley, T., and T. Persson. 2009. The origins of state capacity: Property rights, taxation, and policy. *American Economic Review* 99: 1218–44.

Besley, T., and T. Persson. 2010. State capacity, conflict and development. *Econometrica* 78: 1–34.

Bohlken, A. T. 2010. Coups, election and predatory state. *Journal of Theoretical Politics* 22: 169–215.

Bornhorst, F., S. Gupta, and J. Thornton. 2008. Natural resource endowments, governance, and the domestic revenue effort: Evidence from a panel of countries. Working paper 170. IMF, Washington, DC.

Brunnschweiler, C. N., and E. H. Bulte. 2009. Natural resource and violent conflict: Resource abundance, dependence and the onset of civil wars. OxCarre Research paper 18. University of Oxford.

Caruso, R. 2010. Butter, guns and ice-cream: Theory and evidence from sub-Saharan Africa. *Defence and Peace Economics* 21: 269–83.

Cederman, L. E., N. B. Weidmann, and K. S. Gleditsch. 2011. Horizontal inequalities and ethnonationalist civil war: A global comparison. *American Political Science Review* 105: 478–95.

Collier, P., and A. Hoeffler. 2005a. Democracy and resource rents. Working paper series 16. Global Poverty Research Group, University of Oxford.

Collier, P., and A. Hoeffler. 2005b. Coup traps: Why does Africa have so many coups d'état? Working paper. Center for the Study of Africa Economies, University of Oxford.

Collier, P., F. Van der Ploeg, M. Spence, and A. J. Venables. 2009. Managing resource revenues in developing economies. OxCarre Research paper 15. University of Oxford.

Dal Bò, E., and R. Powell. 2009. A model of spoils politics. *American Journal of Political Science* 53: 207–22.

Deacon, R. T. 2009. Public good provision under dictatorship and democracy. *Public Choice* 139: 241–62.

De Groot, O. J. 2011. Spillovers of institutional change in Africa. *Kyklos* 64: 410–26.

Economist Intelligence Unit. 2011. Democracy Index 2010. The Economist Intelligence Unit Limited, London.

Fearon, J. D., and D. D. Laitin. 2003. Ethnicity, insurgency and civil war. *American Political Science Review* 97: 75–90.

Freedom House. 2009. *Freedom in Sub-Saharan Africa 2009: A Survey of Political Rights and Civil Liberties*. Washington DC.

Geddes B. 2010. How the military shapes dictatorships. Mimeo. University of California, Berkeley.

Gandhi, J. 2008. *Political Institutions under Dictatorship*. New York: Cambridge University Press.

Ghosn, F., G. Palmer, and S. Bremer. 2004. The MID3 Data Set, 1993–2001: Procedures, coding rules, and description. *Conflict Management and Peace Science* 21: 133–54.

Gonzalez, F. M. 2005. Effective property rights, conflict and growth. *Journal of Economic Theory* 137: 127–39.

Gonzalez, F. M. 2010. *The Use of Coercition in the Society. Oxford Handbook of the Economics of Peace and Conflict*. Oxford: Oxford University Press.

Hammond, R. A., and R. Axelrod. 2006. The evolution of ethnocentrism. *Journal of Conflict Resolution* 50: 926–36.

Heston, H., R. Summers, and B. Aten. 2009. Penn World Tables Version 6.3. Center for International Comparisons of Production, Income and Prices at the University of Pennsylvania.

Huntington, S. 1957. *The Soldier and the State: The Theory and Politics of Civil-Military Relations*. Cambridge: Belknap Press of Harvard University.

Huntington, S. 1995. Reforming civil-military relations. *Journal of Democracy* 6: 9–17.

Jackman, R. 1978. The predictability of coups d'état: A model with African data. *American Political Science Review* 72: 1262–75.

Jenkins, J., and A. Kposowa. 1990. Explaining military coups d'état: Black Africa, 1957–1984. *American Sociological Review* 55: 861–75.

Johnson, T., R. Slater, and P. McGowan. 1984. Explaining African military coups d'état, 1960–1982. *American Political Science Review* 78: 622–40.

Kimenyi, M. S., and J. M. Mbaku. 1996. Rents, military elites, and political democracy. *European Journal of Political Economy* 11: 699–708.

La Porta, R., F. Lopez-de-Silanes, A. Shleifer, and R. Vishny. 1999. The quality of government. *Journal of Law Economics and Organization* 15: 222–79.

Lunde, T. K. 1991. Modernization and political instability: Coups d'état in Africa 1955–85. *Acta Sociologica* 34: 13–32.

McGuire, M. C., and M. Olson. 1996. The economics of autocracy and majority rule. *Journal of Economic Literature* 34: 72–96.

Montalvo, G. J., and M. Reynal-Querol. 2005. Ethnic polarization, potential conflict and civil war. *American Economic Review* 95: 796–816.

Montalvo, G. J., and M. Reynal-Querol. 2010. Ethnic polarization and the duration of civil war. *Economics of Governance* 11: 123–43.

O'Kane, R. 1993. Coups d'état in Africa: A political economy approach. *Journal of Peace Research* 30: 251.

Ricciuti, R., and J. Costa. 2010. State capacity, manufacturing and civil conflict. *Economic Bulletin* 30: 3038–43.

Stewart, F. 2008. *Horizontal Inequalities and Conflict: Understanding Group Violence in Multiethnic Societies*. Basingstoke: Palgrave Macmillan.

Tangerås, T. P., and P. N. Lagerlöf. 2009. Ethnic diversity, civil war and redistribution. *Scandinavian Journal of Economics* 111: 1–27.

Tusalem, R. F. 2010. Determinants of coups d'état events, 1970–90: The role of property rights protection. *International Political Science Review* 31: 345–65.

Unctad 2010. World Investment Report 2010. UNCTAD, Genève.

Verbeek, M. 2000. *A Guide to Modern Econometrics*. Hoboken, NJ: Wiley.

Weede, E. 1986. Rent seeking, military participation, and economic performance in LDCs. *Journal of Conflict Resolution* 30: 291–314.

Wintrobe, R. 1990. The tin pot and the totalitarian: An economic theory of dictatorship. *American Political Science Review* 84: 849–72.

Wintrobe, R. 1988. *The Political Economy of Dictatorship*. Cambridge: Cambridge University Press.

6 Sociopolitical Conflict and Economic Performance in Bolivia

Jose Luis Evia, Roberto Laserna,
and Stergios Skaperdas

Many existing approaches to understanding economic performances in low-income countries have not been particularly useful (see Easterly 2001 for a critical review of the various approaches). With all the technological and organizational advances that have occurred over the past half century, let alone the advances that had taken place earlier than that, it would be difficult to understand the economic stagnation of countries like Bolivia if one were to rely solely on economic factors as explanatory variables.

It has therefore become increasingly evident that social and political variables, as well as economic ones, are crucial to improving economic performance.[1] Recent research has pointed to the significant role of conflict (and the roles that governance and institutions assume in reducing conflict) in determining economic performance.[2] Bolivia has high levels of particular types of conflict that may well be distinct from those in other countries of the Americas. The conflicts are among unusually highly developed collective organizations—organized along economic, regional, or ethnic dimensions—that seek to improve their positions through lobbying and influence, strikes, protests, and other forms of collective action. The state appears to have a limited capacity in containing these conflicts, although that capacity has fluctuated over the years.

In this chapter we first describe the landscape of social and political conflicts in Bolivia, the main participating organizations and actors, and how these have evolved in the past few decades. We introduce a dataset on conflicts in Bolivia since 1970 that was constructed by Roberto Laserna, and that we employ in the chapter.

We then examine how appropriative conflict, governance, and economic performance interact. In particular, we argue that conflict in Bolivia affects economic performance in a number of distinct ways.

First, the different types of conflict have direct economic costs that take away resources from production, consumption, and investment. Second, conflict changes the incentives that would normally be expected in a frictionless world of markets so that production, investment, and innovation are distorted in ways that significantly impinge on economic performance. How conflict and growth are related, however, depends on the sources of growth. Conflict and growth generated through investment are negatively related because of the aforementioned negative incentive effects associated with insecurity. Growth that is generated purely from external sources (e.g., from changes in the terms of trade, or from official transfers from abroad) are positively correlated with conflict, as such external sources of growth tend to intensify rent-seeking and other types of appropriative competition. Third, conflict and the levels of resultant economic activity affect investments in "institutions," "governance," or "property rights," which in turn affect future levels of conflict and economic performance.

We provide economic explanations by delineating and developing models that make these different points, and we offer some preliminary evidence in support of some of the hypotheses that we develop. In section 6.1, we present the different dimensions of sociopolitical conflict in Bolivia, introduce the dataset on conflict, and make some preliminary assessment of the effects of conflict. In section 6.2, we develop a simple model that relates the two different types of growth to levels of conflict and develop hypotheses that we examine in section 6.3, where we present estimates of the direct costs and some spillover costs of conflict as well. Section 6.4 concludes.

6.1   Social and Political Conflict in Bolivia

The types of conflicts that have been taking place in Bolivia are qualitatively different from the violent conflicts and civil wars that have taken place in many low-income countries since World War II (see Collier et al. 2003), including those in Latin American countries like Colombia.[3] In Bolivia, conflict takes the form of protests, strikes, boycotts, roadblocks, and other similar "appropriative" activities that are undertaken by well-organized groups. The influence of government policies through other political channels that may not involve any overtly observable appropriative activities also takes place. What is probably unique among other Latin American countries (and perhaps most other low-income countries as well) is the very high level of collective organization of various groups along economic, regional, or ethnic dimensions.[4]

6.1.1   On the Different Dimensions of Conflict

Economic Dimensions and Cleavages   Obviously, collective organizations that articulate economic interests are central actors in the types of conflicts that exist in Bolivia. They include ordinary workers' unions, associations and cooperatives, as well as business groups.

Unions include the *Confederación de Trabajadores en Salud* (health workers' union), the *Confederación Sindical de Maestros* (teachers' union), and the *Central Obrera Boliviana (COB)* (see table X.1 in Robinson 2005). In addition self-employed taxi, microbus, bus, or truck drivers have their own associations, just as *cocaleros* and miners do. Furthermore both wage workers (*Federación Sindical de Trabajadores Mineros*) and individual, small entrepreneurs organize in cooperatives (*FENCO-MIN*). These unions and associations have instruments of public pressure that could be categorized as appropriative and include demonstrations, strikes, work stoppages, and road blockades.

Business groups include the *Confederación de Empresarios Privados de Bolivia* (CEPB) and its nine departmental *Federaciones*, the regionally oriented *Cámara de Industria, Comercio, Servicios y Turismo* de Santa Cruz (CAINCO), and special entrepreneurial *Cámaras* in every department grouping industrial, commerce, construction and other sectors (again, see table X.1 in Robinson 2005) as well as more informal groupings one could find within other organizations, from political parties to civic clubs and associations. Such groups have influence through the credible threat of stopping to pay taxes (as argued in Robinson 2005, an instrument that seldom has been used), their connections with politicians, or their partial ownership of media.

Regional Cleavages   City or regional associations (*Comités Cívicos* and *Juntas Vecinales*) have been important independent actors in policy determination. Most were founded as voluntary organizations of the elite to promote modernization in the first half of the twentieth century, but gained momentum during the national revolution of the 1950s when the Santa Cruz committee managed to claim a permanent, proportional share in hydrocarbons exploitation: an 11 percent royalty on the production value of hydrocarbons for the region.[5] Public investment decided by regional authorities and funded with royalties soared in the region and partially explains the rapid economic growth of Santa Cruz, which became somewhat of a model for other regions.

During military governments, civic committees established themselves as participatory channels, developing consensus-building practices within the regions and negotiating public works and, in some cases, policies, with the government.[6]

Cochabamba, Tarija, Chuquisaca, Beni, Potosí, and other regions or cities like El Alto organized civic associations capable of mobilizing their constituents for demonstrations, strikes, road blockades, as well as for less overt forms of political action. Such civic association action has been instrumental in the past two presidents of the country losing their office.

The discovery of sizable hydrocarbon deposits in Tarija and the existence of a relatively more developed market economy in the eastern part of the country, the so-called half-moon states (Pando, Beni, Santa Cruz, and Tarija), have created in recent years tensions with the central government in La Paz and other more centralist, state-dependent regions, regarding the policies of exploitation and use of the benefits of these deposits, and the more general institutional structure of the country. Regions with more defined identities as such and stronger civic organizations demand more decentralization in the form of autonomous states.

The civic groups and associations are playing, and can be expected to continue to play, prominent roles in the staking of positions and political maneuvering so as to be in better bargaining positions.

Ethnic Dimensions   Another dimension that can be a source of contention is that of ethnicity. The main cleavage that could be identified is that between indigenous communities and what is perceived as a Spanish-derived culture. Organizations like the *Confederación Sindical Única de Trabajadores Campesinos Tupac Katari* (CSUTCB), the *Confederación de Indígenas del Oriente Boliviano* (CIDOB), and the National Council for indigenous communities (*Consejo Nacional de Ayllus y Markas del Qollasuyo*) exert political pressures through demonstrations and road blockades, developing an ethnic identity against what they call internal colonialism that continued during the republic and after independence from Spanish colonial rule (1825).[7]

For a long time in Bolivia, the class divisions were almost coincidental with ethnic divisions. There was an overlapping whereby the poor were mostly indigenous, the upper classes were mostly white and in between, as the real middle class, integrated by truck drivers and middlemen, were the mestizo or cholo groups. This overlapping was reinforced both by discriminatory policies aimed to the economic exploitation of the indigenous labor force that were put in motion during colonial times, but also by successful movements of cultural resistance that lead to the official recognition of specific areas where indigenous groups were capable of preserving their traditional institutions, albeit at the cost of isolating them from the process of modernization with subsequent disadvantages for the participation of members of the group in the market economy and urban life.[8]

The coincidence among the two structures of social differentiation started to crumble after the Nationalist Revolution of the 1950s. The agrarian and educational reforms opened processes of urbanization and social mobility that changed dramatically the economic structure, removing partially the economic "explanations" of ethnic differentiation and discrimination. When some cholos, quechuas, and aymaras became wealthy, they realized that exclusion was not only economic but also cultural, while at the same time those at the lower levels were able to see that being indigenous should not inevitably mean being poor. In both cases, ethnic cleavages became more visible and easy to perceive, so that appealing to them made viable the development of politics of identity and the emergence of ethnic movements. Paradoxically, when structures of discrimination began to change, ethnicity became a hot political issue and a source of major tensions in Bolivia.

Simplistic views on Bolivia, exposed in the political discourse of the emerging groups and uncritically accepted in the media, tend to forget the long history of ethnic mixture within indigenous groups and between them with Western groups. The "mestizaje" was an accepted policy during most of the Colonial period and was officially promoted during the national revolution with the support of social movements, in an attempt to create a unified, national culture and to expand political and economic participation through educational, agrarian, and electoral reforms. The objective of empowering indigenous groups was so successful that it led some of them to a more radical belief: that they do not need to share power, but to control it and recover what has been supposedly lost during the past five centuries. The risk of ethnic conflict arose basically from this way of understanding the issue, which is not general but it is certainly powerful to mobilize feelings of resentments and revenge.

Besides overt political pressures, preexisting or constructed differences in ethnicity can reduce productivity in the workplace, and if widespread can impinge of economic performance.[9]

Lobbying and rent-seeking in the proverbial smoke-filled room is another form or activity that remains covert and almost impossible to measure. What has been measured in Bolivia are different types of overt conflictual activities, in the dataset collected by one of the authors.

6.1.2 Description and Preliminary Analysis of Bolivian Conflict Data

The data on conflict was systematically collected from the most important national newspapers from January 1970 up to the present.[10] The data proved to broaden our understanding of social conflict in Bolivia, while providing quantitative indicators of social disruption, participation, motives, and tools used to exert pressure on governments and the rest of the population.

Every collective event was recorded in a form where the event is described by a phrase and the main and secondary participants are identified as well as the adversary as defined by the protest leaders. The duration and results of the event were also recorded, as were other variables such as place, dates, and coverage. Since the data come from newspapers, not all have the same information, so the information was compared, contrasted, and complemented, and the data polished and refined to one data sheet per event. Once the forms had been completed and duplicates discarded, the information was codified and entered in a computer.

An event is a social, collective action that disrupts production, trade, transportation, or the delivery of public services, including the proper functioning of institutions by infrastructure takeovers or sit-ins. Therefore, for analytical purposes, it must be remembered that a social conflict is not only a recorded event but may have been expressed by a single event or by a chain of events, involving one or many groups. For a deeper understanding of a specific social conflict, the database is clearly insufficient. But it has value as a juncture of social forces and for quantitative analysis.

The dataset used in this chapter contains information on 11,247 events registered between January 1970 and September 2006, in 17 variables plus aggregations that can be made for analytical purposes. There were 25.5 events registered per month during the 441 months covered so far by the data, but the number of events varied considerably from none in some very repressive periods to more than

Figure 6.1
Bolivia: Number of social conflicts per year, 1970 to 2005. Source: Social Conflicts Watch
Program—CERES (Bolivia).

90 during the first postauthoritarian government. In this chapter we
use this database mostly aggregating data per year up to 2005, so that
the periods match those used in economic statistics. The graph in figure
6.1, which shows conflictive events per year, provides a first glimpse
of the past few decades.

After a period of political instability, in August 1971 a faction of the
army took control of the government and abolished civil liberties until
1978, when social protests and international pressures forced general
elections. This period coincided with an improvement in the terms
of trade that enabled Bolivia to achieve an average rate of growth of
5.5 percent.

During these years GDP increased and the number of conflicts
decreased. Although there could be a relationship between growth and
the reduction of the number of conflicts, the abolition of civil liberties
in a nondemocratic regime is a relevant explanatory factor in the low
number of conflicts in this period, since political parties and unions
were banned and thousands of leaders and intellectuals fled to exile.
Also the acute increase in conflicts at the end of the 1970s could be
explained by political reasons: the struggle for democracy and civil
liberties. But also the growth of output in the 1970s could have engi-
neered a struggle for the distribution of income that was masked and
presented as a struggle for democracy.

The period between 1978 and 1982 was one of social unrest, frus-
trated elections, and coups d'état, in which nine civilian and military

governments alternated in power. This period ended with the democratic transition, when a civilian coalition of leftist inspiration took office. The return to democracy unleashed social claims, which the government was unable to control. The deterioration of the world economy, natural disasters that affected agricultural production, and high levels of social conflict generated a hyperinflation that forced the government to shorten its period, calling for early elections in 1985. The average rate of growth between 1978 and 1985 was minus 1.1 percent.

In these years of social instability and short-term governments, declining output accompanied increasing social conflict. The inverse relationship between conflict and growth could be understood differently, depending on the direction of causality. The fall in output could induce increasing social conflicts. But there also could be the possibility that the pattern of more conflict and less output was the outcome of the previous period: the increase of output generated a distributive fight, which damaged growth. The economic crisis that emerged reduced output, and ended the distributive conflict: growth may contain the seeds of its own destruction. If this is the case, this has strong implications for growth in Bolivia: growth could only be sustainable if it spreads its benefits to the whole society.

In 1985 a new government took office and implemented its "New Economic Policy," liberalizing most of the productive and service activities, and pushing for an open market economy. This period of democracy and market-oriented economy ended in 2003, when the president was forced to leave the country in the middle of a violent turmoil. In this period the average rate of growth for the Bolivian economy was of 3.5 percent and, until 1997, the levels of conflict declined. To what extent could growth explain the reduction of conflicts between 1986 and 1997 or could the reduction of conflicts explain growth? The relationship reversed from then on with increasing conflict and social instability, as well as declining growth.[11]

Going back to the data shown in figure 6.1, there are two periods with low conflict and with high peaks in 1970, 1985, and 2004, and the second low-conflict period being longer than the first. A major difference between those two periods lies in the political regimes ruling those periods. While the first was mostly run by the military (1970 to 1982, with disruptions and several coups d´etat), the second was fully democratic, with free elections to renew governments and parliament operating uninterruptedly.

The least intense year was 1981, soon after the military interrupted a democratic opening and imposed a violent authoritarian regime, closely tied with drug trafficking.[12] And the highest peak corresponds to 1984, when there was an escalation of conflicts and mobilizations that, at the end, shortened the Siles Zuazo government by one year.

After general elections, Congress appointed Paz Estenssoro as president in 1985, starting a process of structural adjustment and institutional reforms that introduced profound changes in the country during the immediate terms of Jaime Paz and Gonzalo Sánchez de Lozada. In a way, this process was interrupted when General Banzer, the military ruler of the 1970s, was elected in 1997. As can be seen in the graph, the number of conflictive events immediately skyrocketed in a trend that continues well into the 2006, hampering governance and weakening democratic institutions. At the end of 2003 President Sanchez de Lozada, elected to his second term in 2002, was forced to quit, and the same happened to his successor, the former Vice President Carlos Mesa, by the middle of 2005. The number of events declined a little during the short administration of Eduardo Rodriguez, the Justice who was appointed by Congress in June 2005 to preside over anticipated elections that took place in December. Evo Morales, a peasant leader from the coca region of Chapare won by a landslide, promising to give the state control over natural resources and to "reverse internal colonialism." His administration began in January 2006 and therefore it is left out of the scope of this chapter.

Based on what is shown in the graph and what is known of the political process, it seems clear that when the military ruled, the number of conflicts signaled how open or closed was the regime to political participation, channeled mostly by overt social actions. When there was civilian rule, the number of conflicts signals the weakening of institutional governance, implying a declining capability of representative bodies to manage social and political conflicts. In both cases the growing number of conflicts can be considered an indicator of a reduced capability of the Executive branch to implement public policies.

The more active groups are from the middle classes. As can be seen in table 6.1, protagonists of the largest percentage of events were public employees followed by students, urban teachers, and university employees.

Aggregating these data into fewer categories, the chart in figure 6.2 shows the predominance of the middle classes in the whole period. However, it is interesting that a major change occurs during the last

Table 6.1
Leading groups in social conflicts, 1970 to 2005

	Frequency	Percent
No information	20	.2
Mining workers	532	4.9
Manufacturing workers	421	3.9
Construction workers	135	1.2
Other manual workers	223	2.0
Traditional peasants	543	5.0
Cocalero peasants	210	1.9
Urban neighbors	513	4.7
Housewives	69	.6
Handicrafters—self-employed manual workers	36	3
Rural teachers	195	1.8
Urban teachers	612	5.6
Banking employees	260	2.4
Students	1,039	9.5
Professionals	196	1.8
Public employees	1,651	15.1
University employees and teachers	444	4.1
Private entrepreneurs	288	2.6
Petty traders	222	2.0
Transportation drivers	315	2.9
Political militants	179	1.6
Citizens in general	825	7.6
Unemployed—fired workers	282	2.6
Veterans—retired workers	176	1.6
Other groups	744	6.8
COB	320	2.9
COD	322	3.0
Indigenous—native	60	0.6
Cívic organizations	68	0.6
Total	10,900	100.0

Source: Social Conflicts Watch Program—CERES (Bolivia).

Leading groups (aggregated)

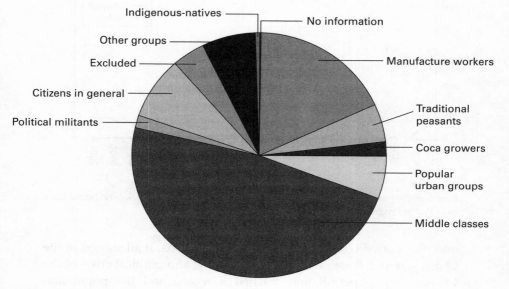

Figure 6.2
Leading groups in social conflicts, 1970 to 2005. Source: Social Conflicts Watch Program—CERES (Bolivia).

years (see figure 6.3). When we differentiate the leading groups of conflictive events in just two categories, formal and informal, based on the type of institutional linkage they have, we can see that informal workers, both rural and urban, have gained in importance since 1998, by being responsible for the majority of events in the last year of the period.

The same trend is observable for groups that cannot be defined in those terms, either because they include both or because their main identity prevents classifying them in terms of formality. What is clear is the declining relevance of social actors linked to the formal economy and the institutional system, which is also signaled by the reduced importance of traditionally powerful organizations, such as the *Central Obrera Boliviana* and the *Federación de Mineros*. The latter is in fact the backbone of the labor movement in Bolivia, and it has had the power to impose policies and ministers to friendly governments, and often also to prevent coups or topple governments they deemed adversarial. The political system between 1932 and 1985 was dominated by the

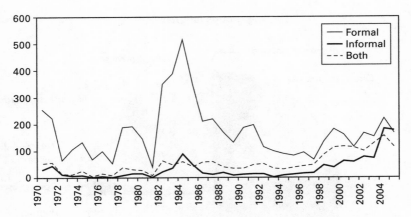

Figure 6.3
Trends in the participation of social groups in conflict, 1970 to 2005. Source: Social Conflicts Watch Program—CERES (Bolivia).

interplay between the Army and the labor unions. It all started in the
Chaco war and remained until the economic and political crisis of the
1980s, when hyperinflation reached a record and the population
expressed demand for order.[13]

In that sense, the current wave of conflicts is very new. Not only
because the nature of the main actors (informal workers, citizens, and
rural peasants) but also because the arena where it is taking place is
quite different.

Democracy is no longer a novelty, as it was for most of the people
in 1982, but a regularity. State-owned companies were privatized and
the fiscal budget was expanded, mostly dedicated to social expenditures. A big part of it was also decentralized in more than 300 municipalities and 9 state governments (*Prefecturas*). The tin crash of 1985
determined the closure of big state-owned mines and an aggressive
plan attracted foreign investments to the hydrocarbons sector, placing
Bolivia at the core of the energy market in South America and completely changing the structure of international trade. In the meantime,
a market-led economy continues its development in the eastern part of
the country, with a dynamic agriculture-producing industrial inputs
like soy beans, cotton, and sugar cane, and the agricultural frontier for
the peasantry has expanded toward the lowlands, supported by the
insatiable cocaine market and, paradoxically, by "alternative development" efforts to control drug trafficking.[14]

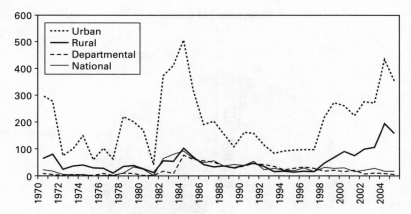

Figure 6.4
Trends of rural/urban participation in social conflicts, 1970 to 2005. Source: Social Conflicts Watch Program—CERES (Bolivia).

Therefore the conflict peaks detected in the plotted series took place in very different scenarios and the shown trends also express those changes. In the graph of figure 6.4, for instance, even though urban conflicts are still dominant, the rural dwellers are leading a growing proportion of events, which demonstrates greater and stronger organizations, despite the declining demographic relevance of rural areas.

In the same figure 6.4 it is also possible to see that the number of events covering a whole department or the whole country have also declined, making visible the process of fragmentation in the social action scene. Conflictive events tend to be smaller, more particularistic, and harder to reach political aggregation, contrary to the case in the 1970s and 1980s. But smaller and particularistic events, lead by fragmented groups, do not mean that they are less disruptive. It may be the opposite.

As figure 6.5 describes, there is a wide variety of pressure tools used in conflictive events. The more frequent are labor strikes, public demonstrations, and hunger strikes, but the number of blockades and takeovers is also very high. When we aggregate the events in wider categories, an interesting picture of the trends emerges.

We find in fact that events can be differentiated according to the required behavior of the participants. We call *active* those types of events that demand that participants to do something different from their normal, regular daily life activities and that has an external effect on other actors. And we call *passive* those events where the participants

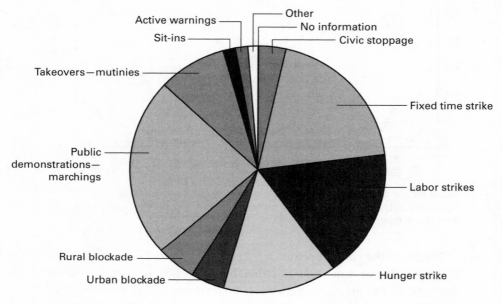

Figure 6.5
Types of conflict, 1970 to 2005. Source: Social Conflicts Watch Program—CERES (Bolivia).

are required to stop doing something that is a daily routine. A road blockade and a demonstration are active events, whereas a labor strike or a civic stoppage is a passive event. Of course, during a civic stoppage there may be a blockade, and during labor strikes there may also be demonstrations. In our database they are registered as secondary manifestations, leaving the dominant one as the main characteristic of the event.

Figure 6.6 plots the whole series aggregating events in just two categories: passive and active events. It is easy to see a change in the declining relevance of passive events and the growing importance of active events. In absolute terms, there are more active events now than there were passive when those were dominant.

This means that social conflicts may now be more disruptive because they are not confined to the place of labor but take the streets and affect the lives of many more people who are unrelated to the matter of conflict. As a result the risk of violence is greater in active events. Some events have turned violent, and have disrupted the lives and work of

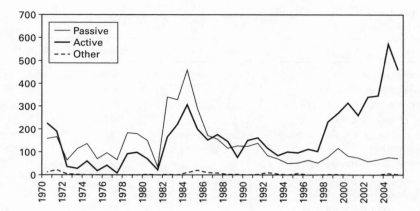

Figure 6.6
Trends of aggregated types of conflict, 1970 to 2005. Source: Social Conflicts Watch Program—CERES (Bolivia).

the rest of the population. Road blockades, for instance, put pressure on innocent civilians to obtain some good or service from the adversary, whether it is the government or a private company. Active events usually try to hit on or to involve a third party in a conflict between two parties, which leads to some level of violence toward the third parties. Not surprisingly, there are often clashes between the active group and the general population. Clashes may end up with people injured or even dead. These risks are even greater when governments refuse to intervene or to regain control of the public spaces used in active events.[15]

6.1.3 On the Politics of Social Conflict

What are, according to our database, the motivations and immediate causes for social conflict in Bolivia? There are two variables that should provide a clue: the stated objectives of the leading groups, provided that their official claims are to be trusted, and the adversary toward whom they address their actions and pressures. Table 6.2 shows the first case.

From the main stated objectives, as described in the table, we see that the largest number of events were related to wages (22.7 percent), followed by more specific demands to participate in nominations or in support of the institution or company. The next largest number, almost 20 percent, was related to public policies or governmental decisions

Table 6.2
Main objectives

Issues	Frequency	Percent
No information	29	0.3
Civil rights and freedom	393	3.6
Human rights—legal justice	302	2.8
Rule of specific laws	577	5.3
Demanding or rejecting nominations and appointment of authorities	715	6.6
Participation in management	124	1.1
Expropiation of properties	360	3.3
To change laws and norms	1,067	9.8
In support of the government	76	0.7
Rejecting government authority or policies	1,052	9.7
Public works for the area	739	6.8
Consumption conditions	380	3.5
Labor conditions	395	3.6
Wage increases	1,224	11.2
Wage payments	1,258	11.5
Labor stability	500	4.6
Organizational—factional conflicts	253	2.3
Solidarity with third parties	402	3.7
Demanding support to a specific company or institution	642	5.9
Other	412	3.8
Total	10,900	100.0

Source: Social Conflicts Watch Program—CERES (Bolivia).

considered to be harmful to the leading group, although often the discourse refers also to "the nation" or "the people."

Crossing this variable with the one that identifies the adversary as defined by the leading group, there is clear dominance of corporatist goals (see crosstab in the annex). Thus the fusion of social actors, political parties, and the state is verified by the data, which according to Touraine would be a basic characteristic of corporatist populism.[16]

A summary of the adversary toward whom a social pressure is addressed shows that the state is the main subject of conflict. When combined with other public institutions, like municipalities or public companies, almost 90 percent of events were directly related to the state. Of course, most were not "against" but "in support of the state, demanding participation or, perhaps more precisely, integration into the political process.

Main forms of action

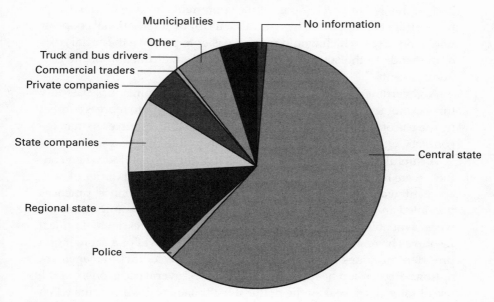

Figure 6.7
Identified adversaries in social conflicts, 1970 to 2005. Source: Social Conflicts Watch Program—CERES (Bolivia).

To a large extent, the relevance of the state as the core of social conflicts in Bolivia suggests, as we have alluded to already, a deeper explanation of the causes of social conflict: rent-seeking or, more generally, appropriation of resources.

A combination of historical, political, and sociological analyses show that the state in Bolivia has had a large role in facilitating access to wealth, mainly to natural resources. Their abundance, from the Potosi silver mountain to the current gas reserves, was only available through political favors, which, in a very unequal society, were instrumental in reproducing inequalities. Only the powerful could get political favors, particularly when institutions were weak and vulnerable. Therefore, no matter what the discourse was or still is, most social conflicts in Bolivia are disguised as political when in fact are just seeking to influence the distribution of existing wealth.[17] From influential lobbies to hunger strikes of policemen's wives, from peasants blockading roads to urban dwellers' demonstrations, from university students to civic committees' requesting support for higher education or a development project, all have a common aspiration: to get a bigger share of a public budget that contains a big part of the contestable income. The Bolivian fiscal budget is supported by natural rents (or by international cooperation), and taxes, which would make it easier to perceive the social costs of demands to the state, are paid only by a small fraction of the economic agents.[18]

A government, when confronted by social pressures, has basically three options: to avoid conflict by giving concessions, to repress conflict by the use of legitimate force, or to use all available resources to manage conflicts. Of course, it may combine them in different ways.

A careful analysis of the data shows that the only period when conflicts were mostly managed within the institutional boundaries of government was between 1985 and 1997. Conflict avoidance practices prevailed in periods that lasted only as long as economic resources were available for the government to make concessions. Political resources have also limitations, but often the removal of a cabinet or a president provides a new opportunity to define conflict management options. Repression has subdued conflicts on several occasions, but the use of force does weaken the political legitimacy of governments when they do not utilize opportunities to experiment with and create other options. Something like this seems to have happened only once, in 1985, when a democratically elected government repressed social movements but immediately opened institutional channels for political conciliation. In other periods, repression led to political weakening of governments, reaching political limits that determined sudden changes in government personnel, through military coups d'état. It may be argued that those changes (cabinet crises and even presidents being forced to quit) helped avoid violence and therefore prevented a deeper and more dangerous weakening of the state as an institutional and normative framework for social, political, and economic life.

The three different models of political management of social conflicts during the period, described above, can be seen in figure 6.8. Indicators on how conflicts were managed are the political regime (authoritarian or democratic) and the information on how many conflicts achieved what they demanded, which may be understood as the probability of success for social conflicts (in the graph, the *Pr(suc)* variable represents the fraction of conflicts that are judged to have succeeded in their organizers' objectives).

The first model spans the period from 1970 to 1982, when low levels of conflict were attained by political repression but where the need for

Figure 6.8
Political management of conflicts

political legitimacy of the authoritarian rulers, since the period was dominated by the military, moved them to combine repression with concessions, raising the probability of success for social conflicts. The second model corresponds to the short period between 1982 and 1985 that may be recognized also after 1997 up to the present. It is a model of high levels of conflict that are in a way stimulated by an increasing probability of success, since governments attempt to avoid conflict by making concessions. And the third model is the one located between 1985 and 1997 signaled by a declining number of conflicts and a declining probability of success during a democratic regime, which suggests that social demands were channeled through institutional means rather than conflicts.

6.2 Thinking about Conflict as an Economic Activity and Its Effects on Income and Growth

Protests, strikes, lobbying, or demonstrations take time, effort, and money that become unavailable for useful production or consumption. Therefore they may be regarded as appropriative activities—a term we will be using for much of the remainder of this chapter. Note also that these activities are not combined cooperatively, as ordinary inputs in production are combined. Instead, they are combined *adversarially*: If one side expends more resources on influencing government policy, it increases the chance that a favorable policy to its side will be adopted and reduces the chance that their adversary will prevail. The more time a union spends organizing and mobilizing its members, advertising its position to the wider public, and building coalitions with other groups, the greater is its chance that it will win a strike and the lower is the chance of its employer. Whereas no strike needs to take place and bargains can be struck that would avoid such eventuality, nevertheless the union and the employers engage in appropriative activities so as to enhance their respective bargaining positions. In a world with perfect commitment, such activities would not be needed.

That is, appropriation takes away resources that could be used for useful production and thus tends to reduce production of all sides, but not necessarily reported incomes since appropriation conflicts take place wherever there are "appropriable resources," that is, resources that are disputable or available for contestation. That happens not only when there are resources and they are concentrated, but when their property rights or norms that regulate their use and access are not clear, so that the control or ownership of those resources are disputed. Therefore incentives for appropriative conflict more than for investment or innovation are closely related with the level of security, and thus impinge negatively on economic growth.

In this section we first present a simple model of appropriation to illustrate the basic ideas regarding the relationship between appropriation and income, and we also derive some hypotheses that we subsequently examine empirically. The model combines features from the static rent-seeking and conflict models in Tullock (1980) and Hirshleifer (1991) with those of dynamic models like those in Grossman and Kim (1996), Lee and Skaperdas (1998), and Gonzalez (2005). However, as indicated by our discussion at the end of the previous section, government policies in Bolivia varied over the period we examine in this chapter. That is, the levels of appropriation depend on the degree of security and, more generally, the quality of governance. In appendix B we examine a model in which the level of security and governance are endogenous and discuss some implications relevant to Bolivia at the end of this section.

6.2.1 A Model of Appropriation and Its Economic Effects

For analytical convenience, we consider two organized groups, A and B, whereby each group has solved the collective action problem within the group and behaves as a unitary actor. Income can be derived from two sources: One that is generated exogenously to the actions of each group and can be due to exports of natural resources or local spending by foreign NGOs, governments, or international organizations. We denote the total income generated from these exogenous sources by T. This income is subject to contestation and capture by the two groups.

The second source of income, Y_i, is generated by each group and at least partly depends on the actions of each group. We can call these actions investments and denote them by I_i, with $Y_i(I_i)$ being an increasing function of I_i. Part of this self-generated income is immune to contestation by the other side. Let σ denote the share of Y_i that is secure. The remainder of own-generated income, $(1 - \sigma)Y_i$, is subject to contestation; that is, $(1 - \sigma)Y_A + (1 - \sigma)Y_B$ is in the same pool with T and is contested by the two groups.

The contested portion of income is divided between the two groups in proportion to their respective levels of appropriative activities. Let a_i ($i = A, B$) denote the level of appropriative activity of $i = A, B$. Then the share of contested income captured by group i is[19]

$$p_i(a_{i,}a_j) = \frac{a_i}{a_i + a_j}, \qquad \text{where } i \neq j, \text{ for } a_i + a_j > 0.$$

The net incomes of the two groups are as follows:

$$V_A = \frac{a_A}{a_A + a_B}[T + (1 - \sigma)Y_A(I_A) + (1 - \sigma)Y_B(I_B)] + \sigma Y_A(I_A) - a_A - I_A,$$

$$V_B = \frac{a_B}{a_A + a_B}[T + (1 - \sigma)Y_A(I_A) + (1 - \sigma)Y_B(I_B)] + \sigma Y_B(I_B) - a_B - I_B.$$

From the point of view of each group, there are two categories of income—the contested part that is captured through appropriation and the secure uncontested part—and two sources of costs, the cost of appropriation and the cost of investing in one's own, partly secure, income. We should emphasize, though, that from the social point of view, investment is productive because it creates wealth, whereas as mentioned earlier, appropriation does not lead to any increase in production as it is a purely redistributive activity of existing wealth.

We suppose that investments I_i are undertaken first so that incomes Y_i are determined before levels of appropriation are chosen.[20] For given level of Y_i's, it can be shown that the Nash equilibrium choice of appropriation are identical and equal:

$$a^* = \frac{T + (1-\sigma)Y_A + (1-\sigma)Y_B}{4} \qquad (6.1)$$

Appropriation levels are increasing in exogenous income T, in endogenous group incomes Y_A and Y_B, and in the degree of insecurity (or, conversely, the lower is the degree of security σ, the higher is the level of appropriation).[21] This is because the higher the contested income is, the harder the parties involved will work to capture it. That is, one simple implication of this analysis is that, if the level of security is kept constant, *conflict and appropriation are positively related to income*. Note that this is a statement about the short run. In the long run, higher levels of insecurity and conflict can be expected to reduce investment, and therefore future income. At the same time, if growth were to be generated by increases in foreign aid or natural gas exports, the appropriation would increase just as it does in the static one-period case.

Subtracting this cost of appropriation, each group's net income as a function of own investment becomes

$$V_A(a^*) = \frac{T + (1-\sigma)Y_A(I_A) + (1-\sigma)Y_B(I_B)]}{4} + \sigma Y_A(I_A) - I_A,$$

$$V_B(a^*) = \frac{T + (1-\sigma)Y_A(I_A) + (1-\sigma)Y_B(I_B)]}{4} + \sigma Y_B(I_B) - I_B.$$

Supposing that returns to investment are diminishing, each group i will choose its investment level, denoted I_i^*, so that

$$\left(\frac{1-\sigma}{4} + \sigma\right)Y_i'(I_i^*) = 1.$$

Note that each group's optimal investment can be shown to be positively related to the security level σ. This is intuitively plausible, as the incentives to increase one's own income through investment should depend on how much of this income can be kept away from others. Since, by (6.1), conflict is negatively related to the same security level, we can conclude that *conflict is negatively related to investment*.

Over time, the growth path of Bolivia's income could be considered to have the two types of sources we have examined in this simple model: exogenous sources that may be due to terms of trade effects, discovery of new natural resources, or foreign aid (represented by T in our model) and internal sources due to productive investment. To the extent that conflict is negatively related to investment, we should also expect *conflict to be negatively related to investment-generated income growth*. However, growth that is exogenously generated can either be not related to conflict (when that growth in unanticipated) or positively related to conflict (when that growth is anticipated).

Thus, from the simple model of conflict and appropriation (which is also consistent with much of the related literature that has examined more elaborate economic environments), we have derived the following implications:

• Conflict reduces the resources available for consumption and production.

• Conflict and (contestable) income are positively related.

• Conflict and investment are negatively related.

• Conflict and endogenously generated growth are negatively related.

• Conflict and exogenously generated growth are either not related or positively related (the latter, when growth is anticipated).

6.2.2 On the Role of Governance

In the model we just examined, the role of government, in terms of the variable σ, has been considered exogenous. However, as we have indicated toward the end of section 6.1, the policies of Bolivian governments have varied since 1970, and to some extent these different policies could be considered as interacting with both the levels of economic performance and appropriation. Even when government has not been a direct participant, it should be considered a critical third party with the potential to greatly influence the outcome of the other disputes in which it had not been directly involved.

In appendix B we examine a model in which governance is endogenous, so as to provide guidance in thinking about the role of governance and its effect on conflict and economic performance. We show there that governance depends on economic variables like the value of contested resources. It is perhaps too obvious, yet important to recognize and emphasize the finding that lower incomes could easily lead to lower expenditures on governance, and therefore more conflict. Reductions in exogenous sources of income, like export revenue or foreign aid, for example, could precipitate a breakdown of either the public sector's capacity or the political process' ability to contain conflicts. However, it would be difficult to attribute changes in the level of security and governance solely to economic factors. Knowledge of the *particular historical development* of Bolivia should be relevant and is likely to be significant. Another variable that is critical in the model of the appendix is *the degree of cooperation between the competing groups* regarding how much they are willing to tax themselves and how to allocate public expenditures to the improvement of governance as well as how the groups are willing to use the normal political process.

6.3   Conflict, Income, and Growth

In this section we examine empirically some of the implications derived above. We use the data on conflict described in section 6.1, and macro-economic data that come from official sources (National Statistics Institute). We first provide rough estimates of the direct and spillover costs of conflict and then attempt to disentangle the correlations between conflict and the two different types of income growth that we laid out in the previous section.

6.3.1   Economic Costs of Conflict

Different incidents of conflict have involved different numbers of participants, and therefore different direct and indirect economic costs. In figure 6.9 we report estimates on the direct costs of conflict (left scale), based on the time cost of the participants. (The method we used to measure these costs is outlined in appendix A.) The average over 35 years was a bit below US$60 million per year (in 2004 prices), or

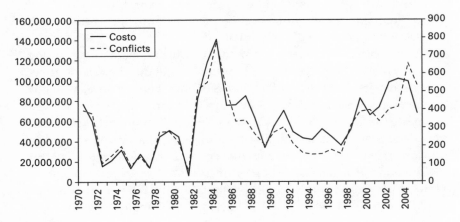

Figure 6.9
Direct costs of conflict

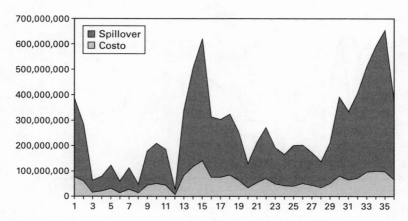

Figure 6.10
Spillover costs of conflict

roughly 1 percent of GDP. As it is evident from figure 6.9, our estimate of their direct costs follows closely the number of incidents of conflict, especially up to the mid-1980s, which denotes that changes in the characteristics of conflict have also economic cost implications.

Different incidents of conflict can in fact also have widely different spillover costs. A strike in a manufacturing plant can affect the output of other downstream and upstream production and a road blockade can bring about wide-ranging disruption in the affected city or region, whereas a sit-in or a protest with few participants does not have much of an effect on economic activity. Based on assumptions of different "multipliers" regarding the spillover effects of different incidents, we have estimated the cost of spillovers and report it in figure 6.10. (Again, for the method used, see appendix A.) The average yearly cost of spillovers was over US$200 million per year (in 2004 prices), which represents more that 3 percent of GDP. As can be seen in figure 6.8, these costs are much higher for the mid-1980s and the 2002 to 2005 period.

Thus the estimated direct and spillover costs significantly reduce GDP, with some years approaching a loss of as much as a tenth of GDP.

6.3.2 Overall Growth and Conflict
Before trying to empirically distinguish between exogenous and endogenous sources of growth, which is a rather difficult task, we first examine any possible relationships between overall growth of GDP

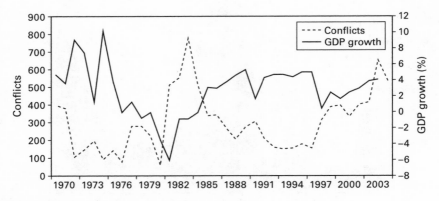

Figure 6.11
Social conflicts and GDP growth, 1970 to 2003
Source: Social Conflicts Watch Program—CERES (Bolivia) and INE.

Table 6.3
Conflict and GDP growth: I

Dependent variable: Conflicts	Constant	Trend	GDP growth lagged	REP	AR(1)	R^2	DW
	218	6.85	−1,723		0.50	0.54	1.95
	(105)	(4.50)	(812)		(0.17)		
	32.81	0.39	−758	132	0.54	0.71	2.06
	(103.72)	(4.27)	(672)	(33)	(0.17)		

Note: Standard errors in parentheses.

and conflict. Figure 6.11 plots GDP growth and conflict, with the correlation between the two variables appearing to be negative.

Econometrically, at first there appears to be a negative relationship between conflict and lagged values of GDP growth, as indicated in table 6.3. (We could not find a relationship between contemporaneous values of GDP growth and conflict.) Adding a discrete variable of the degree of government repression (REP), however, reduces both the effect and the statistical significance of the growth variable.[22] We also regressed GDP growth on lagged values of conflict, with the results shown in table 6.4. Note that the addition of the REP variable in the regression changes neither the quantitative nor the statistical significance of the conflict variable on growth.

The Granger causality test reported in table 6.5 favors the hypothesis that conflict Granger-causes GDP growth. Given our hypotheses about the two opposite expected relationships between growth and conflict,

Table 6.4
Conflict and GDP growth: II

Dependent variable: GDP Growth	Constant	Trend	Conflicts lagged	REP	AR(1)	R^2	DW
	3,262.5	(96.6)	−0.805		0.495	0.39	2.15
	(2,268)		(0.380)		(0.168)		
	89.4						
	(2,268)						
	5,900	170	−0.814	−1,900	0.332	0.48	2.15
	(2,000)	(80)	(0.322)	(900)	(0.200)		

Table 6.5
Granger causality

Null hypothesis:	Observed	F-Statistic	Probability
CONFLICTS do not Granger cause GDPGRO	33	3.211	0.0555
GDPGRO does not Granger cause CONFLICTS		2.532	0.0976

it appears that the negative effect from conflict to lower (endogenously generated) growth predominates.[23] Since the overall growth rate contains both exogenously and endogenously generated components, this is fairly strong, though indirect, evidence of the negative effect that conflict might have on economic growth.

6.3.3 Conflict and Exogenously Generated Income

We now turn to examining the possible effect of exogenous income growth on conflict, as hypothesized in section 6.2. Since Bolivia is a small country, its terms of trade can be safely considered exogenous and changes in income that accompany changes in the terms of trade can be considered exogenous. We will examine the effect on conflict of two variables that can be considered exogenous: the terms of trade themselves and the "trade gain," a variable that measures changes in income due to changes in the terms of trade.

Figure 6.12 shows that the terms of trade, which generally depend on the price of Bolivia's primary exports, are positively correlated with the level of conflict. The changes in income due to shifts in the terms of trade can be referred to as the *trade gain*. The trade gain is calculated as the difference between the current trade balance deflated by a price

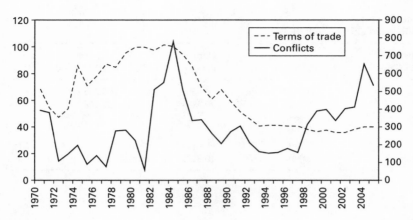

Figure 6.12
Social conflict and terms of trade, 1970 to 2005. Source: Social Conflicts Watch Program—
CERES (Bolivia) and INE.

index minus the trade balance calculated at the export and import
prices of a reference year (base year):

$$T = \left(\frac{X - M}{P}\right) - \left(\frac{X}{P_x} - \frac{M}{P_m}\right),$$

where T is the trade gain, X and M are exports and imports at current
prices, P_x and P_m are the price index for export and imports, respectively, and P is a price index.

The trade gain measures changes of purchasing power of the trade
balance that are partly due to changes in the terms of trade. It must be
remembered that the selection of variables refers to the specific Bolivian
case, where exports are mainly composed of raw materials with little
industrial value added, and where minerals and hydrocarbons provided relevant export revenues, not only for the country's economy but
also, through fiscal rent capture, for public spending.

To calculate the trade gain, we need to choose a base year and a price
index (deflator). We calculated the trade gain with 1990 as base (taking
the prices of exports and imports that prevailed in 1990 as the reference), and using the Consumer Price Index (IPC) as the deflator (measuring the purchasing power in terms of the consumer basket). One
can interpret the trade gain as representing the "rents," if one considers
that the base year reflects the situation without these "rents." Figure
6.13 shows the trade gain as percentage of the GDP. (For 1990 the trade
gain is zero, because we chose this year as the base year).

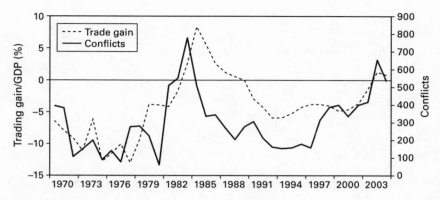

Figure 6.13
Trade gain and social conflict, 1970 to 2005. Source: Social Conflicts Watch Program—CERES (Bolivia) and INE.

Table 6.6
Conflict and exogenous income

Dependent variable: Conflict	Constant	Trend	Terms of trade	Trade gain	Trade gain lagged	REP	AR(1)	R2	DW
	−232.54 (222.72)	14.57 (5.87)	4.18 (2.07)				0.53 (0.15)	0.51	2.07
	−191.27 (189.29)	4.96 (5.50)	2.62 (1.82)			110.72 (34.17)	0.50 (0.17)	0.65	1.98
	263.11 (114.22)	4.93 (4.42)		9.6e-05 (5.6e-0.5)			0.48 (0.18)	0.51	1.95
	125.7 (53.7)	−5.66 (2.31)		0.00012 (2.5e-05)		169.75 (27.2)	0.13 (0.175)	0.75	1.56
	−281.5 (73.2)	25.1 (3.03)			0.00018 (3.1e-05)		−0.076 (0.204)	0.81	1.83

In table 6.6 we regress conflict on our measures of exogenous income. In all cases the sign is as hypothesized—increases in all our measures of income induce increases in conflict. In the case of no statistical significance—as is the case of the trade gain variable—the addition of the REP variable improves it, in addition to increasing explanatory power.

6.3.4 Conflict and Investment

In our discussion and model of the previous section, endogenously generated growth and conflict are mediated through investment. That

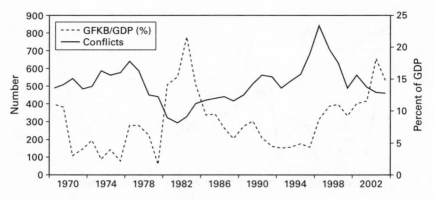

Figure 6.14
Social conflict and investment, 1970 to 2005. Source: Social Conflicts Watch Program—
CERES (Bolivia) and INE.

is, higher conflict tends to reduce investment which, in turn, tends to
reduce that source of growth. The graph in figure 6.14 shows the evolution of investment in the economy, measured through the gross fixed
capital (as percentage of GDP), and social conflict.

The relationship between investment and conflict appears to be
negative for most of the period. We tried several specifications, including lagged values of investment, but the hypothesis of no correlation
between investment and social conflict could not be rejected. The
hypothesis of no co-integration could not be rejected either. It is possible that a large part of investment is not productive investment (e.g.,
in plant and equipment) but housing and other investment that does
not enhance future income, and is partly an outcome of increases in
exogenously generated income.

The graph in figure 6.15 shows the gross fixed capital building for
the private and the public sector, as percentage of GDP for the period
1970 to 2002 (the statistical institute has not released data for later
periods yet). Private capital building was depressed during the 1980s,
contemporaneous with the hyperinflation, and expanded after the stabilization plan. In the late 1990s, the effect of the capitalization program
is clearly recognizable. The capitalization program, the Bolivian scheme
of the Bolivian privatization, consisted of handing the control of public
enterprises to private companies that made the highest investment
offer for the company in a public auction. The company had to invest
resources pledged to the company according to an investment plan, in

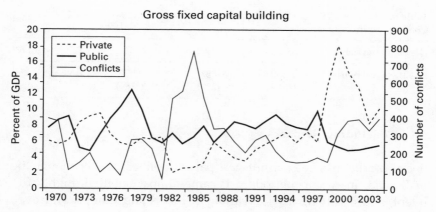

Figure 6.15
Gross fixed capital building

theory doubling its value. In exchange for that, the company received 51 percent of the enlarged company while the rest of the shares went to a trust fund that benefited all Bolivians older than 21 years at the moment of the capitalization, with a yearly payment once they turned 65. As could be expected, this program stimulated private investment. But the process increased private investment much more than the investment pledged by the capitalization only.

Since the bigger companies were acquired by the private sector, public investment decreased following the capitalization program. But not only had the capitalization program increased private investment, it also generated an important reaction in some groups of society. The privatization program was accompanied with significant public criticism and demonstrations against the process, not just from the left but also from the more on the right ADN party.

To assess the relationship between private investment and conflicts, we regressed private investment on conflicts, but only for the period 1970 to 1996. We did not consider the period 1997 to 2002 in the regression because of the capitalization process. The results are shown in table 6.7.

Conflict has a clear negative effect on private investment. As we hypothesized, more conflict had the effect of depressing private investment in the period studied.

Table 6.7
Conflict and investment

Dependent variable	Constant	Conflicts	AR(1)	R2	DW
Private investment	1,125,185	−887	0.581	0.68	1.93
	(111,114)	(287)	(0.184)		

6.4 Concluding Remarks

Social conflict has been an integral part of political and economic life in Bolivia. In certain periods it became almost habitual, highly frequent, and involving a wide variety of issues and groups. However, there have also been times of a more stable social environment, when the frequency of conflict declined and institutions had been working better. The strength of social organizations, whose tradition goes back to the beginning of the twentieth century and became particularly relevant after the National Revolution of the 1950s, partially explain this central feature of Bolivian politics, which is enough to justify our analysis of the likely relationship between conflict and economic growth.

The direct and immediate spillover costs of conflict in Bolivia amount to at least several percentages of GDP, and in some years they have approached a tenth of GDP. Such costs are significant for any country, let alone for a low-income country like Bolivia. The actual impact may even be larger, since the information on conflict comes from written media reports, which is much lower than the real figures. Other sources of appropriation and rent-seeking, not approximated by the data examined here, are also excluded from our estimates. Of course, the effects of conflict are not confined to just these costs, for conflict can affect the incentives for production, investment, and innovation, and therefore affect future growth.

In fact growth seems to reduce conflict when endogenously generated, while it seems to cause conflict when exogenously generated. After specifying a simple model that generates hypotheses that take into account these two different types of growth, we found evidence consistent with the hypotheses. In particular, variation in incomes due to changes in the terms of trade can be considered exogenous, and we find that increases in such income induce greater conflict. However, greater conflict tends to reduce private investment, at least some of which could be considered to be a main source of future (endogenously generated) growth. Finally, the degree of government repression tends, not surprisingly, to reduce conflict.[24]

A corollary of our approach is that a reduction in conflict would increase economic growth in Bolivia, provided that such a reduction is not diverted to some other (perhaps equally) costly appropriative activities. Taking the fight from the streets to the halls of parliament and ministries can be expected to reduce, though not eliminate, the costs of appropriation, provided that the distortions introduced through the normal political process are not much greater than those that have prevailed for the past four decades or so.

Building what has been variously described as "institutions," "governance," or "property rights" is certainly very important, even from a strictly economic point of view, but little is known about how it can be done in practice. However, both history and theory suggest that the main contending groups and their elites could, in principle, agree on greater cooperation, regardless of external conditions and economic influence, and dramatically improve the ways in which the economic pie is divided without dramatically changing the pie itself and the prospects for future growth. Again, though, little is known about how such an elite compact could be practically achieved.

Appendix A: Estimation of Labor Days Lost and Economic Losses due to Social Conflicts

Labor Days
Based on observation and experience, we assigned an estimate of the mean number of participants in the events according to the social group and location registered in the database. For example, for an event led by traditional peasants in La Paz, we assigned 10,000 participants, but only 5,000 in Cochabamba and 2,000 if the event took place elsewhere. If the event was led by the cocaleros, we estimated only 2,000 if the movement took place in La Paz but 5,000 in Cochabamba. For events that took place at national level, bigger parameters were assigned.

We aggregated the data in 27 categories for social groups and 4 categories for location. The assigned parameters we used to estimate the number of individuals participating are shown in table 6.8. Since August 1985 the database registers how many days each event lasted, so we estimated the number of lost days by multipliying the estimated number of participants using the parameters of the previous table times the duration. Missing data was assigned just one day.

Table 6.8
Estimates of event participation

	La Paz	CBB SC	Rest	Nation
1 Mining workers	5,000	1,000	5,000	10,000
2 Manufacturing workers	5,000	4,000	1,000	10,000
3 Construction workers	8,000	4,000	2,000	15,000
4 Other workers (SEMAPA, YPFB, FFCC)	4,000	2,000	500	0
5 Traditional peasants (highlands, valleys, lowlands)	10,000	5,000	2,000	17,000
6 Cocalero peasants and colonists	2,000	5000	500	7,500
7 Urban dwellers and neighborhood committees	10,000	7,000	4,000	21,000
8 Housewives (marginal neighborhoods, workers wives)	2,000	1,000	500	3,500
9 Handicrafters and other nonwage workers	5,000	5,000	2,000	12,000
10 Rural teachers	10,000	7,000	4,000	21,000
11 Urban teachers	15,000	10,000	5,000	230,000
12 EmploIyees of the financial system	2,000	1,000	500	3,500
13 Students (high school–universities)	20,000	15,000	5,000	40,000
14 Professionals (including LAB pilots)	400	200	100	700
15 Public employees	15,000	10,000	200	30,000
16 University teachers and employees	1,000	500	1,000	1,700
17 Private sector employees	5,000	4,000	2,000	10,000
18 Petty traders	10,000	6,000	5,000	18,000
19 Truck drivers	10,000	10,000	500	25,000
20 Party militants	4,000	2,000	20,000	6,500
21 Citizens in general and civil committees	50,000	50,000	100	120,000
22 Unemployed/jobless/fired workers	1,000	500	500	1,600
23 Veterans—retired workers	2,000	1,000		3,500
24 Other groups				
25 Bolivian Central Union of Workers COB				50,000
26 Central unions at regional level	20,000	20,000	20,000	
27 Indigenous, "originarios"	10000	5000	2000	17000

For the period before 1985, we assigned the average number of days that the events with information lasted (2.2 days).

Economic Losses

From the 2004 Household Survey we obtained the average monthly income obtained from labor by occupation and estimated a daily rate in US dollars for each social group category. They ranged from 2.3 dollars per day in the case of poor peasants to 9.6 dollars per day in the case of public servants and private employees.

Multiplying the lost labor days times the daily income rate, we have the estimated economic losses of each event. By using means comparisons by year, it was possible to obtain the total number of days lost in conflict and an estimation of their economic significance expressed in 2004 US dollars.

Economic losses should also take into account the spillover effects of social conflicts. When a group of mining workers blocks a road, not only their labor days are lost but the blockade also has an impact on the productive day of other people. We estimated these costs using the following criteria.

For each type of event we assigned a multiplier effect, so that the total cost of an event would be the previous estimation multiplied by the multiplier effect (see table 6.9). Some types of events are much more costly for the society than others, and the predominance of certain events over other types may signal levels of disruption that are not necessarily reflected in the number of conflicts. These parameters were used to estimate the spillover effect, by multipliying them to the estimated number of days lost or the economic cost of the conflicts.

Appendix B: Modeling Conflict and Governance as Economic Activities

In this appendix we relax the assumption of perfect and costless enforcement of property rights in a variation of the model of section 6.2. Though simple, the model allows for the endogenous costly determination of governance, conflict, and income, all as functions of economic endowments and the valuation of such endowments in international markets. We show that governance depends on economic variables like the value of contested resources. However, governance also can critically depend on norms of cooperation as well as on historical contingencies. Thus it would be difficult to attribute changes in the

Table 6.9
Multipliers for different events

Code	Type of event	Multiplier effect	Criteria
1	Cívic stoppage	2	What happens in one region partially affects the neighboring regions.
2	Strike for a defined period	2.77	To stop working affects the company, its providers and its suppliers. We assign a multiplier that is the reverse of the labor cost of the industry. The labor cost in Bolivia is estimated at a similar percentage of the household consumption over the total demand (36 percent), so that the multiplier effect is $100/36 = 2.77$
3	Strike for undefined period	2.77	
4	Hunger strike	2.77	
5	Urban blockade	12.5	Due to the population density in cities, we estimate that every individual participating in an urban blockade affects 100 more individuals, but not for the same amount of time of the blockade, since people have other options to move around. So we assigned one hour loss per individual suffering a blockade in the city. This is $1/8$ of a labor day, so that the final effect is $100 \times 1/8 = 12.5$
6	Rural blockade	10	Rural blockades affect less people but for more time, since they do not have much more options to drive around and avoid the blockade. In our case we estimated that for every person blocking a road, 20 people are affected for at least 4 hours or half a labor day. So the final effect is $20 \times 4/8 = 10$
7	Marchings and walks	3.12	Marchings and walks on streets and avenues have a similar effect as urban blockades but they last less, so we estimated its impact to be one-fourth of the urban blockade: 3.12 (no difference between urban and rural)
8	Take obres	5.54	Take obres usually involve those participants in the action and those individuals affected by the takeover of an institution or a company. So we estimate its multiplier effect to be twice as the labor strike.
9	Strike on site	2.77	The impact is similar to that of a strike but, of course, with more publicity since workers remain in the building or the company's place.
10	Emergency	0	It does not affect more people.
11	Other	4.737	Since this category involves a variety of events, we assign to it the average of the rest.

level of security and governance solely on economic factors. Knowledge of the particular historical development of Bolivia should be relevant and is likely to be significant.

We continue to consider two organized groups, A and B, each as a unitary actor. Again, income can be derived from two different types of endowments: One that is contestable and exogenous and another is endogenously generated. Let each group initially possess T units of the contestable endowment and have Y units of the secure endowment. Then, in the absence of any conflict or governance costs, the gross value of each group's endowment is

$R = T + Y$.

The parts of the government's budget that consist of transfers to each group and that can be fought over in the future can be considered part of this category of income. That is, to keep our analysis simple, we include in T all the economic resources, including those of the government's budget, that the two groups can be expected to fight over.

The nature and costliness of fighting over the contestable part of each group's income will be examined in detail next. Broadly, the two groups make the following two sets of decisions:

1. The level of government protection of each group's contestable income is determined by past and current taxation and other decisions.

2. Taken the level of protection as given, each group engages in appropriative activities that determine each group's final allocation and income.

That is, we consider a setting in which both governance and conflict are costly economic activities. We begin with the analysis of the second stage of appropriation and conflict.

Conflict

We model insecurity in a somewhat more sophisticated way than we did in section 6.2. Each group could engage in appropriative activities in order to defend its own contestable income, T, or to challenge that of its adversary. Let a_{ij} denote the level of appropriation that group i engages in relation to the contestable income of group j. Note that if $j = i$, then this is the level of appropriative activity in defending own income, and if $j \neq i$, then this is the challenging level of appropriation against i's adversary.

Appropriative activities determine the probability of winning or, equivalently, the share of each contested income[25] in the following fashion:

$$p_{ii}(a_{ii}, a_{ij}) = \frac{\phi a_{ii}^m}{\phi a_{ii}^m + (1-\phi)a_{ij}^m} \qquad (m \in (0,1]),$$

$$p_{ij}(a_{ii}, a_{ij}) = \frac{(1-\phi)a_{ij}^m}{\phi a_{ii}^m + (1-\phi)a_{ij}^m}, \qquad i \neq j \text{ and } \phi \in \left[\frac{1}{2}, 1\right].$$

Here $p_{ii}(a_{ii}, a_{ij})$ is the share of its contested income that the defending group i keeps, and $p_{ij}(a_{ii}, a_{ij})$ is the attacker's share of the defender's contested income. Such functions, commonly called contest success functions, have been used in many different areas of economics, including in rent-seeking, political campaigning, lobbying, as well as in the economics of conflict. In its defense/offense interpretation, this functional form has been used extensively by Herschel Grossman (e.g., Grossman 2001).

The critical parameter that determines the security of property rights is ϕ. The closer to 1 is ϕ, the more secure the property rights of the defender are, whereas the closer the value of that parameter is to 1/2, the more insecure property rights are, with the limiting case of $\phi = 1/2$ being one in which there is no advantage to being a defender relative to the challenger. For our purposes here, we can broadly think of ϕ as being determined by the strength of the courts, the state agencies and bureaucracies, and the political apparatus of the country as a whole. How easy is it for the holder of the (uncertain) property right to argue against the challenger in front of a court, bureaucrats, politicians, or the public at large so as to convince such audiences that the defender is right and not the challenger? The closer ϕ is to 1, the easier it is for the defender and the more difficult it is for the challenger to do so. Also, the more professional are the courts and the bureaucracy, and the greater are the checks and balances in politics, the closer would ϕ be to 1.

Another parameter of interest is m. It can be thought of as a measure of the ease or *effectiveness* of producing appropriative effort.[26] Working directly through the political process and the state (the courts, the bureaucracy, or the halls of parliament) would entail a lower m to fighting it out in the streets or even in the court of public opinion.

In this subsection we take ϕ as well as m as given. Given the level of security, the payoff functions of the two groups are the following:

$$V_A^c(a) = \frac{\phi a_{AA}^m}{\phi a_{AA}^m + (1-\phi)a_{AB}^m} T + \frac{(1-\phi)a_{BA}^m}{\phi a_{BB}^m + (1-\phi)a_{BA}^m} T + Y - a_{AA} - a_{BA},$$

$$V_B^c(a) = \frac{(1-\phi)a_{AB}^m}{\phi a_{AA}^m + (1-\phi)a_{AB}^m} T + \frac{\phi a_{BB}^m}{\phi a_{BB}^m + (1-\phi)a_{BA}^m} T + Y - a_{AB} - a_{BB},$$

where $a = (a_{AA}, a_{BA}, a_{BB}, a_{AB})$ are the strategies of the two groups, one each for defense of own endowment and challenge of the other group's endowment.

Given the sharing functions and the identical endowments that the two groups have, it can be shown that the (Nash) equilibrium levels of appropriation are identical for defense and challenge and across the two groups:[27]

$$a_{AA}^* = a_{BA}^* = a_{BB}^* = a_{AB}^* = \phi(1-\phi)mT.$$

Note that the closer ϕ is to 1 (i.e., the better governance is), the lower is the level of appropriation. ($\phi(1-\phi)$ is minimized at 1 and reaches its maximum at 1/2.) Each group keeps a ϕ fraction of its own contested endowment and receives a $1-\phi$ fraction of its adversary's contested endowment. Given the level of security, the equilibrium payoff of each group equals:

$$V_i^c \equiv V_i^c(a^*) = \phi pT + (1-\phi)T + R - 2\phi(1-\phi)mT$$

$$= [1 - 2\phi(1-\phi)m]T + R$$

$$= \sigma T + R \text{ where } \sigma \equiv 1 - 2\phi(1-\phi)m. \tag{6.A1}$$

As can be expected, the lower is the level of protection ϕ, the lower is the equilibium payoff of each group. Note how, with security given, changes in the value of the endowment T (e.g., by the discovery of new tradable resources, the exhaustion of old ones, or the change in the international price of existing resources) lead to monotonic changes in appropriation and in equilibrium payoffs. In particular, for fixed levels of security, a reduction in T reduces appropriation and increases equilibrium payoff. We next examine how security can be determined by current and past conditions in stage 1 of the two-stage process we have outlined above.

Endogenous Governance

The level of ϕ (as well as of m), and therefore the fraction σ of the contestable endowment that each group eventually keeps, would in general depend on the societal and political norms, but more important for the case of modern, anonymous property rights on the country's political development and the fiscal choices and organizational decisions that have been made in the past as well as those made in the present. Many of these choices can be expected to depend on the country's characteristics. As a first approximation, its current conditions can be considered both similar to those in the past, and to the extent that the conditions might have changed, current conditions can be expected to have considerable influence on current governance. In particular, the resources available for paying and training judges, civil servants, or the police can have an immediate impact on the quality of governance and property rights. These resources are largely determined by the taxing ability of the state, which could in turn greatly depend on the ability of the two contending groups to agree on taxation. Past decisions on taxation also have impact on the quality of governance through the educational level of not just government employees but also of others in the country (lawyers, politicians, engineers, citizens in general) and through other collective-good investments from court buildings to university budgets.

Thus we consider the level of security to be a function of past and present investments on governance so that

$$\sigma = \sigma(g_o + g_A + g_B),$$

where g_o denotes the inherited investments in governance and g_A and g_B are the current contributions to governance by the two groups. We suppose that security is strictly increasing in its argument ($\sigma' > 0$) at a decreasing rate ($\sigma'' < 0$).

How the level of governance expenditures—which we suppose to equal total taxes—is determined is of course an important issue. Security here is a public good, and in the provision of public goods through taxation, there are two focal regimes: One in which public good provision maximizes total welfare and the other in which its provision is noncooperative and generally inefficient. We examine both types of provision regimes and discuss their implications and their relation to Bolivia.

The welfare-maximizing choice of governance expenditures solves the following problem:

$$\max_{g_A + g_B} V_A^c + V_B^c - g_A - g_B$$

$$= 2\sigma(g_o + g_A + g_B)T + 2Y - g_A - g_B.$$

Under the condition that the optimum is interior, or that the inherited level of governance is not too high and there are no liquidity constraints,[28] the welfare-maximizing level of governance expenditures satisfies the following first-order condition:

$$2\sigma'(g_o + \hat{g}_A + \hat{g}_B)T - 1 = 0. \tag{6.A2}$$

It is clear that total optimal expenditure $\hat{g}_A + \hat{g}_B$ can be distributed in many different ways between the two groups (and that in itself can be a source of contention that makes optimal provision difficult to implement). It is clear that $\hat{g}_A + \hat{g}_B$ is positively related to the value of the contested resource T and inversely related to the inherited investments in governance g_o.

The noncooperative contributions to governance are determined as the Nash equilibirum of the game with the following payoff functions:

$$V_A(g_A, g_B) = \sigma(g_o + g_A + g_B)T + Y - g_A,$$

$$V_B(g_A, g_B) = \sigma(g_o + g_A + g_B)T + Y - g_B.$$

It is straightforward to show that the equilibrium is characterized by the same condition for both groups (and also results in determining only the total and not the particular distribution of expenditures between the two groups):

$$\sigma'(g_o + g_A^* + g_B^*)T - 1 = 0. \tag{6A3}$$

As in the case of optimal expenditures, Nash equilibrium expenditures are positively related to T and inversely related to inherited investments in governance g_o. From a comparison of (6.A2) to (6.A3) and given the strict concavity of $\sigma(\cdot)$, we have expenditures in governance under the Nash equilibrium that are lower than optimal expenditures ($g_A^* + g_B^* < \hat{g}_A + \hat{g}_B$). That is, under Nash equilibrium, each group only cares about its own welfare and no weight is put on the adversary's payoff.

We are particularly interested on the effect of a reduction in the terms of trade (a reduction in T) on the levels of security and appropriation. The reason is that volatility and significant reductions in the price of Bolivia's major exports—from silver early in its history to tin during the 1980s—could have been important for government stability, security of property rights, and the level of sociopolitical conflict, with all affecting directly and indirectly economic performance. That is, the external shock of a price reduction in exportables could have had effects on income that go far beyond the direct effect of the price reduction itself.

Considering the case of the noncooperative provision of security, where $\sigma^* \equiv \sigma(g_o + g_A^* + g_B^*)$, and noting from (6.5) that $\alpha_{ii}^* = \phi(1-\phi)mT = T[(1-\sigma^*)/2]$, the overall effect of the value of the contestable endowment on equilibrium appropriation can be shown to be the following:

$$\frac{\partial a_{ii}^*}{\partial T} = \frac{(\sigma^{*'})^2}{2\sigma^{*''}} + \frac{1-\sigma^*}{2}. \tag{6.A4}$$

The first term is negative since $\sigma'' < 0$, whereas the second term is positive. The first term is negative because it reflects the effect on appropriation via governance—a reduction in T reduces governance and security and increases appropriation (i.e., $\phi(1-\phi)m$ increases as a result of a reduction in governance expenditures). The second effect is positive because it is the direct effect on appropriation. Overall, the effect of the value of T on equilibrium appropriation is ambiguous. If the governance effect (first term of equation 6.A4) dominates, the total effect is negative; if the direct, value-of-prize effect dominates, the total effect is positive:

$$\frac{(\sigma^{*'})^2}{\sigma^{*''}} + 1 - \sigma^* < 0,$$

or when

$$-\frac{\sigma^{*''}}{\sigma^{*'}} > \frac{\sigma^{*'}}{1-\sigma^*},$$

which occurs when $-\sigma^{*''}/\sigma^{*'}$ is large enough or when σ is sufficiently concave.

Regardless of whether the two groups choose the optimal or noncooperative levels of governance, the qualitative effects on security and appropriation are similar. Of course, when the choices are noncooperative, the negative effects of a reduction in T are higher on levels of security, on appropriation, and on real income.

However, the level of T might also have an independent effect on the choice of governance expenditures. If, for example, the two groups were to originally have the norm of choosing the optimal level of governance but suddenly face a shortfall in their expected incomes, they might refrain from that optimal level of governance expenditures and decide on a lower level or even the noncooperative level of governance expenditures. Such a choice might come about because of internal disputes within groups as well as between the groups that are often precipitated by reductions in incomes or other crises. Allowing for a continuous effect of T on the level of cooperation between the groups regarding governance expenditures, we can posit that these expenditures are a convex combination of the optimal and noncooperative choices:

$$g_i^\gamma = \gamma(T)\hat{g}_i + (1 - \gamma(T))g_i^*, \qquad \text{where } \gamma'(\cdot) > 0 \text{ and } i = A, B. \tag{6.A5}$$

Then the total effect on appropriation of changes in pT becomes

$$\frac{\partial a_{ii}^*}{\partial T} = -\frac{\gamma'(T)\sigma^{\gamma'}(\hat{g} - g^*)}{2} + \frac{\sigma^{\gamma'}}{2}\left[\gamma\frac{\hat{\sigma}'}{\hat{\sigma}''} + (1 - \gamma)\frac{\sigma^{*'}}{\sigma^{*''}}\right] + \frac{1 - \sigma^\gamma}{2}, \tag{6.A6}$$

where

$$\sigma^\gamma \equiv \sigma(g_o + g_A^\gamma + g_B^\gamma), \quad \hat{g} \equiv \hat{g}_A + \hat{g}_B, \quad g^* \equiv g_A^* + g_B^*, \quad \text{and}$$
$$\hat{\sigma} \equiv \sigma(g_o + \hat{g}_A + \hat{g}_B).$$

The last two terms of (6.A6) are qualitatively similar to those of the two terms in (6.A4). The first term in (6.A6) is new and is due to the change in the level of governance choices induced by a change in T; that effect is negative since $\gamma'(T) > 0$, $\sigma^{\gamma'} > 0$, and $\hat{g} > g^*$. Recapitulating, a reduction in the value of the contested resource T has three effects:

1. a tendency to reduce appropriation because the value of the contestable resource is reduced (represented by third term in (6.A6);

2. a tendency to increase appropriation because it reduces the governance expenditures and security—represented by second term in (6.A6);

3. a tendency to increase appropriation because it reduces the degree of cooperation on the choice of governance expenditures between the groups—represented by the first term in (6.A6).

Of course, the opposite effects are present on the real final income of the groups. In addition each group's income is reduced directly since T is part of income, but which is counterbalanced by the reduction in governance expenditures as a result of a reduction in T. Final real income for each group is

$$Y_i^r = \sigma(g^\gamma(T))T + R - g_i^\gamma(T).$$

Overall, the effect of the size of contested resources on incomes is ambiguous and depends on the *degree of cooperation* among the groups, which in turn can critically depend on *historical contingencies*. Economic factors are important but can only be a part of the story. History and elite norms of cooperation can be important as well. We provide an overview of these noneconomic factors in Bolivia in section 6.4.

Acknowledgments

We would like to thank participants at a conference on Bolivia, held at the Kennedy School of Government, for their comments, and especially Francisco Rodriguez for his detailed suggestions. For discussions, comments, and background information, we are also very grateful to Eduardo Antelo, Viviana Caro, Nathan Fiala, Horst Grebe, Gary Milante, Herbert Muller, Suresh Naidu, Oswaldo Nina, Henry Oporto, Guido Riveros, Jim Robinson, Carlos Toranzo, and anonymous referees.

Notes

1. North (1990) has been an early advocate of the centrality of institutions in determining economic performance. Olson (2000) has been emphasizing the role of governance and power, whereas Greif (2006) provides a historical perspective informed by modern game theory. Acemoglu, Johnson, and Robinson (2005) have spearheaded the recent push in establishing the centrality of the social and political determinants of economic growth. An early precursor to such approaches who introduced the possibility of conflict and appropriation in modeling economic growth but who received almost no attention is Haavelmo (1954).

2. In empirical studies, Rodrik (1999) has examined the effect of social conflict and the institutions that control conflict on economic performance, Easterly and Levine (1997) have assessed the role of ethnic divisions in Africa's low growth, Alesina et al. (2003) have extended the analysis (but with ambiguous results), whereas Abadie and Gardeazabal (2003) have focused on the measurement of the differential performance between Basque regions and other regions of Spain. Hirshleifer (1989, 1991, Grossman (1991,, Skaperdas (1992), Skaperdas and Syropoulos (2002) have allowed for the possibility of conflict in otherwise regular economic models and shown how resource allocation differs significantly from those in which conflict is not possible. Garfinkel and Skaperdas (2007) provide an overview of the literature. Miguel et al. (2004) show how exogenous shocks to growth induce conflict, whereas Collier et al. (2003) synthesize much research on civil wars and their relationship to economic development.

3. For an overview of new data in conflict research, see Bernauer and Gleditsch (2012); with few exceptions, these data concern violent types of conflict, not the types of mostly nonviolent conflicts (and their effects) that we examine. For methods that exploit the spatial distribution of (violent) conflicts, see Cederamn et al. (2011) and Weidmann and Ward (2010).

4. This high level of collective organization could be part of the legacy of the active efforts in encouraging such organization that lead to the nationalist revolution in the 1950s, which in turn promoted grassroots organizations in order to favor participatory populist politics over formal democracy. See Lora (1967–1980), Dunkerley James (1984, Lavaud Jean Pierre (1998), and Calderón and Smukler (2000).

5. Roca (1980) read Bolivian history as produced through regional conflicts and Calderón and Laserna (1983) collected analysis of the contemporary role of regional movements.

6. See Laserna (1987).

7. See particularly Calderón and Dandler (1984), Rivera (1984), and Hurtado (1986).

8. See Albo, Greaves, and Sandoval (1981), Loayza (2004), and Laserna (2005).

9. Gellner (1983) has described nation-building as a process of cultural homogenization that essentially plays the role of homogenizing labor for ultimately economic purposes. In the absence of such homogenization, communication and collaboration within the modern workplace becomes difficult according to Gellner, and reduces overall economic performance.

10. There have always been at least three major newspapers, one from each of the main Bolivian cities. In La Paz we started with *Presencia* and moved to *La Razon* when the first ceased publication. In Cochabamba with *Los Tiempos* and in Santa Cruz with *El Deber*. The same forms and definitions have been used for the whole time to make sure that the data, no matter when is collected, remain compatible. Before coding the forms, they are compared and the information completed, making sure that each event is registered only once. Not all conflictive events reach the newspapers, and we found that the higher the frequency, the greater is the proportion of small conflicts not registered in the media. This means that estimates based on this database are conservative, but analyses based on long-term trends are quite accurate.

11. For a review of the whole period, see Laserna (2004).

12. Gen. Luis García Meza was condemned to thirty years in prison, and Cnl. Luis Arce Gómez, his Interior Minister, was sentenced to jail in the United States for drug trafficking. Both are in jail.

13. See Malloy (1989), Klein (1968), and Zavaleta (1970).

14. Coca leaves production in Bolivia is part of a diversified, domestic economy of small peasants. They are, of course, trying to take advantage of high prices but also are stimulated by the seemingly endless market and the agricultural features of coca cultivation (a permanent plant that allows for three to four crops a year and is resistant to plagues and soil depletion). However, it is very unusual to find peasants dedicated only to coca cultivation, since most emphasize risk reduction more than economic profit. Alternative development projects made the coca areas the most attractive due to the concentration of public investments there. See Sanabria (1993)

15. During the last years, the Banzer (1997–2001), Mesa (2003–2005) and Morales (2006) governments made explicit vows not to use repression in social conflicts, in an attempt to gain or to preserve popularity while making concessions to appease the conflictive groups. As we will see, this policy backfired, encouraging ever more conflicts since the costs or risks of being part of them declined. Before Banzer's quitting due to a fatal ailment, there were already voices asking for his resignation, and Mesa was actually forced to resign in the middle of a social upheaval. Morales's popularity, immense at the

beginning, has been declining as social conflicts arise, but his fate may certainly be different. Sanchez de Lozada's second term (2002–2003) was interrupted by social conflicts, even though he tried to keep control by using the police and the army, when fragmentation and internal conflicts had been already eroding those institutions just as the rest of the government institutions.

16. See Touraine (1987, pp. 12ff).

17. From this perspective it is not surprising to find a very high correlation between the number of conflicts and the publicly known natural gas reserves, which are indicators of rent expectations.

18. In fact 0.3 percent of the taxpayers provide 56.2 percent of all collected taxes, and 77.2 percent pay 0.1 percent of all taxes. Moreover there are only 508 thousand tax payers for an economically active population of around 4.5 million people. Data collected by CAINCO (2004).

19. This a function that was first used by Tullock (1980) and many other since then in literatures as varied as those on rent-seeking, conflict, patent races, law and economics, tournaments, and even in sports economics. For properties of this and other functional forms, see Hirshleifer (1989).

20. Different sequences of moves yield similar results. We have avoided the introduction of a truly dynamic model for simplicity, but the main ideas regarding the effect of appropriation on growth can be conveyed with the device of including investments in the static model here.

21. In appendix Bwe develop a model in which security is endogenous, and examine some of its implications in section 6.4.

22. The variable takes the value of 1 when the government has been considered predominantly repressive in dealing with conflict, the value of 2 if it has been moderately repressive, and the value of 3 when the government has been judged to be reluctant to use force in dealing with conflict. For a justification of using such a variable, see our discussion in the last part of section 6.1.

23. Strictly speaking, in the model of section 6.2 it is insecurity that causes both the levels of appropriative conflict and growth, rather than appropriative conflict directly causing growth.

22. Of course, greater repression could well divert appropriation into other, less overt forms (e.g., the distribution of rents among those who are close to the government).

25. Probabilities of winning and shares are equivalent under risk neutrality and divisibilty of incomes. For exposition purposes, we will employ the share interpretation in the remainder of this chapter.

26. Note that m is the elasticity of the "impact" function a^m; that is, $m = (\partial a^m / \partial a)/(a^m / a)$. Also Jia (2005) provides a stochastic derivation of contest success function, where the output of each side's effort is stochastic, with m being a parameter that reduces the variability of output as a function of effort (with higher m reducing that variability).

27. If endowments for the two groups were different, the levels of appropriation would be higher for the endowment that is higher but the levels of the defense and challenge would still be identical.

28. In practice, especially for low-income countries like Bolivia, we can expect the liquidity constraints to be more likely to be binding, especially for the case of welfare-maximizing provision.

References

Abadie, Alberto, and J. Gardeazabal. 2003. The economic costs of conflict: A case-control study for the Basque country. *American Economic Review* 93 (1): 113–32.

Acemoglu, D., S. Johnson, and J. A. Robinson. 2005. Institutions as the fundamental cause of long-run growth. In P. Aghion and S. Durlauf, eds., *Handbook of Economic Growth*, vol. 2. Amsterdam: North Holland, 385–472.

Albo, Xavier, Thomas Greaves, and Godofredo Sandoval. 1981. *Chukiyawu, la cara aymara de La Paz*, 3 vols. La Paz: Cipca.

Alesina, Alberto, Arnaud Devleeschauwer, William Easterly, Sergio Kurlat, and Romain Wacziarg. 2003. Fractionalization. *Journal of Economic Growth* 8: 155–94.

Bernauer, Thomas, and Nils Petter Gleditsch. 2012. Preface: New event data in conflict research. *International Interactions* 38 (4): 375–81.

CAINCO. 2004. *Cámara de industria, comercio y turismo de Santa Cruz. "Lo que el Estado recauda de la economía boliviana" (Msc.).* Santa Cruz: Cainco.

Calderón, Fernando, and Roberto Laserna. 1983. *El Poder de las regiones*. Cochabamba: Ceres.

Calderón, Fernando, and Alicia Smukler. 2000. *La Política en las calles*. Cochabamba-La Paz: Ceres-Plural-Uasb.

Calderón, Fernando, and Jorge Dandler, eds. 1984. *La Fuerza histórica del campesinado*. Cochabamba: Unrisd-Ceres.

Cederman, L.-E., N. B. Weidmann, and K. S. Gleditsch. 2011. Horizontal inequalities and ethno-nationalist civil war: A global comparison. *American Political Science Review* 105 (3): 478–95.

Collier, Paul, V. L. Elliott, Havard Hegre, Anke Hoeffler, Marta Reynal-Querol, and Nicholas Sambanis. 2003 *Breaking the Conflict Trap; Civil War and Development Policy*. Washington, DC: World Bank and Oxford University Press.

Dunkerley, James. 1984. *Rebellion in the Veins: Political Struggle in Bolivia*. London: Verso.

Easterly, William, and Ross Levine. 1997. Africa's growth tragedy: Policies and ethnic divisions. *Quarterly Journal of Economics* 112 (4): 1203–50.

Easterly, William. 2001. *The Elusive Quest for Growth*. Cambridge: MIT Press.

Garfinkel, Michelle R., and Stergios Skaperdas. 2007. Economics of conflict: An oveview. In T. Sandler and K. Hartley, eds., *Handbook of Defence Economics*, vol. 2. Amsterdam: North Holland, 649–709.

Gellner, Ernest. 1983. *Nations and Nationalism*. Ithaca: Cornell University Press.

Gonzalez, Francisco M. 2005. Insecure property and technological backwardness. *Economic Journal* 115: 703–21.

Greif, Avner. 2006. *Institutions and the Path to the Modern Economy: Lessons from Medieval Trade*. New York: Cambridge University Press.

Grossman, Herschel I. 1991. A general equilibrium model of insurrections. *American Economic Review* 81: 912–21.

Grossman, Herschel I. 2001. The creation of effective property rights. *American Economic Review, Papers and Proceedings* 91 (2): 347–52.

Grossman, Herschel I., and Minseong Kim. 1996. Predation and accumulation. *Journal of Economic Growth* 3 (1): 333–50.

Haavelmo, Trygve. 1954. *A Study in the Theory of Economic Evolution*. Amsterdam: North-Holland.

Hirshleifer, Jack. 1989. Conflict and rent-seeking success functions: Ratio vs. difference models of relative success. *Public Choice* 63: 101–12.

Hirshleifer, Jack. 1991. The paradox of power. *Economics and Politics* 3: 177–200.

Hurtado, Javier. 1986. *El Katarismo*. La Paz: Ed Hisbol.

Jia, Hao. 2005. *A Stochastic Derivation of Contest Success Functions*. Irvine: University of California.

Klein, Herbert. 1968. *Orígenes de la revolución nacional*. La Paz: Juventud.

Laserna, Roberto. 1987. *Movimientos sociales regionales. Apuntes para la construccion de un campo empirico*, vol. 10. Madrid: Pensamiento Iberoamericano.

Laserna, Roberto. 1997. *20 (Mis)conceptions on coca and cocaine*. La Paz: Clave.

Laserna, Roberto. 2005. *Ciudades y pobreza*. Cochabamba: Umss.

Laserna, Roberto. 2004. *La democracia en el ch'enko*. La Paz: Milenio.

Lavaud, Jean, Pierre. 1998. *El embrollo boliviano. Turbulencias sociales y desplazamientos politicos*. La Paz: Ifea-Cesu-Hisbol.

Lee, Jaewoo, and Stergios Skaperdas.1998. Workshops or barracks? Productive versus enforcive investment and economic performance. In M. R. Baye, ed., *Advances in Applied Microeconomics*, vol. 7. Stamford, CT: JAI Press, 103–13.

Loayza Bueno, Rafael. 2004. *Halajtayata, Etnicidad y racismo en Bolivia*. La Paz: Fundemos.

Lora, Guillermo. 1967, 1969, 1970, 1980. *Historia del Movimiento Obrero*, 4 vols. Cochabamba: Los Amigos del Libro.

Malloy, James. 1989. *La Revolución inconclusa*. Cochabamba: Ceres.

Miguel, Edward, Shanker Satyanath, and Ernest Sergenti. 2004. Economic shocks and civil conflict: An instrumental variables approach. *Journal of Political Economy* 112 (4): 725–53.

North, Douglass C. 1990. *Institutions, Institutional Change, and Economic Performance*. New York: Cambridge University Press.

Olson, Mancur. 2000. *Power and Prosperity*. New York: Basic Books.

Rivera, Silvia. 1984. *Oprimidos pero no vencidos, luchas del campesinado aymara y quechua 1900–1980*. La Paz: Hisbol.

Robinson, James A. 2005.The political economy of decentralization in Bolivia. Harvard School of Government.

Roca Jose, Luis. 1980. *Fisonomía del regionalismo boliviano*. Cochabamba, La Paz: Los Amigos del Libro.

Rodrik, Dani. 1999. *The New Global Economy and Developing Countries: Making Openness Work*. Washington, DC: Overseas Development Council.

Sanabria, Harry. 1993. *The Coca Boom and Rural Social Change in Bolivia*. Ann Arbor: University of Michigan Press.

Skaperdas, Stergios. 1992. Cooperation, conflict, and power in the absence of property rights. *American Economic Review* 82 (4): 720–39.

Skaperdas, Stergios, and Constantinos Syropoulos. 2002. Insecure property and the efficiency of exchange. *Economic Journal* 112 (476): 133–46.

Touraine, Alain. 1987. *Actores sociales y sistemas políticos en América Latina*. Santiago: PREALC.

Tullock, Gordon. 1980. Efficient rent seeking. In J. M. Buchanan, R. D. Tollison, and G. Tullock, eds., *Toward a Theory of the Rent Seeking Society*. College Station: Texas A&M University Press, 355–72.

Weidmann, Neils B., and Michael D. Ward. 2010. Predicting conflict in space and time. *Journal of Conflict Resolution* 54 (6): 883–901.

Zavaleta, René. 1970. *Bolivia: el desarrollo de la conciencia nacional*. Montevideo: Marcha.

7 Occupational Choices and Insurgency in Afghanistan's Provinces

Vincenzo Bove and Leandro Elia

7.1 Introduction

Afghanistan is a landlocked, mountainous, and sparsely populated country, with an area of 647,500 square kilometers, the same size as Texas, and bordered by Iran, the People's Republic of China, and the Central Asian republics of Turkmenistan, Uzbekistan, and Tajikistan. Afghanistan is strategically positioned between Central Asia and the Middle East and is crucial for the political stability of the entire region, given its particular geographic location. It has been historically inhabited by a tribal society, divided into several tribes and clans. Afghanistan is also one of the world's poorest countries; its population, estimated at almost 30 million, is largely rural and mostly uneducated. Development indicators published by the World Bank and the UN rank Afghanistan at the bottom of virtually every category, including nutrition; infant, child, and maternal mortality; life expectancy; and literacy. The country is also at the lowest levels of global human security, according to the Human Development Index. Over the last two decades, Afghanistan has been ravaged by civil conflicts and foreign interventions. In 1979, over 100,000 Soviet troops invaded the country and withdrew after a prolonged war against the Mujahedeen and other Afghan resistance groups, backed by the United States. After 1992, when the Mujahedeen took Kabul, the local warlords fought a destructive internal war to consolidate their economic activities, fragmenting the country in a series of subconflicts. In the mid-1990s, the disintegration of the country and the dissatisfaction among the population about greedy "warlordism" encouraged the rise of the Taliban. From their stronghold in the south, in the Kandahar province, the Taliban conquered the country. By September 1996, they had captured Afghanistan's capital, Kabul. Under the fundamentalist Taliban group,

Afghanistan became a haven for terrorists. After the terrorist attacks of September 11, 2001, the United States and a coalition of its allies invaded Afghanistan and removed the Taliban from power. Following the Taliban's removal, the coalition began the process of establishing a new Afghan government. However, despite eleven years of external assistance, humanitarian aids and external military intervention to support a fragile government, unemployment rates remain high and a large segment of the population does not have access to basic services.

Opium is the country's biggest export—Afghanistan provides 93 percent of the global supply of opium and over 90 percent of the heroin trafficked into the United Kingdom, according to the several reports from the United Nations Office for Drugs and Crime. The primary route is overland from Afghanistan via Iran, Pakistan, Turkey, the Balkans, and the Netherlands. Many factors contributed to the development of opium cultivation in the country, in particular, the almost complete collapse of central government after the Soviet withdrawal; the warring tribes' need for sources of financing; and the fact that opium is a crop well adapted to the prevailing weather conditions. Indeed opium is relatively drought-resistant, and due to a limited irrigation system in many areas, its cultivation is preferable to wheat. Average yield in Afghanistan is about 40 kg/ha compared to 10 kg/ha in Burma, the former major global producer of illicit opium (UNODC 2008). Moreover dry opium is easy to store and transport; the poor state of roads and stocking facilities in the country give it an advantage over other crops (Martin and Symansky 2006). Following the fall of the Taliban, enduring insecurity and widespread corruption among government officials contributed to further development of this illicit activity.[1] The persistence of poverty is another important driver of poppy cultivation. As any labor-intensive crop, opium is particularly appropriate for a labor-rich and capital-poor country. It generates jobs in on-farm casual work (e.g., weeding and harvesting) and in the non-farm rural sector. According to the United Nations Office for Drug and Crime, in 2009 poppy cultivation created 5.6 jobs per hectare (UNODC 2009a), thus sustaining the livelihoods of millions of rural Afghans. In particular, one in seven Afghans is reportedly involved in some aspect of the trade, with 6.5 percent of the population involved in growing poppy (UNODC 2009b).

Ever since their return as insurgents into southern Afghanistan in 2005, the Taliban—and other antigovernment forces—have derived enormous profit from the opium trade. Although the magnitude is subject to debate, the total drug-related funds accruing to insurgents and warlords were estimated at $200–400 million in 2006 to 2007 and at $450–600 million between 2005 and 2008 (UNDOC 2009b). These estimates included incomes from four sources: levies on opium farmers, protection fees on lab processing, transit fees on drug convoys, and taxation on imports of chemical precursors. Even though Taliban insurgents levy taxes on all other forms of trade and agriculture, opiates are the highest value product on the market. The drugs trade is supposed to pay for soldiers, weapons, and protection, and is also a source of patronage. By providing protection to farmers and traffickers (e.g., preventing interdiction and eradication efforts), they delegitimize the central government and reconsolidate the political influence in areas under their control. For this reason ISAF forces consider opium eradication a "strategic threat" for the long-term security of the country, while the UN finds "a strong link between insecurity and opium cultivation" (UNODC 2009b).

In a comprehensive review of the literature on civil war, Blattman and Miguel (2010, p. 8) argue that the causal line from poverty to conflict should be treated with caution; because this line can be drawn in reverse, war devastates life, health, and living standards, devastates physical infrastructure and human capital, and may alter social and political institutions. In our context, violence and a state of lawlessness may well affect the production and trafficking of opium. Indeed, in 2006, UNODC published a study on the socioeconomic and psychologic factors influencing the variations of opium poppy cultivation the country (UNODC 2006). Among the motivations for opium cultivation, they found that a lack of rule of law and a high level of insecurity were important factors affecting the choice to grow opium. Therefore we do not only question the ability of the Taliban-led insurgency to finance war expenditures through the drug economy; we investigate whether the (perceived) lack of security makes illegal activities more profitable. If a positive conflict-induced opium prices mechanism and an opium-for-weapons mechanisms work at the same time, the combination would create a vicious circle: violence stimulates high prices enabling insurgents to finance their military campaigns, which in turn would further escalate the conflict.

Yet the survey also reported that the role of legal revenue opportunities is an important disincentive toward illegal cultivation. In fact both a lack of employment affecting basic needs and a lack of water affecting agricultural infrastructure were put forward as explaining the striking level of opium cultivations. Both substitution-effect and opportunity-cost calculations are at play when choosing between peaceful activities (e.g., farming, whether legal or illegal) and insurgency. In fact opium cultivation is not the main occupational opportunity in the Afghan economy. Almost half of Afghan households depend on income from agriculture, 33 percent on non–farm labor, 23 percent on livestock, and 4 percent on opium production (UNODC 2009a).

Since many Afghans in rural areas rely on diversified livelihood strategies to generate household income, we will undertake a micro-level data analysis to identify the relation between different occupational choices—and thus revenue opportunities and violence.

To sum up, this chapter explores empirically whether opium prices induce subsequent violence; whether a reverse mechanism coexists; and whether alternative measures of the relative income can help explain the spread of insecurity in Afghanistan. To this end, we have gathered a unique dataset with monthly information on opium prices, security incidents and the prices of four alternative commodities from 15 Afghan provinces over the period 2004 to 2009. Our baseline analysis assumes the endogeneity of the variables; therefore we use a vector autoregression, VAR, to estimate a system in which both income and violence are functions of their own lag, and then the lag of the other variable in the system. The geographic disaggregation of our data enables us to exploit variations across provinces and over time. Section 7.2 describes the unobvious relationship between revenues—or occupational choices—and violence drawing from the economic literature and a preliminary descriptive analysis of our data. The section focuses on the difficulties of identifying a clear pattern among opium, alternative measures of income and the insurgency. Section 7.3 describes our dataset, and section 7.4 presents the empirical strategy and our evidence. Section 7.5 concludes the chapter.

7.2   Revenues and Violence in Theory and Practice

The economic theory on conflict suggests two opposite relations between income and violence. The first branch suggests that wage and income shocks increase the incentives for peace through the reduction of labor supplied to conflict activities. The higher the returns to (legal) productive activities relative to the returns to fighting activities, the higher is the amount of citizens' time devoted to peaceful activities

(Grossman 1991). According to a second branch, the contest model, the greater the national wealth, the greater is the effort devoted to fighting relative to production (Hirshleifer 1995; Garfinkel and Skaperdas 2007). The nexus between income and violence is not so clear-cut also in the empirical evidence. While Besley et al. (2008) show that positive price shocks to imported and exported commodities make civil war more likely, Bruckner and Ciccone (2010) find that a civil war is more likely in those sub-Saharan countries where the value of export commodities is decreasing.

In their recent cross-country survey of conflict, Blattman and Miguel (2010) find severe shortcomings, and suggest that researchers should take a "more systematic approach to understanding war's economic consequences"; the most promising avenue for new empirical research is on the subnational scale. In fact country-level analyses are growing at fast pace: a number of works on the Colombian conflict and the drug–violence nexus finds a positive effect of coca production on conflict both through a microeconometric (Angrist and Kugler 2008) and a macroeconometric approach (Gonzales and Smith 2006). Dube and Vargas (2008) find that both a price drop in labor-intensive activities and a rise in capital-intensive commodities have the same effect of intensifying attacks by Colombian guerrillas. To the best of our knowledge, there are only three quantitative analyses of the Afghanistan conflict and the nexus drugs–violence.

Two of them (i.e., Lind et al. 2011; Clemens 2008) used indicators of opium production, provided by UNODC, but available online. They used data on the location and extent of opium cultivation and opium eradication efforts. Data are annual and based on satellite image acquisition.

While Lind et al. (2011) show that ISAF has a significant impact on annual opium production, Clemens (2008) explores the potential for source-country drug-control policies to reduce opium production. He suggests that substantial increases in crop eradication would be needed to achieve moderate reductions in production. Why do we use prices rather than opium production? We believe that prices (and price movements) in the opium economy are of greater interest for three important reasons.

First, prices are a critical determinant of the overall level of opium/opiate revenues across the provinces, and of the distribution of revenues within the drug industry, that is, how much goes to farmers and traders. As in other market activities, prices provide market-based signals to producers, traders, and insurgents that influence their decisions.

Second, since opium is a durable good and is widely held as an asset, opium prices directly affect asset values, capital gains, and decisions on building, holding, and selling inventories (Byrd and Jonglez 2006). And finally, the large amount of opium-denominated debt in Afghanistan's rural economy (hundreds of millions of dollars by all accounts) means that prices can have an effect on the level of opium-related debt and associated adverse consequences including for rural poverty (Byrd and Jonglez 2006). This chapter builds on our preliminary analysis of the opium–violence nexus (Bove and Elia 2012). However, opium cultivation is only a tiny part of the occupational opportunity set available in the Afghan economy. While in our previous analysis we focused exclusively on illegal opportunities, we now include measures of legal income and legal occupational choices. Legal commodity prices and wages may shed light on the characteristics of the labor markets and the agricultural sector, including pastoralism. The aim is to explore whether legal occupational opportunities and higher wages may lower conflict through the opportunity-cost effect and how this mechanism compare to the drug-violence nexus. We also provide a broad discussion of the security and development situation in the country and give policy indications on how to tackle the development challenges that the country faces more effectively.

By most measures, insecurity in Afghanistan has dramatically increased in the last seven years. This is primarily a result of the insurgency's growing strength. The Afghan National Army, the Afghan National Police, and ISAF forces are the most frequent targets, but there have also been a substantial number of civilian casualties. In 2008 and 2010, many Afghanistan's provinces registered a record number of attacks (figure 7.1), ranging from suicide bombings to coordinate assaults on military compounds to kidnapping of government officials and contractors. Much of the violence occurred in southern Afghanistan (e.g., Kandahar and Helmand), but insecurity has also spread eastward (e.g., Kunduz), to cover the majority of Afghan provinces.

Most of the violent events are usually attributed to the Taliban-led insurgency. Yet it is very difficult to distinguish among terrorist movements, insurgencies, and organized crime (linked to the drug trade or otherwise), since their tactics and funding sources are increasingly similar. As a label, "AGE" (antigovernment elements) brings under one umbrella a complex mixture of groups and shifting alliances. This mix

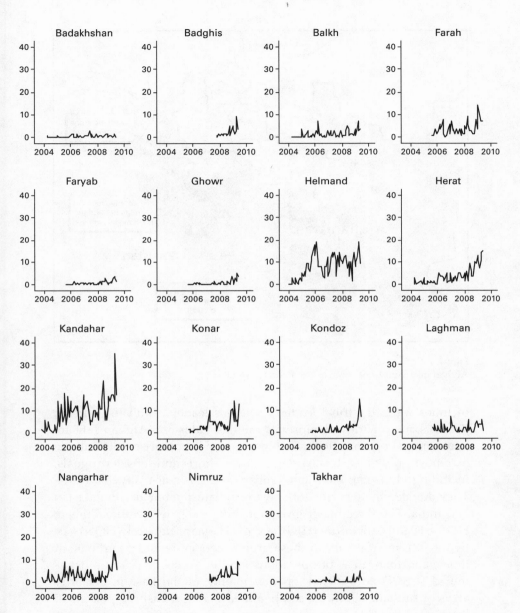

Figure 7.1
Number of security incidents. Author's calculation based on records from the Worldwide Incidents Tracking System, US National Counterterrorism Center, and from the UNODC Statistics and Survey Section.

Figure 7.2
Afghan insurgent front. Source: The Rand Corporation.

includes warlords, tribal leaders, religious leaders (mullahs), foreign jihadists, mercenaries/semiprivate militias, Pakistani/Afghan Taliban, and criminal organizations. The insurgency is comprised of multiple extremist groups, each pursuing its own short- and long-term goals, including al Qaeda, Pakistani Taliban, and Lashkar-e Tayyiba (LeT). They threaten the security not only in Afghanistan but also in Pakistan and India. The three major groups include the Quetta Shura Taliban, Hezb-e Islami Gulbuddin (HIG), and the Haqqani Network (HQN) (see figure 7.2). In Afghanistan these groups cooperate and coordinate at times, and their areas of operations tend to be geographically determined (USDD 2010). They operate mainly in the Pashtun-majority areas of Afghanistan in the south and east, and in Pashtun pockets in the north. The US Department of Defense says that "The common goals of these groups are to expel foreign forces from Afghanistan and to undermine the central government "(USDD 2010, p. 22).

The most devoted insurgents—those who want to take over the government and expel ISAF troops—associate themselves with the

Taliban or Al-Qaeda. Defining the borders between the ideologically driven Taliban and the criminal groups in the opium business is beyond the scope of this chapter.

To what extent is regional instability and insurgency fueled by the Afghan opiate industry? According to a number of sources and reports by the UNODC, extortions fund AGE through two forms of local-levied taxes: *ushr*, a 10 percent tax on agricultural products and *zakata*, a 2.5 percent wealth tax applied to traders (Kalfon et al. 2005). The 2007 Afghanistan Opium Survey says that almost all the farmers in the southern and western regions pay the *ushr*. Between 2005 and 2008, the total estimated farm-gate value of opium produced by those regions was US$2 billion. That means approximately US$ 200 million paid as *ushr* by farmers. Taliban also levy taxes on laboratories producing morphine and heroin (UNODC 2009a). Hence the narcotic trade seems to be crucial in supporting antigovernment element through the acquisition of weapons and the payment of "salaries" to the militia. Theoretically the mechanism is complex and bidirectional; there is a strong revenue-appropriation mechanism or "greed" effect on lootable resources (e.g., Collier and Hoeffler 2004): violence might be over the opium cultivation and controlling the plantation can finance the insurgency. Figure 7.3 shows that at the aggregated national level, monthly opium prices and attacks do not show a similar trend. Since 2004, there

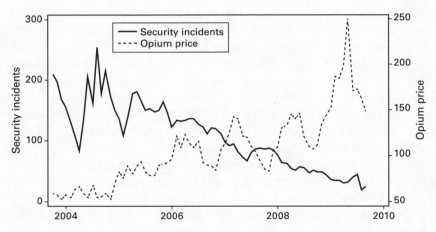

Figure 7.3
Opium prices and number of security incidents. Source: Author's calculation based on records from the Worldwide Incidents Tracking System, US National Counterterrorism Center, and from the UNODC Statistics and Survey Section.

has been a notable increase in the number of security incidents in Afghanistan in parallel with a decrease in opium prices. This suggests that there is a negative correlation between opium prices and violence, although at this level of aggregation we cannot say anything about causation.

As can be seen from figure 7.4, opium is an extremely volatile commodity. The large discrepancies in opium prices across provinces may well reveal some interesting dynamics and may explain how and why violence affects differently these prices; and whether violence itself responds to idiosyncratic variations in the level of revenue generated by the opium trafficking.

As we said, the theoretical literature on economic conditions and warfare highlights the role of the illegal returns in the decision to fight: an increase in the return to crime increases the labor supplied to criminals, therefore increasing the level of violence (Grossman 1991). Thus the opportunity-cost effect is a main factor motivating civil wars. The theory is supported by empirical evidence of the link between criminal activities and economic conditions also in non–war environments (Hidalgo et al. 2010). Therefore better legal occupational opportunities and higher wages should reduce the labor supplied to both opium production and criminal activities, including the insurgency. As a matter of fact, opium cultivation and trafficking are not the main occupational opportunities in the country. In principle, individuals can choose between opium cultivation and legal activities (e.g., wheat and cereal production, or sheep-farming), or they can join an antigovernment group (e.g., Taliban, insurgency linked to Al-Qaeda or nonideological organized crime). Frequently individuals have such choices and the farmers decide what to plant and how to allocate labor and land on their own. For example, in the 2003 to 2004 season, 87 percent of poppy growers and 81 percent of non–poppy growers decided independently on the allocation of land between opium and wheat (UNODC 2004). There are obviously some geographical variations; land ownership also varies across the country, as well as sharecropping, which is more common in the northeastern and eastern regions (UNODC 2004).

Agriculture is the major source of income for the majority of the population. The theory mentioned above would suggest a correlation between the relative income—or the purchasing power—and the level of violence in Afghanistan's provinces. A healthy licit agricultural sector can generate long-term employment and foster economic and political stability.

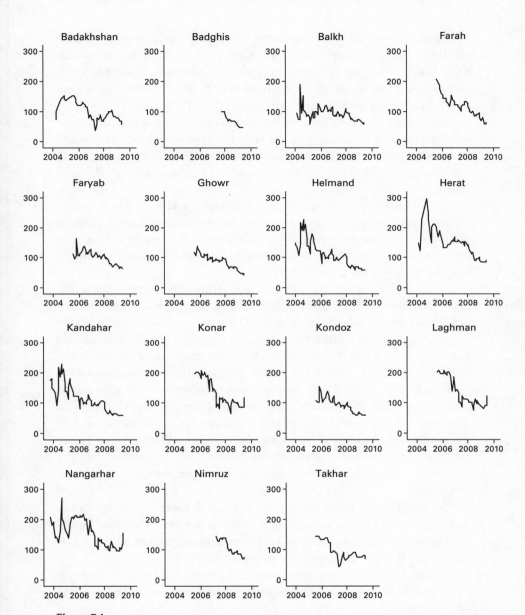

Figure 7.4
Monthly prices of dry opium at farm-gate level. Source: UNODC Global Illicit Crop Monitoring Program, Statistics and Survey Section.

Indeed sustainable economic growth, with particular emphasis on creating a large number of new jobs in the private sector, is a key priority of the Afghan government; "providing economic opportunities and sustainable livelihoods for all Afghans is critical to counter the appeal of the insurgency and reduce instability" (USDD 2010, p. 59).

Household surveys demonstrate the centrality of wheat and livestock prices in the economy of the country. Wheat, in particular, is the main legal crop in rural Afghanistan. It is also a key staple food, accounting for over half of the population's caloric intake (Persaud 2010).

But we also look at the price of one day of unskilled labor to proxy for the purchasing capacity of households relying on casual labor as main income. The price of one-year-old female sheep is an indicator of the purchasing capacity of those households that are mainly reliant on income from livestock (pastoralists).

In figure 7.5 all our indicators show an increasing trend over the period 2004 to 2009, in conjunction with increasing insurgents' activities. In particular, the period 2006 to 2008 witnessed an unprecedented surge in global agricultural prices, and wheat prices in Afghanistan followed the global trend.[4] Since 2008, the dramatic increase in the number of security incidents seems to have been accompanied by peaking prices. While sheep and labor prices follow idiosyncratic variations across provinces, with pronounced differences in the level of revenues between provinces, wheat prices are highly seasonal, and all the provinces we analyze show similar patterns. While wheat prices tend to move together over the eleven provinces, comovements among provinces are less clear when we consider other price levels such as sheep and labor (see figure 7.6).

The breakdown by month reveals general hikes in wheat prices around harvesting times in spring and autumn. Certainly wheat prices in Afghanistan are correlated to international market prices, thus explaining this common trend across provinces.

Overall, the effect of the occupational choices on the level of violence is not obvious. And although the link between income and violence is among the most robust in the economic literature, the direction of causality remains another serious concern. The recent literature has focused on addressing the causal identification problem, in a search for exogenous measures (e.g., Miguel et al. 2004). Are changes in prices caused by some underlying security factors? And to what extent livelihood strategies are affected by the number of insurgency attacks in the

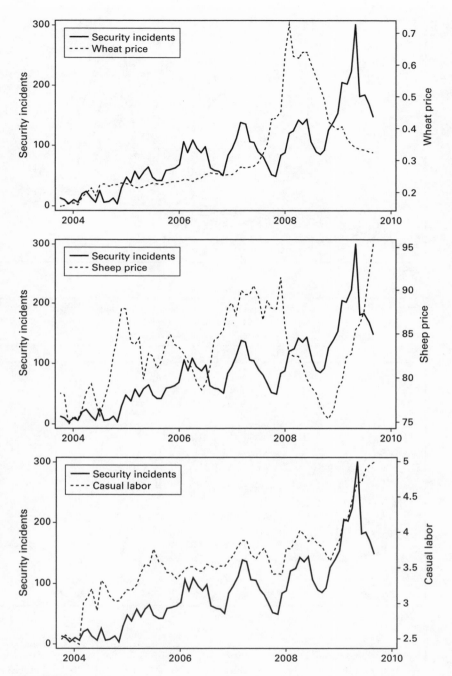

Figure 7.5
Income and security incidents in Afghanistan. Author's calculation based on records from *Vulnerability Analysis and Mapping (VAM) Market Data* from Afghanistan main cities, from World Food Program, and from the *Worldwide Incidents Tracking System* (WITS), US National Counterterrorism Center.

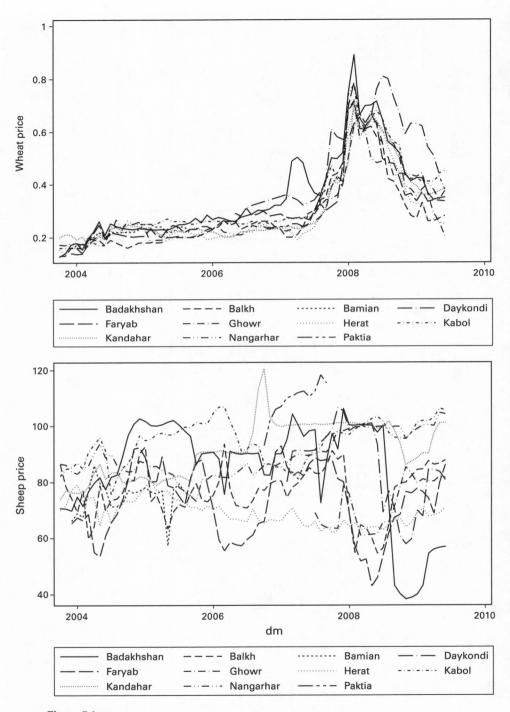

Figure 7.6
Analysis of prices in Afghanistan's provinces. Source: *Vulnerability Analysis and Mapping (VAM)* market data from Afghanistan main cities, World Food Programme.

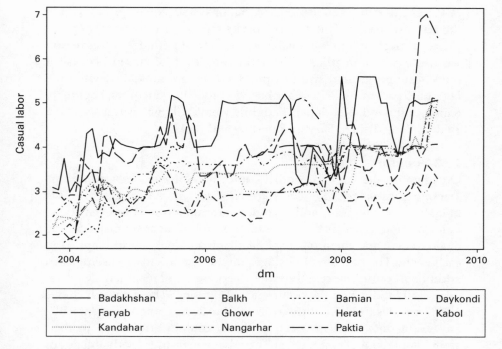

Figure 7.6
(continued)

country? This ambiguous relation between relative income and the political/military situation prevailing on the ground needs to be tested with sophisticated empirical techniques, using data disaggregated at the provincial level.

7.3   Data

7.3.1   Opium
Monthly prices of opium have been kindly provided by the *UNODC Global Illicit Crop Monitoring Programme, Statistics and Survey Section*. These price data are based on inquiries in major opium-producing areas (interviews with some 170 farmers and 160 traders) on a monthly basis. They recorded farmer and trader prices of dry and fresh opium. Farmer refers to the farm-gate price of opium, trader refers to the local trading level, dry opium refers to air-dry opium, and fresh opium to "wet" opium shortly after harvest—or kept "fresh" by plastic wrapping to avoid moisture loss.

Prices are subject to seasonal variations, with lower prices during the harvest season. This is particularly true for fresh ("wet") opium prices, as fresh opium is available in the harvest period. For this reason we use dry opium prices. The farm-gate level is chosen because it reflects supply factors and risk premia. Data are broken down at the level of 15 provinces. Prices have been recorded in Nangarhar, Laghman, Kunar, Hilmand, Kandahar, Badghis, Herat, Ghowr, Farah, Nimroz, Takhar, Badakhshan, Faryab, Kunduz, and Balkh.

7.3.2 Conflict

Our data on the Afghan conflict comes from the *Worldwide Incidents Tracking System (WITS), US National Counterterrorism Center*. This dataset is event-based, and includes information on the event type, date, location, whether the perpetrator is an Islamic extremist, a Sunni, or unknown, and the number of deaths, wounded, and kidnapped in each event. The number of hostages might be particularly useful as an additional control, since it indicates the presence of insurgents without necessarily indicating the occurrence of fighting. The dataset includes 6,080 episodes in 34 provinces from 2004 to 2009. Our conflict data, like any event data used in social research, contain errors due to their sources and coding techniques. The advantages and disadvantages of event data have been extensively studied and discussed by scholars in the last few years (for an extensive review, see the special issue edited by Schrodt 2012). Coding errors are particularly problematic due to the discrepancy between events on the ground and the evaluation of a statistical model. Daily reports on incidents in the country, in particular, on the nonlethal episodes, might only be a fraction of all of the events that occur daily, and they may be nonrandomly selected by reporters at times. The value added by additional sources is still disputed (Schrodt 1994, 2012). Yet the lack of a diversity of sources in this war-torn region makes it difficult for us to assess the accuracy of the data collection and the coding methods.

7.3.3 Market Prices

We gathered monthly US$ prices of 1 kg of wheat; a one-year-old female sheep; and 1 day of unskilled labor. Prices are from the *Vulnerability Analysis and Mapping (VAM) Market Data, World Food Programme*. Prices have been recorderd in 11 provinces: Badakhshan, Balkh, Bamian, Daikondi, Faryab, Ghowr, Herat, Kabul, Kandahar, Nangarhar, and Paktia.

7.4 Estimates

There are almost certainly unobserved common factors influencing all parameters, and to allow for this the estimation and testing approach is based on the Common Correlated Effects (CCE) method advanced by Pesaran (2006). The approach consists of approximating the linear combinations of the unobserved factors by cross-sectional averages of the dependent and explanatory variables, and then running our regressions augmented with these cross-sectional averages. An advantage of this method is that it yields consistent estimates in a variety of situations such as serial correlation in errors, unit roots in the factors, and contemporaneous dependence of the observed regressors with the unobserved factors (Pesaran and Tosseti 2009).

To see the motivations for this procedure, consider a general model of this form

$$y_{it} = \alpha_i + \beta_i x_{it} + \gamma_i f_t + \varepsilon_{it},$$

where f_t represents the unobserved factors, which may influence each unit differently and which may be correlated with the x_{it}. The average across units gives

$$\bar{y}_t = \bar{\alpha} + \bar{\beta}\bar{x}_t + \bar{\gamma} f_t + \bar{\varepsilon}_t + N^{-1}\sum(\beta_i - \bar{\beta})x_{it},$$

$$f_t = \bar{\gamma}^{-1}[\bar{y}_t - \bar{\alpha} + \bar{\beta}\bar{x}_t + \bar{\varepsilon}_t + \sum(\beta_i - \bar{\beta})x_{it}],$$

so the $\bar{y}_t$ and $\bar{x}_t$ provide a proxy for the unobserved factor. The CCE generalizes to many factors and lagged dependent variables. We hope that any seasonality is captured by this means (seasonality is a common factor).

We consider an economic variable—our proxy for income/occupational choices—for province i in month t (P_{it}) and the number of security incidents (I_{it}), such that

$$P_{it} = a_{11}^i P_{it-1} + a_{12}^i I_{it-1} + \sigma_{11}\bar{P}_t + \sigma_{12}\bar{I}_t + \varepsilon_{it},$$

$$I_{it} = a_{21}^i P_{it-1} + a_{22}^i I_{it-1} + \sigma_{21}\bar{P}_t + \sigma_{22}\bar{I}_t + \varepsilon_{it},$$

with $\bar{P}_t$ and $\bar{I}_t$ being the cross-sectional averages of the prices and security incidents, respectively. Besides the parameters in the equation, our econometric specification includes a constant term and two lags.

We consider alternative measures of P_{it} in the context of the bivariate VAR above. Due to a lack of a large T (we only have a maximum of 67 time series observations for some provinces, and less than 30 for a couple of provinces), we do not consider VARs in more variables. The economic variables we use are (1) the revenue from opium (i.e., opium prices) in table 7.1, (2) the purchasing capacity of households relying on legal agriculture (i.e., wheat prices) in table 7.2, (3) the purchasing capacity of households relying on livestock (i.e., sheep prices) in table 7.3, and (4) the purchasing capacity of household relying on casual labor in table 7.4.

To summarize our results, we use the mean group (MG) estimator proposed by Pesaran and Smith (1995). The MG estimator is defined as the simple average of the coefficients a_{11}, a_{12}, σ_{11}, and σ_{21}. Given a coefficient a_{11}, we compute the MG coefficients and standard errors, respectively, using the following formulas:

$$a_{11}^{MG} = \bar{a}_{11} = \frac{\sum_{k=i}^{N} a_{11}^i}{N},$$

$$se(a_{11}^{MG}) = \frac{\sqrt{\sum_{k=i}^{N} (a_{11}^i - \bar{a}_{11})/N - 1}}{\sqrt{N}}.$$

The MG estimator can produce consistent estimates of the average of the parameters. The first column of each table shows the results for the MG estimator.

We start with table 7.1, where we find almost no effects of lagged opium price on subsequent number of incidents. The mean group estimator confirms no effects: even though we achieve statistical significant, the coefficients are very close to zero. This finding runs counter to the growing economic literature on civil conflict, which demonstrates that insurgencies have the capability of exploiting drug money for funding, such as the FARC in Colombia.

The strong and highly significant effect of the cross-sectional average of the number of attacks suggests the persistence of unobservable common factors. As one would expect, accounting for common correlated effects decreases the effects of the other variables in the equation. The lagged number of security incidents in the opium price equation is negative and significant for most of the provinces. The mean group estimator also shows a negative impact of violence on opium prices, suggesting that violence may disrupt the opium trade.

The fact that violence induces lower opium prices can be explained by two simultaneous mechanisms, a demand-side and a supply-side

Table 7.1
Security incidents (I_{it}) and opium price (P_{it})

	Mean group	BDS	BDG	BAL	FRA	FYB	GHO	HEL	HER	KAN	KNR	KDZ	LAG	NAN	NIM	TAK
Security incident equation																
I_{it-1}	**0.02**	-0.14	-0.26*	-0.05	0.08	0.17	0.09	0.27**	0.23*	-0.10	0.09	0.24	-0.28**	-0.07	0.24	-0.12
	(0.05)	(0.14)	(0.15)	(0.12)	(0.15)	(0.15)	(0.13)	(0.12)	(0.13)	(0.09)	(0.16)	(0.15)	(0.13)	(0.11)	(0.17)	(0.15)
I_{it-2}	**-0.05**	-0.00	-0.76***	-0.00	-0.01	0.04	-0.26	0.21*	0.12	-0.07	0.15	-0.16	-0.18	-0.02	0.29	-0.09
	(0.06)	(0.14)	(0.22)	(0.11)	(0.15)	(0.15)	(0.16)	(0.12)	(0.13)	(0.11)	(0.17)	(0.17)	(0.13)	(0.11)	(0.24)	(0.14)
P_{it-1}	**-0.02***	-0.02*	-0.07	-0.00	-0.03	-0.01	-0.03	-0.02	-0.01	-0.03	0.01	-0.01	-0.01	-0.00	-0.11*	-0.03**
	(0.00)	(0.01)	(0.07)	(0.01)	(0.04)	(0.01)	(0.02)	(0.03)	(0.02)	(0.02)	(0.03)	(0.02)	(0.02)	(0.01)	(0.06)	(0.02)
P_{it-2}	**0.01***	0.02*	0.01	-0.00	0.01	-0.00	0.02	0.01	-0.00	0.01	-0.00	0.01	0.04***	0.00	0.01	0.03**
	(0.00)	(0.01)	(0.05)	(0.01)	(0.04)	(0.01)	(0.02)	(0.02)	(0.02)	(0.02)	(0.03)	(0.02)	(0.02)	(0.01)	(0.05)	(0.02)
I_{CCE}	**0.97***	0.03	0.93***	0.65***	0.98***	0.15	0.53***	1.28***	0.98***	3.38***	0.46	1.22***	0.96***	1.66***	0.98***	0.42***
	(0.20)	(0.09)	(0.19)	(0.16)	(0.32)	(0.11)	(0.12)	(0.37)	(0.25)	(0.40)	(0.34)	(0.27)	(0.22)	(0.26)	(0.25)	(0.16)
P_{CCE}	**0.01**	-0.01	0.02	0.01	0.01	-0.00	0.00	0.03	-0.01	0.05*	-0.05	-0.02	-0.03	0.03**	0.24***	-0.00
	(0.01)	(0.01)	(0.08)	(0.01)	(0.03)	(0.01)	(0.01)	(0.03)	(0.02)	(0.03)	(0.05)	(0.02)	(0.03)	(0.01)	(0.08)	(0.01)
cons	**-0.51**	1.53*	2.90	-0.17	0.43	1.86	-0.44	-1.55	2.49	-1.20	5.91	-0.48	-1.01	-4.70*	-12.92**	-0.34
	(1.08)	(0.91)	(4.42)	(1.58)	(2.66)	(1.29)	(1.07)	(3.05)	(2.37)	(3.26)	(4.00)	(2.14)	(2.08)	(1.87)	(6.00)	(1.27)

Table 7.1
(continued)

	Mean group	BDS	BDG	BAL	FRA	FYB	GHO	HEL	HER	KAN	KNR	KDZ	LAG	NAN	NIM	TAK
Opium price equation																
I_{t-1}	**-0.54*****	0.82	-0.86**	-0.66	-0.80*	-2.29	-1.61	-1.01**	0.35	-0.87**	-1.44*	-0.41	0.61	1.97**	-1.52***	-0.41
	(0.28)	(1.82)	(0.34)	(1.45)	(0.48)	(1.84)	(1.02)	(0.44)	(1.13)	(0.34)	(0.84)	(0.67)	(1.15)	(0.87)	(0.57)	(1.37)
I_{t-2}	**-0.37***	1.85	-0.01	-0.51	-0.78	-0.85	-0.50	-0.79*	-1.70	-0.46	-0.62	-0.29	0.02	-0.44	-0.88	0.33
	(0.20)	(1.87)	(0.49)	(1.37)	(0.49)	(1.79)	(1.25)	(0.44)	(1.11)	(0.40)	(0.87)	(0.76)	(1.19)	(0.91)	(0.78)	(1.29)
P_{t-1}	**0.44*****	0.85***	0.38**	0.10	0.64***	0.20	0.37**	0.36***	0.29*	0.35***	0.35*	0.48***	0.40**	0.53***	0.47**	0.89***
	(0.05)	(0.14)	(0.16)	(0.11)	(0.15)	(0.13)	(0.15)	(0.09)	(0.17)	(0.09)	(0.14)	(0.11)	(0.16)	(0.10)	(0.19)	(0.15)
P_{t-2}	**-0.06***	-0.00	-0.26**	0.14	-0.14	-0.02	0.01	-0.16*	0.12	-0.17**	0.04	-0.28***	0.06	-0.01	-0.03	-0.17
	(0.03)	(0.14)	(0.11)	(0.11)	(0.12)	(0.12)	(0.12)	(0.09)	(0.14)	(0.08)	(0.13)	(0.10)	(0.14)	(0.09)	(0.16)	(0.15)
I_{CCE}	**0.71***	-0.93	-0.68	0.87	-0.96	-0.50	-1.20	0.72	-2.91	0.68	4.66***	1.04	2.89	4.67**	0.39	1.96
	(0.55)	(1.16)	(0.42)	(1.92)	(1.06)	(1.36)	(0.91)	(1.39)	(2.11)	(1.52)	(1.75)	(1.21)	(2.00)	(2.14)	(0.83)	(1.48)
P_{CCE}	**0.65**	0.07	1.16***	0.35***	0.42***	0.56***	0.45***	0.80***	0.49***	0.84***	1.00***	0.72***	0.98***	0.79***	0.87***	0.29**
	(8.08)	(0.10)	(0.18)	(0.10)	(0.11)	(0.10)	(0.09)	(0.09)	(0.14)	(0.10)	(0.27)	(0.09)	(0.28)	(0.11)	(0.25)	(0.13)
cons	**-3.40**	7.01	-30.72***	26.99	22.01**	27.85*	10.64	3.08	41.86**	-1.44	-36.99*	-7.17	-46.53**	-41.64***	-12.55	-13.50
	(7.01)	(12.04)	(9.91)	(19.03)	(8.79)	(15.81)	(8.26)	(11.30)	(20.30)	(12.33)	(20.61)	(9.58)	(18.96)	(15.15)	(19.82)	(11.67)
N	15	50	19	62	45	45	45	65	56	67	45	45	45	67	26	45

Note: Standard errors in parentheses * $p < 0.10$, ** $p < 0.05$, *** $p < 0.01$.

dynamic. On the demand side, we should expect antigovernment elements to fight over the extraction of revenues from the opium trade, which in turn causes a disruption of the opiate business and reduces the level of demand. In fact both government and antigovernment militia have been ending up in second-order conflicts over the extraction of revenues from the opium trade in recent years. This might explain a conflict-induced disruption of the opium trading, which in turn results in lower opium prices. On the supply side, conflicts strengthen the level of lawlessness—indeed opium is more likely to be cultivated where the influence of the central authority is weak—and therefore we should expect to observe higher productions in those areas and lower prices. Common correlated effects are again those showing more statistical significance and the mean group estimator confirms the presence of common factors driving the dynamics of violence and opium prices.

Tables 7.2 to 7.4, on the purchasing capacity of household relying on different income sources, show mixed results. We use the wheat, sheep, and casual labor prices to proxy for different income sources. We have information on prices for eleven provinces; however, in the table of estimates, we drop two provinces, Bamian and Paktia, due to an insufficient number of monthly observations and an insufficient variation of the security incidents series over time. Our mean group estimates rely therefore on nine provinces.

The bivariate VAR of table 7.2 shows no significant correlation between the security incidents and the wheat prices series, not for the single provinces nor for the mean group estimates. While in some provinces worsening economic conditions are followed by increasing levels of violence, in others there seems to be a positive relation between these two variables. In the majority of provinces the coefficients are not statistically different from zero.

In table 7.3 the VAR considers as a source of revenue—or occupation—the livestock (pastoralists). Even in this case the effect of lagged prices on incidents are not strong. We have a negative effect of lagged sheep price on incidents only for two of the nine provinces considered and no significant relationship in the mean group estimates, even if the sign is in the direction expected. When sheep prices are the dependant variables, most of the variation in the sheep price series is explained by its own lags and by common factors.

Finally, the estimates of table 7.4 show a similar pattern. We find no strong and significant correlation between the lags of the casual labor

Table 7.2
Security incidents (I_{it}) and wheat price (P_{it})

	Mean group	BDS	BAL	DAY	FYB	GHO	HER	KAB	KAN	NAN
Security incident equation										
I_{it-1}	0.02	-0.13	-0.12	-0.05	0.16	0.03	0.37***	0.15	-0.10	-0.08
	(0.05)	(0.11)	(0.12)	(0.18)	(0.12)	(0.16)	(0.12)	(0.11)	(0.10)	(0.11)
I_{it-2}	-0.06	-0.04	-0.03	-0.19	0.10	-0.44**	0.21*	-0.01	-0.08	-0.07
	(0.06)	(0.11)	(0.11)	(0.18)	(0.11)	(0.21)	(0.12)	(0.12)	(0.12)	(0.12)
P_{it-1}	2.69**	0.11	3.40	-1.45	1.22	6.23	-1.98	0.59	8.52	7.61
	(1.31)	(1.92)	(5.23)	(2.59)	(2.64)	(4.71)	(9.75)	(6.58)	(14.81)	(8.06)
P_{it-2}	-0.04	3.70**	5.05	0.28	1.03	-7.36*	3.49	0.71	-4.27	-3.00
	(1.36)	(1.58)	(4.02)	(2.43)	(1.94)	(4.16)	(6.51)	(4.57)	(11.89)	(5.65)
I_{CCE}	0.98***	0.14**	0.76***	0.24**	0.26***	0.71***	0.84***	0.92***	3.41***	1.63***
	(0.34)	(0.06)	(0.14)	(0.09)	(0.07)	(0.15)	(0.23)	(0.18)	(0.45)	(0.26)
P_{CCE}	-4.40***	-3.71**	-8.95**	0.27	-1.32	-3.31	-1.08	-2.10	-6.96	-12.47**
	(1.40)	(1.71)	(4.45)	(1.33)	(1.87)	(2.77)	(6.53)	(5.36)	(8.65)	(6.14)
cons	0.89**	0.23	0.31	0.10	-0.38*	1.09	-0.44	0.94	3.84***	2.39***
	(0.46)	(0.21)	(0.39)	(0.53)	(0.22)	(1.18)	(0.60)	(0.64)	(1.24)	(0.74)

Table 7.2
(continued)

	Mean group	BDS	BAL	DAY	FYB	GHO	HER	KAB	KAN	NAN
Wheat price equation										
I_{it-1}	**0.00**	0.01	0.00	0.00	−0.01	−0.01	−0.00	0.00	−0.00	0.00
	(0.00)	(0.01)	(0.00)	(0.01)	(0.01)	(0.01)	(0.00)	(0.00)	(0.00)	(0.00)
I_{it-2}	**0.00**	0.01	−0.00*	0.04***	−0.01	0.00	−0.00**	0.00	−0.00	0.00
	(0.00)	(0.01)	(0.00)	(0.01)	(0.00)	(0.01)	(0.00)	(0.00)	(0.00)	(0.00)
P_{it-1}	**0.49***	0.55***	0.68***	0.81***	0.60***	1.08***	0.15*	0.08	0.39***	0.09
	(0.11)	(0.11)	(0.13)	(0.12)	(0.11)	(0.15)	(0.08)	(0.08)	(0.09)	(0.10)
P_{it-2}	**−0.17***	−0.26***	−0.34***	−0.04	−0.34***	−0.55***	0.00	−0.10	0.01	0.02
	(0.06)	(0.09)	(0.10)	(0.11)	(0.08)	(0.14)	(0.06)	(0.06)	(0.07)	(0.07)
I_{CCE}	**−0.00**	0.00	−0.00	−0.01**	0.01*	0.00	−0.01***	0.00*	−0.00	−0.01*
	(0.00)	(0.00)	(0.00)	(0.00)	(0.00)	(0.00)	(0.00)	(0.00)	(0.00)	(0.00)
P_{CCE}	**0.68***	0.75***	0.64***	0.27***	0.68***	0.35***	0.91***	1.04***	0.62***	0.93***
	(0.08)	(0.10)	(0.11)	(0.06)	(0.08)	(0.09)	(0.06)	(0.07)	(0.05)	(0.07)
cons	**0.00**	0.01	−0.00	0.03	0.01	0.03	−0.01*	−0.00	−0.00	−0.02*
	(0.00)	(0.01)	(0.01)	(0.03)	(0.01)	(0.04)	(0.01)	(0.01)	(0.01)	(0.01)
N	9	67	67	29	65	22	67	67	67	67

Note: Standard errors in parentheses * $p < 0.10$, ** $p < 0.05$, *** $p < 0.01$.

Table 7.3
Security incidents (I_{it}) and sheep price (P_{it})

	Mean group	BDS	BAL	DAY	FYB	GHO	HER	KAB	KAN	NAN
Security incident equation										
I_{it-1}	**0.01**	-0.18	-0.09	-0.00	0.04	0.02	0.33***	0.09	-0.09	-0.02
	(0.04)	(0.12)	(0.12)	(0.19)	(0.13)	(0.18)	(0.12)	(0.11)	(0.09)	(0.11)
I_{it-2}	**-0.06**	-0.04	-0.00	-0.20	0.05	-0.42**	0.19	-0.04	-0.09	-0.01
	(0.05)	(0.11)	(0.11)	(0.19)	(0.12)	(0.21)	(0.12)	(0.11)	(0.11)	(0.12)
P_{it-1}	**-0.00**	-0.03**	0.04	0.01	-0.00	0.06	0.09	0.00	-0.20*	-0.05
	(0.03)	(0.01)	(0.03)	(0.02)	(0.02)	(0.04)	(0.08)	(0.07)	(0.12)	(0.12)
P_{it-2}	**-0.00**	0.03***	-0.04	-0.00	-0.02	0.01	-0.12	0.09	0.13	-0.08
	(0.02)	(0.01)	(0.02)	(0.02)	(0.02)	(0.05)	(0.08)	(0.08)	(0.11)	(0.13)
I_{CCE}	**0.94*****	0.22***	0.65***	0.23**	0.35***	0.50***	0.90***	0.78***	3.32***	1.53***
	(0.32)	(0.06)	(0.13)	(0.10)	(0.07)	(0.17)	(0.22)	(0.17)	(0.42)	(0.26)
P_{CCE}	**-0.00**	0.00	-0.00	0.01	0.02	0.03	-0.10*	0.01	0.15	-0.16**
	(0.03)	(0.02)	(0.04)	(0.04)	(0.03)	(0.05)	(0.05)	(0.06)	(0.11)	(0.06)
Cons	**1.51**	-0.65	0.12	-1.55	0.08	-7.66	10.16	-7.48	-3.59	24.24***
	(3.33)	(1.66)	(3.03)	(2.80)	(1.84)	(4.69)	(6.55)	(6.68)	(8.40)	(7.70)

Table 7.3
(continued)

	Mean group	BDS	BAL	DAY	FYB	GHO	HER	KAB	KAN	NAN
Sheep price equation										
I_{it-1}	-0.03	-0.89	-0.68	0.00	1.54	0.20	-0.20	-0.05	-0.05	-0.13
	(0.22)	(1.23)	(0.58)	(1.60)	(0.98)	(0.83)	(0.17)	(0.18)	(0.09)	(0.11)
I_{it-2}	-0.18	-1.32	0.01	-2.20	0.94	0.61	0.33**	-0.09	0.09	-0.06
	(0.32)	(1.18)	(0.53)	(1.60)	(0.91)	(0.99)	(0.17)	(0.18)	(0.11)	(0.11)
P_{it-1}	0.90***	0.86***	0.73***	0.62***	1.14***	1.10***	0.63***	1.05***	1.07***	0.94***
	(0.06)	(0.12)	(0.12)	(0.19)	(0.12)	(0.20)	(0.12)	(0.12)	(0.12)	(0.12)
P_{it-2}	-0.13***	-0.09	-0.14	0.08	-0.38***	-0.43*	0.23**	-0.19	-0.25**	-0.01
	(0.07)	(0.12)	(0.12)	(0.17)	(0.13)	(0.24)	(0.12)	(0.13)	(0.11)	(0.13)
I_{CCE}	0.09	-0.84	0.58	0.37	-0.91	0.46	-0.25	0.35	0.53	0.59**
	(0.20)	(0.61)	(0.60)	(0.81)	(0.56)	(0.80)	(0.30)	(0.27)	(0.41)	(0.26)
P_{CCE}	0.32***	0.80***	0.34*	0.98***	0.53**	0.01	-0.00	0.06	0.17	0.04
	(0.12)	(0.24)	(0.20)	(0.32)	(0.21)	(0.22)	(0.08)	(0.09)	(0.11)	(0.06)
cons	-8.96	-43.99**	2.65	-57.00**	-25.72*	20.38	9.74	9.04	1.78	2.45
	(8.92)	(17.35)	(14.52)	(23.81)	(14.21)	(21.61)	(9.04)	(10.83)	(8.29)	(7.52)
N	9	67	67	27	65	22	67	67	67	67

Note: Standard errors in parentheses * $p < 0.10$, ** $p < 0.05$, *** $p < 0.01$.

Table 7.4
Security incidents (I_{it}) and casual labor wage (P_{it})

	Mean group	BDS	BAL	DAY	FYB	GHO	HER	KAB	KAN	NAN
Security incident equation										
$I_{it\text{-}1}$	**0.02**	−0.09	−0.11	−0.05	0.15	0.05	0.30**	0.12	−0.06	−0.10
	(0.04)	(0.12)	(0.12)	(0.19)	(0.12)	(0.21)	(0.12)	(0.12)	(0.10)	(0.12)
$I_{it\text{-}2}$	**−0.06**	−0.00	−0.02	−0.24	0.11	−0.42*	0.14	0.01	−0.07	−0.07
	(0.05)	(0.11)	(0.11)	(0.19)	(0.12)	(0.22)	(0.12)	(0.12)	(0.11)	(0.12)
$P_{it\text{-}1}$	**0.54**	−0.52***	−0.49	0.23	0.17	0.89	1.25	2.69	2.93	−2.26
	(0.54)	(0.19)	(0.65)	(0.88)	(0.20)	(0.71)	(1.45)	(1.92)	(2.89)	(2.02)
$P_{it\text{-}2}$	**−0.55**	0.40**	1.01	0.94	−0.30	−0.68	0.72	−1.19	−3.90	−2.03
	(0.54)	(0.18)	(0.67)	(0.88)	(0.19)	(0.87)	(1.37)	(1.66)	(2.64)	(2.08)
I_{CCE}	**0.91***	0.12	0.88***	0.09	0.14	0.55*	0.88***	0.85***	3.25***	1.50***
	(0.33)	(0.10)	(0.21)	(0.16)	(0.11)	(0.30)	(0.30)	(0.30)	(0.60)	(0.31)
P_{CCE}	**0.07**	0.39	−0.97	0.80	0.93	0.39	−1.11	−1.38	0.03	1.59
	(0.34)	(0.48)	(0.86)	(0.89)	(0.61)	(1.76)	(1.35)	(1.69)	(2.88)	(1.67)
cons	**−0.21**	−0.46	1.40	−7.62	−2.66	−2.90	−2.54	0.38	5.69	6.81
	(1.49)	(1.37)	(2.74)	(5.33)	(1.71)	(5.10)	(3.82)	(4.02)	(7.41)	(4.16)

Table 7.4
(continued)

	Mean group	BDS	BAL	DAY	FYB	GHO	HER	KAB	KAN	NAN
Casual labor wage equation										
I_{it-1}	**-0.01***	-0.00	-0.01	-0.01	-0.08	0.00	0.02	-0.01*	-0.00	-0.01
	(0.00)	(0.07)	(0.02)	(0.04)	(0.08)	(0.05)	(0.01)	(0.01)	(0.00)	(0.01)
I_{it-2}	**-0.00**	-0.02	-0.04**	0.02	-0.03	0.03	-0.01	0.00	-0.01	-0.01
	(0.00)	(0.07)	(0.02)	(0.04)	(0.07)	(0.06)	(0.01)	(0.01)	(0.00)	(0.01)
P_{it-1}	**0.56***	0.64***	0.78***	0.17	0.80***	-0.04	1.01***	0.46***	0.53***	0.74***
	(0.11)	(0.12)	(0.12)	(0.17)	(0.12)	(0.18)	(0.12)	(0.11)	(0.11)	(0.12)
P_{it-2}	**-0.14***	-0.12	-0.09	-0.19	-0.22*	-0.55**	-0.23**	-0.02	0.11	0.01
	(0.06)	(0.11)	(0.12)	(0.17)	(0.12)	(0.22)	(0.11)	(0.09)	(0.10)	(0.12)
I_{CCE}	**0.00**	-0.06	0.05	-0.06*	0.06	-0.09	0.02	0.04***	0.05**	0.01
	(0.02)	(0.07)	(0.04)	(0.03)	(0.07)	(0.08)	(0.02)	(0.02)	(0.02)	(0.02)
P_{CCE}	**0.51***	0.78**	-0.08	0.44***	0.65*	1.54***	0.20*	0.46***	0.43***	0.18*
	(0.15)	(0.30)	(0.16)	(0.17)	(0.38)	(0.45)	(0.11)	(0.09)	(0.11)	(0.10)
cons	0.36	-0.47	1.14**	2.58**	-0.70	0.51	-0.02	0.34	-0.27	0.13
	(0.33)	(0.87)	(0.50)	(1.01)	(1.06)	(1.30)	(0.32)	(0.22)	(0.28)	(0.24)
N	9	67	67	27	65	22	67	67	67	67

Note: Standard errors in parentheses * $p < 0.10$, ** $p < 0.05$, *** $p < 0.01$.

and the level of insurgency, but only significant effect of the labor lags in the labor equation.

To sum up, the results suggests that income effects on violence are overall neither stronger nor more significant than the reverse mechanism. Lagged income levels have sometimes a significant effect on the number of incidents, whereas lagged incidents have no significant effects on prices. Common effects are strong in both equations, and the mean group estimator seems to confirm this finding. This result was expected since common correlated effects, such as weather conditions, seasonality, and world prices, have an impact on yields, agricultural production, and pastoralism and therefore influence the prices. In conclusion, the number of attacks at provincial level is only affected by common correlated factors, while all others coefficients are mostly insignificant. The strong impact of the correlated common factors may explain the lack of statistical significance of our variables in many provinces.

7.5 Conclusions

This chapter has examined how different sources of revenues interact with the level of violence in Afghanistan. We treat relative income and violence as endogenous, and consider a vector autoregressive model (VAR) that describes the dynamic evolution of income and violence in a system. Using detailed data at provincial level over a five-year period, we show that unobservable common channels prevail in determining how income and conflict dynamics interact. The relation between opium prices and violence in some provinces suggests that opium can play a role in affecting the level of violence, although not in the expected magnitude and significance. Our study reveals that opium prices do not have a main role in exacerbating the level of insurgency activities, measured by the number of security incidents; however, the opposite dynamic holds, and we find that the violence, and its intensity, has a negative impact on the level of opium prices. A conflict-induced opium production and a simultaneous conflict-induced demand for opiates—which drive the prices—seem to play a bigger role. In particular, we explain this interaction through a simultaneous effect of the insurgency strength on the demand and supply for opiates: Antigovernment elements fight over the extraction of revenues from the opium trade, which in turn causes a disruption of the opiate business and reduces the level of demand. Lower levels of demand depress the prices, which in fact, at an aggregate level, are plummeting in conjunction with sky-rocketing and unprecedented high levels of violence. On the supply side, conflict strengthens the level of lawlessness, which fosters higher productions, therefore causing lower prices.

Since 2004, the nexus of drugs and insurgency has become stronger, and as a result the potential transnational threat posed by Afghanistan's opium has become more acute. Drug production and drug trafficking are effects as well as causes of political instability. They flourish under weak states and sustain that weakness by financing insurgency and warlordism, and by corrupting the officials of enforcement agencies and security forces. Afghanistan is a primary instance of this complex of economic and political pathologies, and needs to be further investigated using novel datasets.

We also look at the interaction between different indicators of well-being and revenue and the level of violence across most of Afghanistan's provinces. In particular, we use commodity prices and wages because their behavior, including the structure, movements, and fluctuations, may shed light on the characteristics of the labor markets and the agricultural sector, which could provide indications on how to respond to the development challenges that the country faces more effectively. The relative value of revenues generated from different sources (e.g., casual labor, pastoralism) shows mixed and not so clear-cut effects on the level of violence. Again, common correlated factors, like weather conditions, seasonality, and world prices for the commodities, together with the strategy chosen by ISAF forces and the AGE at the country level, are the main drivers of both violence and relative income. Results are preliminary, and any conclusion is only tentative because the time span is quite short; data collection in a war region is inevitably subject to many errors of measurement. Due to a lack of reliable and comparable data, we cannot evaluate the robustness of these conclusions. How the level of income and other observable and unobservable factors interact to produce the value-to-violence relationship in the Afghanistan provinces is an important avenue for further research on this topic.

Acknowledgments

We are grateful to the UNODC Statistics and Survey Section for generously providing the dataset on opium prices. We wish to thank Ron Smith for helpful advices and Tilman Brück, Antonio Giustozzi,

Kristian Skrede Gleditsch, Marijke Verpoorten, and three anonymous referees for their insights. We also thank HiCN's Workshop participants at the Universidad de los Andes, seminar participants at the Institute of Development Studies, conference participants at the Global Economic Costs of Conflict Conference, CSAE Conference 2011 and CESifo Venice Summer Institute for their comments. Financial support from the AXA Research Fund is greatly acknowledged.

Notes

1. According to press reports, Afghan government officials are involved in 70 percent of opium trafficking and a quarter of the 249 members of the Afghan Parliament have connections with the drug trade. Members of the police force are allegedly involved in the opium trade as facilitators, protectors and even consumers (Pothier 2009).

4. According to the IMF's Heavily Indebted Poor Country paper published in February 2010, inflation in Afghanistan has been "appropriately managed." After a period of high inflation due to high fuel and commodity (e.g., wheat) prices, inflation is back down to manageable levels in Afghanistan—around 6 percent for the first quarter of 2010. Except for a spike in inflation during the drought-stricken years of 2007 to 2008, when global commodity prices also surged, inflation in Afghanistan has in general remained below 10 percent.

Bibliography

Angrist, J. D., and A. D. Kugler. 2008. Rural windfall or a new resource curse? Coca, income, and civil conflict in Colombia. *Review of Economics and Statistics* 90 (2): 191–215.

Besley, T. J., T. Persson, and H. Street. 2008. The incidence of civil war: Theory and evidence. Working paper 14585. NBER, Cambridge, MA.

Blattman, C., and E. Miguel. 2010. Civil war. *Journal of Economic Literature* 48 (1): 3–57.

Bove, V., and L. Elia. 2012. Drugs and violence in Afghanistan: A panel VAR with unobserved common factor analysis. *Defence and Peace Economics. Special Issue on the Economic Costs of Conflict.* http://www.tandfonline.com/doi/abs/10.1080/10242694.2012.72315 7#.Uf-W59Kmguc.

Bruckner, M., and A. Ciccone. 2010. International commodity prices, growth and the outbreak of civil war in sub-Saharan Africa. *Economic Journal* 120 (544): 519–34.

Byrd, W. A, and O. Jonglez. 2006. Prices and market interactions in the opium economy. In W. A. Byrd, and D. Buddenberg, eds., *Afghanistan's Drug Industry: Structure, Functioning, Dynamics, and Implications for Counter-Narcotics Policy*. Washington, DC: World Bank, 117–54.

Clemens, J. 2008. Opium in Afghanistan: Prospects for the success of source country drug control policies. *Journal of Law and Economics* 51 (3): 407–32.

Collier, P., and A. Hoeffler. 2004. Greed and greviance in civil war. *Oxford Economic Papers* 56 (4): 563–95.

Dube, O., and J. Vargas. 2008. Commodity price shocks and civil conflict: Evidence from Colombia. Unpublished manuscript. Harvard University.

Garfinkel, M. R., and S. Skaperdas. 2007. Economics of conflict: An overview. *Handbook of Defense Economics* 2: 649–709.

Gonzales, T., and R. Smith. 2006. Drugs and violence in Colombia: A VECM analysis. Working paper n0906 in economics and finance. Birbeck, London.

Grossman, H. I. 1991. A general equilibrium model of insurrections. *American Economic Review* 81 (4): 912–21.

Hidalgo, F. D., S. Naidu, S. Nichter, and N. Richardson. 2010. Occupational choices: Economic determinants of land invasions. *Review of Economics and Statistics* 92 (3): 505–23.

Hirshleifer, J. 1995. Anarchy and its breakdown. *Journal of Political Economy* 103: 26–52.

Kalfon, T., Schaetzen, B., Bennett, A., Dicks-Mireaux, L., Fischer, F., and Rooden, R. 2005. *Reconstructing Afghanistan.* Washington, DC: IMF.

Lind, J., K. O. Moene, and F. Willumsen. 2011 Opium for the masses? Conflict-induced narcotics production in Afghanistan. Working paper. ESOP, Washington, DC..

Martin, E., and S. Symansky. 2006. Macroeconomic impact of the drug economy and counter-narcotics efforts. In W. A. Byrd and D. Buddenberg, eds., *Afghanistan's Drug Industry: Structure, Functioning, Dynamics, and Implications for Counter-Narcotics Policy.* Washington, DC: World Bank, 25–46.

Miguel, E., S. Satyanath, and E. Sergenti. 2004. Economic shocks and civil conflict: An instrumental variables approach. *Journal of Political Economy* 112 (41): 725–53.

Persaud, Suresh. 2010. Price volatility in Afghanistan's wheat market. Outlook report WHS-10d-01. US Department of Agriculture, Economic Research Service.

Pesaran, M. H. 2006. Estimation and inference in large heterogeneous panels with a multifactor error structure. *Econometrica* 74 (4): 967–1012.

Pesaran, M. H., and R. Smith. 1995. Estimating long-run relationships from dynamic heterogeneous panels. *Journal of Econometrics* 68 (1): 79–113.

Pesaran, M. H., and E. Tosseti. 2009. Large panels with spatial correlations and common factors. *Journal of Econometrics* 161 (2): 182–202.

Pothier, F. 2009. Opium in Afghanistan, a reality check. IDEAS report SU 001. London School of Economics.

Schrodt, Philip A. 1994. Statistical characteristics of events data. *International Interactions* 20 (1–2): 35–53.

Schrodt, Philip A. 2012. Precedents, progress, and prospects in political event data. *International Interactions: Empirical and Theoretical Research in International Relations* 38 (4): 546–69.

UNODC. 2004. Farmers Intentions Survey 2003/2004. United Nations, Office on Drugs and Crime, Vienna.

UNODC. 2006. Socio-economic and psychological assessment of fluctuations and varia-tions of opium poppy cultivation in key provinces in Afghanistan. United Nations, Office on Drugs and Crime, Vienna.

UNODC. 2008. World Drug Report 2008. United Nations, Office on Drugs and Crime Vienna 2008.

UNODC. 2009a. Addiction, crime and insurgency: The transnational threat of Afghan opium. United Nations, Office on Drugs and Crime, Vienna.

UNODC. 2009b. Afghanistan Opium Survey 2009. United Nations, Office on Drugs and Crime, Vienna.

USDD. 2010. Report on progress toward security and stability in Afghanistan. US Depart-ment of Defense. Report to Congress. Washington DC.

8 Social Unrest in the Wake of IMF Structural Adjustment Programs

Caleb Stroup and Ben Zissimos

8.1 Introduction

The Structural Adjustment Programs (SAPs) of the International Monetary Fund (IMF) have long been criticized for allegedly worsening well-being in the countries where they are imposed.[1] It is claimed that they may reduce welfare, exacerbate income inequalities, and ultimately provoke social unrest as those in society hit by the SAPs lash out in response. Stiglitz (2002) provides an account of the possible effects of SAPs when he writes: "For decades, people in the developing world have rioted when the austerity programs imposed on their countries [by the IMF] proved to be too harsh . . ." (p. 3). "For the peasants in developing countries who toil to pay off their countries' IMF debts or the businessmen who suffer from higher value added taxes upon the insistence of the IMF, the current system run by the IMF is one of taxation without representation. . . . Left with no alternatives, no way to express their concern, to press for change, people riot" (p. 20). Yet, despite widespread acknowledgment that there is a link between the imposition of SAPs and the occurrence of social unrest, we still do not have a clear understanding of the forces that drive this link.

The purpose of this chapter is to try to understand the relationship between the imposition of SAPs and the occurrence of social unrest. We identify a well-defined set of circumstances under which the imposition of an SAP can be expected to lead to social unrest and find support for this in the data. Our testable prediction is that if a country has an SAP, it will also tend to experience social unrest if it has a comparative advantage in primary products and at the same time undergoes deeper (i.e., greater/increased) trade integration.

This prediction builds on an analytical framework developed and tested empirically in our prior work, Stroup and Zissimos (2011, henceforth SZ). Since the present chapter builds on that paper, it is worth reviewing the key features of the framework we set up in SZ. In that previous paper, we show how the effects of a ruling elite's attempts to maintain political stability on efficiency depend on underlying factor endowments. If a country's endowments are such that it has a comparative advantage in primary products, and if the elite predominantly owns the land used to produce primary products, trade integration is potentially destabilizing. The reason is because the conjunction of a comparative advantage in primary products and trade liberalization raises the value of primary products and hence the land on which they are produced. This raises the incentives for the rest of society to try to seize control of the elite's land in a popular uprising. This in turn mandates an increase of government spending in general and government employment in particular, through which the elite make transfers to the rest of society in a bid to maintain political stability.[2] The general equilibrium effects of increasing government employment are to draw resources away from the more efficient manufacturing sector, potentially reducing overall economic efficiency. If a country's endowments are such that it has a comparative advantage in manufactures then the elite's incentives are reversed, and trade integration enhances economic efficiency.

The testable prediction that arises from the theoretical model in that earlier paper is as follows: an increase in trade integration leads to an increase in government employment in countries with a comparative advantage in primary products, but to a decrease in government employment in countries with a comparative advantage in manufactures. Our econometric analysis in that paper, which conditions on a variety of country-specific factors and persistence in the size of government, provides support for this prediction across a variety of specifications.

The testable prediction of the present chapter is then derived as follows: the conditionality of an SAP requires a country to liberalize trade while at the same time undertaking privatization, involving a process of rolling back the state and reducing government employment.[3] But in the context of the framework set out by SZ, if the country has a comparative advantage in primary products, the rest of society has an incentive to mount a revolution precisely in situations where trade liberalization occurs and so inequality increases. Without the constraints imposed by an SAP, the elite would respond by increasing government employment in order to undertake redistribution and thus defuse the incentive for political unrest. But the constraints imposed by the SAP to privatize and roll back the state constrain the elite in their ability to undertake redistribution through expansion of government employment. This results in the rest of society's incentive to mount a revolution remaining undefused. Therefore the testable prediction of the present chapter is a surprising implication of SZ that we did not pursue in the earlier paper. It is that when a country has a comparative advantage in primary products, trade liberalization in the presence of an SAP makes the country 'vulnerable to revolution.'

How do we capture vulnerability to revolution in the data? The lead up to a revolution usually unfolds gradually. There is often a protracted period between when the incentive to mount a revolution arises and when a revolution actually occurs, assuming the ruling elite do successfully avert its occurrence. Ellis and Fender (2010) have modeled this process as an information cascade whereby members of the rest of society signal to one another their desire to mount a revolution. Adapting Ellis and Fender's framework to the present context, the types of social unrest that have arisen in response to SAPs may be construed in terms of such signals: for example, strike activity, violent demonstrations, large-scale peaceful protest. We will refer to these forms of social unrest as indicating vulnerability to revolution.[4]

The specific process through which a ruling elite may defuse vulnerability to revolution is as follows: once a situation arises where a country may become vulnerable to revolution, there is a window of opportunity within which the elite can respond with measures, such as increasing government employment, that restore the status quo. The elite accept the constraints on government employment imposed by an SAP, through which vulnerability to revolution may arise, since it is usually the elite who have most to gain from the SAP's successful imposition. The reason is that the SAP generally determines a country's future access to world capital and goods markets, which benefit the elite. To the extent that the rest of society is unable to access capital markets and unable to afford traded goods, its benefit from the imposition of an SAP is less clear. So a country's elite is likely to support the imposition of an SAP to the fullest extent possible while the rest of society may be against it. But the elite will have an incentive to relax its terms if the SAP appears to be creating vulnerability to revolution. Governments generally have sufficient leeway, and in any case the sovereignty, to renege on the terms of an SAP if needed (Easterly 2005).

We are able to obtain measures of various types of social unrest across a broad range of countries from the Cross National Time Series (CNTS) data archive. And we proxy trade liberalization using a standard measure of economic openness. Our results show that for a country that has a comparative advantage in primary products and an SAP in place, an increase in economic openness relative to the size of government does increase vulnerability to revolution and hence the likelihood of social conflict. This relationship holds for six out of eight measures of social conflict in the CNTS. We take this to represent support in the data for our framework's prediction. As we will discuss below, this observed relationship is robust to a broad range of salient alternative hypotheses.

The key difference between the present chapter and SZ can be understood in terms of differences in the time frame of the analysis. An underlying assumption in SZ is that sufficient time passes within a period that the elite are able to resolve any vulnerability to revolution using adjustments to government employment. In that paper, social unrest is not actually observed on the equilibrium path. In the present chapter, the time frame within a period is assumed to be sufficiently short that vulnerability to revolution may indeed arise, reflected in social unrest. This difference in approach makes it possible for us to study the causes of social unrest in the present chapter, where this was not possible in SZ.

The past literature in economics evaluating the impact of IMF SAPs has tended to focus overwhelmingly on their impact on economic growth, not least because the stated intention of SAPs is to improve it. The results from a wide range of studies, by the IMF and by independent researchers, have found positive, zero, and negative effects of IMF lending on growth. Easterly (2005) first reviews the literature and reports it to be inconclusive, and then undertakes his own analysis to show a significantly negative effect of SAPs on economic growth. There is similarly mixed evidence of SAPs on policies (see the survey by Killick, Gunatilaka, and Marr 1998). There is a small academic literature on the effects of SAPs on conflict, which is nicely summarized by Guimond (2007). This literature studies the efficacy of SAPs in countries that have had social conflict in the past, focusing on civil war, at reducing the likelihood that conflict will break out again in the future.

As with the literature on the impact of SAPs on growth, conclusions are varied with no clear pattern emerging.[5]

There is also a literature in political science and sociology on how structural adjustment or the policies attributed to IMF conditionality affect social unrest. Walton and Seddon (1994) were among the first to systematically explore the significant fluctuations in commodity prices that ultimately gave way to the first Latin American debt crisis of the 1980s, prompting intervention by the IMF in a bid to restore economic and political stability. They document that it was the wave of unrest that came about as a result of these events that prompted the term "IMF riot." Similarly to the literature in economics on the relationship between IMF conditionality and growth, the line of enquiry exploring IMF conditionality and conflict has largely been inconclusive; see Hartzell, Hoddie and Bauer (2010), who find that IMF structural adjustment programs increase the likelihood of civil war, and the literature cited therein. Hartzell et al. is related to our chapter in that the discussion emphasizes how IMF conditionality creates gainers and losers while at the same time constraining the government's ability to make transfers that could mitigate social unrest. But neither they nor the literature that they cite focus on comparative advantage as a way to distinguish among the circumstances under which the rest of society is likely to resort to social unrest as we do here. The key novel point we are therefore making is that comparative advantage plays a decisive role in predicting the circumstances under which IMF conditionality leads to social unrest.

The rest of the chapter is structured as follows: Section 8.2 provides details of the empirical setup. Section 8.3 describes the data in more detail. Section 8.4 presents the estimation results, and section 8.5 discusses the extent to which the estimates might be given a causal interpretation. Conclusions are drawn in section 8.6.

8.2 Empirical Setup

We now set out an econometric formalization of the economic framework described informally in the previous section. In SZ, an elite maintains the status quo by ensuring that a "no-revolution constraint" (NRC) binds. From a situation where the NRC is binding, it would fail to bind if the country had a comparative advantage in primary products and trade integration deepened. The elite would then make the NRC bind again by increasing government employment. In any country

i and period t, the NRC depends directly on the elite's choice variable, which is the size of government employment, B_{it}, as well as on trade integration, O_{it}, and comparative advantage, C_i.[6] We can express the reduced form of the NRC as $\psi(C_i, O_{it}, B_{it})$.

We will say that the country in question becomes vulnerable to revolution when its NRC fails to bind. The NRC fails to bind if $0 < \psi(C_i, O_{it}, B_{it})$. In this state, members of the rest of society signal to one another that they would like to engage in a revolution by undertaking various types of social unrest. To formalize this social unrest, denote its probability in country i and period t by c_{it}. Given that idiosyncratic income shocks, ε_{it}, influence the probability of social unrest, we can express the probability of social unrest as follows:

$$c_{it} = \begin{cases} 0 & \text{if } 0 \geq \psi(C_i, O_{it}, B_{it}) + \varepsilon_{it}, \\ 1 & \text{if } 0 < \psi(C_i, O_{it}, B_{it}) + \varepsilon_{it}. \end{cases} \tag{8.1}$$

Consider a country that has a comparative advantage in primary products ($C_i = 1$). For $C_i = 1$, increased trade integration increases vulnerability to revolution; $\partial\psi/\partial O_{it} > 0$. At the same time, an expansion of government employment has an offsetting effect; $\partial\psi/\partial B_{it} < 0$. The opposite effects hold for countries with a comparative advantage in manufactures, where the term "manufactures" will be used as a short-hand for "all goods other than primary products." An unconstrained elite will usually be able to offset changes in trade integration with changes in government employment, thus heading off social unrest.[7] This specification captures in a simple way the econometric framework of SZ. Note that the framework of SZ does not allow for the increased likelihood of social unrest if the country is bound by an SAP that is the concern of the present chapter.

Where an SAP is imposed, an elite may be constrained from increasing government employment, at least in the first instance, thus creating vulnerability to revolution and increasing the probability of social unrest. Vulnerability comprises three necessary conditions for the NRC to fail. First, a country must have a comparative advantage in primary products ($C_i = 1$). Second, the country must have an SAP, brought about by the occurrence of a balance of payments (BOP) crisis ($BOP_{it} = 1$). Finally, we require an inverse relationship between trade integration and the size of government employment, which is given by the fact that the country has a comparative advantage in primary products. This is formalized by the function $f(O_{it}, B_{it})$, whereby $\partial^2 f_{it}/\partial O_{it}\partial B_{it} < 0$. We thus measure vulnerability to revolution as follows:

$$v_{it} = \begin{cases} 0 & \text{if } BOP_{it} = 0, \\ f(O_{it}, B_{it}) & \text{if } C_i = 1 \,\&\, BOP_{it} = 1. \end{cases} \tag{8.2}$$

This setup suggests a straightforward estimating approach via the following equation:

$$c_{it}^j = \beta_1^j v_{it} + \Theta_{it} + a_i + \tau_t + \varepsilon_{it}, \tag{8.3}$$

where the variables are defined as follows: c_{it}^j is a specific measure of social unrest such as strike activity or the occurrence of violent demonstrations, v_{it} indexes the vulnerability to revolution in terms of the probability that the NRC may fail to bind, Θ_{it} is a vector of time-varying country-specific controls, a_i is a vector of country-specific fixed effects, and τ_t are year effects.[8]

It might be suggested that we implement (8.3) using a binary response model such as logit or probit by imposing the assumption of normally distributed errors. However, fixed effects in such frameworks must be computed individually, leading to the incidental variables problem in which the number of parameters increases in proportion to the number of countries, thus generating inconsistent parameter estimates. We want to take the simplest possible approach and estimate (8.3), using a linear-probability model estimated via OLS, which allows for feasible computation of individual country fixed effects. Our focus is not on the precise marginal effects of vulnerability to social unrest but rather the presence or absence of the predicted effect. Therefore we view the robustness conferred by using country-specific fixed effects as strongly outweighing the requirement that estimated marginal effects be interpreted as a linear approximation of the true effects.

8.3   Data

To construct the dataset for this study, we combined the dataset from SZ with the Cross National Time Series (CNTS) dataset to provide measures of economic activity in conjunction with indicators of domestic social unrest. The measures of domestic social unrest in CNTS are as follows (followed by an abbreviation in parentheses):[9] (1) politically motivated assassinations (assassinations), (2) a strike of one thousand or more industrial workers (strikes), (3) armed activity by independent bands of citizens or irregular forces aimed at the overthrow of the present regime (armed activity), (4) a rapidly developing situation that threatens the downfall of the present regime (threatened regimes),

(5) systematic elimination of opposition politicians by jailing or execution (opposition elimination), (6) violent demonstration or clash of
more than one hundred citizens involving the use of physical force
(violent demonstrations), (7) any actual or attempted illegal or forced
change in the top government elite including armed rebellion (revolution—pos. attempted), and (8) any peaceful public gathering of at least
one hundred people for the purpose of voicing opposition to government policies or authority (peaceful demonstrations). For each of the
eight measures, indexed by $j = 1 \ldots 8$, we construct a dummy variable
that takes a value of 1 if, for a particular country in a particular year,
there is an occurrence of social unrest.

We measure government employment, B_{it}, using the log of annual
data for central government spending on wages and salaries (1972 to
2008 in millions of real US dollars) from the International Monetary
Fund's (IMF's) Government Finance Statistics database. A full list of
countries is given in table 8.1.[10]

We employ the measure of revealed comparative advantage (RCA)
due to Balassa (1965), and construct it from World Bank trade flows.[11]
Measurement of trade integration presents us with a difficulty when it
comes to estimation. On the one hand, our discussion of IMF/SAP
conditionality at the start of this chapter suggests that tariffs would be
the appropriate way to measure this. After all, the Washington Consensus calls for trade liberalization through adjustments to economic
policy. However, tariffs are also understood to be endogenously determined, making them unsuitable for use on the right hand side of a
regression. Consequently we measure trade integration with the grav-
ity-based measure used by Rose (2004), and Hijzena, Gorg, and Munchin
(2008), among others, which is the distance-weighted average of all
trading partners' GDPs.[12] First define Y_{it} as country i's GDP in year t
expressed in millions of constant dollars and let δ_{ij} be the distance
between countries i and j. This measure of trade integration is
$O_{it} = \sum_{j \neq i} Y_{jt} / \delta_{ij}$. Unlike other measures of trade integration such as
tariffs and the terms of trade, which are clearly endogenous, most
countries' governments have limited if any influence over (the distance-weighted average of) their trading partners' GDPs. Therefore
variation in O_{it} plausibly extracts identifying variation in relative prices.

The variable v_{it} is measured as follows: First, $v_{it} = 0$ when either
C_i or BOP_{it} are equal to zero and $v_{it} = f(O_{it}, B_{it})$ otherwise, so that $v_{it} =$
$f(O_{it}, B_{it}) \times C_i \times BOP_{it}$, where the latter two are binary variables. Second,

Table 8.1
List of countries

Albania	Egypt	Lesotho	Portugal
Australia	El Salvador	Liberia	Romania
Austria	Estonia	Lithuania	Rwanda
Barbados	Finland	Luxembourg	Senegal
Belarus	France	Madagascar	Seychelles
Belgium	Gabon	Malaysia	Singapore
Benin	Georgia	Mali	Slovenia
Bhutan	Greece	Malta	Spain
Bolivia	Guinea	Mauritius	Sri Lanka
Brazil	Haiti	Mexico	Sweden
Bulgaria	Honduras	Moldova	Switzerland
Burundi	Hungary	Mongolia	Tajikistan
Cameroon	Iceland	Morocco	Tanzania
Chad	India	Netherlands	Thailand
Chile	Indonesia	Nicaragua	Togo
Colombia	Ireland	Niger	Tunisia
Costa Rica	Italy	Norway	Turkey
Croatia	Jamaica	Pakistan	Ukraine
Cyprus	Kazakhstan	Paraguay	Uruguay
Denmark	Latvia	Peru	Vanuatu
Djibouti	Lebanon	Poland	Zambia
Dominica			Zimbabwe

Note: This table provides a list of in-sample countries for which there exists unrest data. The unbalanced panel spans the years 1972 to 2008.

since our fixed-effects estimation procedure identifies model parameters off of variation *within* a country across time, we approximate $f(O_{it}, B_{it})$ with O_{it}/B_{it}. This satisfies the requirement (specified above) that $\partial^2 f_{it}/\partial O_{it}\partial B_{it} < 0$.

Balance-of-payments crises are likely to induce social unrest in a variety of ways not directly tied to the theoretical model presented in SZ. To control for these, we also include BOP_{it} by itself in the regressions. Similarly we include C_i, B_{it}, and O_{it} in levels in all equations, along with all pairwise interactions among these variables. We also include the full vector of interaction combinations within the set $\{O_{it}, B_{it}, C_i, BOP_{it}\}$; this will be referred to in the tables as the "interaction vector." Finally, we control for observable determinants of total government employment that may be correlated with trade integration, comparative advantage, and BOP crises. For example, larger economies may tend to have both a comparative advantage in manufacturing and to experience larger responses of total government employment to changes in trade integration. If larger economies tend to be more developed, they may also be less subject to BOP crises. To capture these economy-size effects, we include total GDP expressed in millions of US dollars (GDP_{it}). Similarly, countries with higher incomes may tend to have higher wage rates and thus higher central government spending on wages and salaries. This may vary systematically by comparative advantage to the extent that countries with a comparative advantage in manufacturing have higher average wage rates than countries with a comparative advantage in primary products. An ideal measure would be middle class wage rates or the minimum wage. Since no such data exist at the annual level for a wide variety of developing countries, we use GDP per capita in thousands of dollars (GDP_{it}/N_{it}) instead. These two series came from the Penn World Tables. Table 8.2 summarizes the unrest measures broken down by the incidence of unrest.

8.4   Empirical Results

Table 8.3 presents results from a simple regression of each of our eight measures of social unrest (introduced at the beginning of Section 8.3) on BOP_{it}. Recall that BOP_{it} captures BOP crises that involved imposition of an SAP. The estimated coefficients are positive and significant at conventional levels across six out of the eight measures, confirming that SAPs are indeed broadly correlated with the occurrence of social unrest, as generally suspected.

In table 8.4 we introduce the measure of vulnerability to revolution, v_{it}, to the specification. From the top row we can see that inclusion of the vulnerability measure leads to substantial attrition in the predictive power of BOP_{it}; in this case it has no predictive power for assassinations (column 1), strikes (column 2), threatened regimes (column 4), and peaceful demonstrations (column 8). This indicates that the observed correlation presented in table 8.3 between BOP_{it} and our eight measures of social unrest is likely to reflect omitted country-specific variables and, in particular, the omission of v_{it} itself. Turning to the coefficient on v_{it}, we can see that for all but two measures the estimated coefficients are negative; in four cases they are negative and significant. In only one case, that of armed activity (column 3) is the estimated coefficient positive and significant.

Table 8.2
Measures of social unrest

	$BOP_{it} = 0$		$BOP_{it} = 1$	
	Mean	S.D.	Mean	S.D.
Assassinations	0.167	0.373	0.243	0.430
Strikes	0.171	0.376	0.261	0.440
Armed activity	0.163	0.370	0.293	0.456
Threatened regimes	0.198	0.399	0.254	0.436
Opposition elimination	0.090	0.287	0.161	0.368
Violent demonstrations	0.199	0.399	0.336	0.473
Revolution (pos. attempted)	0.132	0.338	0.318	0.466
Peaceful demonstrations	0.271	0.444	0.376	0.485
N	1,257		279	

Note: This table presents summary statistics for conflict indicators defied at the country-year level. Assassinations takes a value of unity for country i in year t if there is a politically motivated murder or attempted murder of a high government official or politician. The remaining variables are defined analogously. Strikes takes a value of unity if there is a strike of 1,000 or more industrial or service workers. Armed activity takes a value of unity if there is any armed activity, sabotage, or bombings carried on by independent bands of citizens or irregular forces and aimed at the overthrow of the present regime. Threatened regimes takes a value of unity if there is any rapidly developing situation that threatens to bring the downfall of the present regime. Opposition elimination takes a value of unity if there is any systematic elimination by jailing or execution of political opposition within the ranks of the regime or the opposition. Violent demonstrations takes a value of unity if the country experiences a violent demonstration or clash of more than 100 citizens involving the use of physical force. Revolutions takes a value of unity if there is any illegal or forced change in the top government elite, any attempt at such a change, or any successful or unsuccessful armed rebellion whose aim is independence from the central government. Peaceful demonstrations takes a value of unity if there is any peaceful public gathering of at least 100 people for the primary purpose of displaying or voicing their opposition to government policies or authority.

As discussed above, the presence of country-specific factors simultaneously correlated with BOP_{it} and v_{it} could lead to biased estimates of the true effect of these variables on the incidence of social unrest. To address this possibility, in table 8.5 we incorporate country-specific fixed effects and the interaction vector. Looking across the first row, which presents the estimated coefficients on v_{it}, we can see that inclusion of these country-specific factors leads to a dramatic change in the estimated coefficients so that v_{it} is positive and statistically significant at the 5 percent level or below for all but two of our measures of social unrest. The exceptions are threatened regimes (column 4, which is only

Table 8.3
Social unrest and IMF SAPs

	(1)	(2)	(3)	(4)	(5)	(6)	(7)	(8)
BOP_{it}	0.073*	0.089***	0.133	0.056**	0.071**	0.144***	0.192***	0.108***
	(0.030)	(0.020)	(0.068)	(0.020)	(0.025)	(0.033)	(0.029)	(0.017)
Constant	0.171***	0.173***	0.161***	0.199***	0.091***	0.193***	0.127***	0.269***
	(0.022)	(0.016)	(0.034)	(0.023)	(0.010)	(0.025)	(0.022)	(0.029)
Year effects	Yes	Yes	Yes	Yes	Yes	Yes	Yes	Yes
Nation effects	No	No	No	No	No	No	No	No
Interaction vector	No	No	No	No	No	No	No	No
Observations	1,493	1,493	1,493	1,493	1,493	1,493	1,493	1,493

Note: This table presents estimates of equation (8.1). The dependent variable takes a value of one for country i in year t if there is a politically motivated murder or attempted murder of a high government official or politician (column 1), if there is a strike of 1,000 or more industrial or service workers (column 2), if there is any armed activity, sabotage, or bombings carried on by independent bands of citizens or irregular forces and aimed at the overthrow of the present regime (column 3), if there is any rapidly developing situation that threatens to bring the downfall of the present regime (column 4), if there is any systematic elimination by jailing or execution of political opposition within the ranks of the regime or the opposition (column 5), if the country experiences a violent demonstration or clash of more than 100 citizens involving the use of physical force (column 6), if there is any illegal or forced change in the top government elite, any attempt at such a change, or any successful or unsuccessful armed rebellion whose aim is independence from the central government (column 7), and if there is any peaceful public gathering of at least 100 people for the primary purpose of displaying or voicing their opposition to government policies or authority (column 8). All equations include year fixed effects. Cluster-robust standard errors at the region level are in parentheses below the estimated coefficients. *, **, and *** denote statistical significance at the 10 percent, 5 percent, and 1 percent levels.

Table 8.4

Social unrest and vulnerability to revolution: Baseline specification

	(1)	(2)	(3)	(4)	(5)	(6)	(7)	(8)
v_{it}	0.008	-0.109**	0.042***	-0.008	-0.014	-0.097**	-0.033	-0.128***
	(0.019)	(0.038)	(0.010)	(0.036)	(0.009)	(0.035)	(0.036)	(0.023)
BOP_{it}	0.075	0.016	0.165**	0.053	0.063*	0.083*	0.171***	0.023
	(0.040)	(0.029)	(0.063)	(0.032)	(0.028)	(0.032)	(0.028)	(0.039)
Constant	0.173***	0.173***	0.163***	0.199***	0.090***	0.192***	0.127***	0.268***
	(0.022)	(0.016)	(0.033)	(0.024)	(0.010)	(0.026)	(0.022)	(0.030)
Year effects	Yes	Yes	Yes	Yes	Yes	Yes	Yes	Yes
Nation effects	No	No	No	No	No	No	No	No
Interaction vector	No	No	No	No	No	No	No	No
Observations	1,459	1,459	1,459	1,459	1,459	1,459	1,459	1,459

Note: This table presents estimates of equation (8.1). The dependent variable takes a value of one for country i in year t if there is a politically motivated murder or attempted murder of a high government official or politician (column 1), if there is a strike of 1,000 or more industrial or service workers (column 2), if there is any armed activity, sabotage, or bombings carried on by independent bands of citizens or irregular forces and aimed at the overthrow of the present regime (column 3), if there is any rapidly developing situation that threatens to bring the downfall of the present regime (column 4), if there is any systematic elimination by jailing or execution of political opposition within the ranks of the regime or the opposition (column 5), if the country experiences a violent demonstration or clash of more than 100 citizens involving the use of physical force (column 6), if there is any illegal or forced change in the top government elite, any attempt at such a change, or any successful or unsuccessful armed rebellion whose aim is independence from the central government (column 7), and if there is any peaceful public gathering of at least 100 people for the primary purpose of displaying or voicing their opposition to government policies or authority (column 8). All equations include year fixed effects. Cluster-robust standard errors at the region level are in parentheses below the estimated coefficients. *, **, and *** denote statistical significance at the 10 percent, 5 percent, and 1 percent levels.

Table 8.5
Social unrest and vulnerability to revolution: Adding country effects and control variables

	(1)	(2)	(3)	(4)	(5)	(6)	(7)	(8)
v_{it}	0.365***	0.279***	0.333***	0.120*	0.232***	0.221***	0.298***	0.026
	(0.032)	(0.013)	(0.009)	(0.059)	(0.010)	(0.043)	(0.030)	(0.108)
BOP_{it}	0.520**	0.271	0.993*	-0.034	-0.095	0.302	0.724***	0.278
	(0.131)	(0.334)	(0.463)	(0.538)	(0.348)	(0.336)	(0.122)	(0.473)
C_{it}	0.266	0.056	0.221	-0.278	0.158	-0.042	0.120	0.476
	(0.224)	(0.393)	(0.337)	(0.243)	(0.298)	(0.313)	(0.272)	(0.449)
B_{it}	0.082	0.008	-0.008	-0.043	0.023	-0.026	0.089**	0.092
	(0.044)	(0.064)	(0.043)	(0.041)	(0.049)	(0.064)	(0.029)	(0.080)
O_{it}	0.227	0.047	-0.354	-0.570	-0.092	-0.268	0.138	0.364
	(0.250)	(0.411)	(0.251)	(0.394)	(0.428)	(0.417)	(0.267)	(0.557)
Year effects	Yes	Yes	Yes	Yes	Yes	Yes	Yes	Yes
Nation effects	Yes	Yes	Yes	Yes	Yes	Yes	Yes	Yes
Interaction vector	Yes	Yes	Yes	Yes	Yes	Yes	Yes	Yes
Observations	1,459	1,459	1,459	1,459	1,459	1,459	1,459	1,459
Number of id	83	83	83	83	83	83	83	83

Note: The dependent variable takes a value of one for country i in year t if there is a politically motivated murder or attempted murder of a high government official or politician (column 1), if there is a strike of 1,000 or more industrial or service workers (column 2), if there is any armed activity, sabotage, or bombings carried on by independent bands of citizens or irregular forces and aimed at the overthrow of the present regime (column 3), if there is any rapidly developing situation that threatens to bring the downfall of the present regime (column 4), if there is any systematic elimination within the ranks of the regime or the opposition (column 5), if the country experiences a violent demonstration or clash of more than 100 citizens involving force (column 6), if there is any illegal or forced change in the top government elite, any attempt at such a change, or any successful or unsuccessful armed rebellion whose aim is independence from the central government (column 7), and if there is any peaceful public gathering of at least 100 people opposing the government (column 8). All equations include year and country-specific fixed effects. Cluster-robust standard errors at the region level are in parentheses below the estimated coefficients. *, **, and *** denote statistical significance at the 10 percent, 5 percent, and 1 percent levels.

significant at the 10 percent level) and peaceful demonstrations (column 8). This indicates that, given a BOP crises and imposition of SAP in a country with a comparative advantage in primary products, a deepening of trade integration relative to the size of government did indeed increase the likelihood of social unrest. For assassinations (column 1) and revolutions (pos. attempted) (column 7), the coefficient on BOP_{it} is positive and significant at the 5 and 1 percent levels, respectively. This suggests that, for these measures of social unrest, a BOP crises and SAP significantly increases the likelihood of social unrest as we might expect.

In table 8.6 we add GDP and GDP per capita to the specification. Inclusion of these variables leads the coefficient on v_{it} to be slightly smaller in magnitude, even though GDP and GDP per capita have no predictive power themselves. This is not surprising since both variables are highly correlated with the time-invariant fixed effects that are present in these specifications. None of the variables have explanatory power for peaceful demonstrations (column 8), possibly because this type of protest is more associated with developed countries where BOP crises accompanied by SAPs are a much rarer occurrence in our dataset.

8.5 Discussion

The estimates obtained from (8.3) are consistent with the underlying causal channel proposed by SZ. We now discuss whether these findings might also be consistent with other salient alternative hypotheses. Of particular importance is that we have controlled for variables that are thought to drive unrest. For example, liberalization by itself may lead to unrest, so we have included O_{it} in the regressions to control for this fact. Similarly, reductions in government employment may lead to unrest, so we have included B_{it} by itself in all regressions. As observed in numerous studies that examine the effect of SAPs, the introduction of these conditionalities may be driven by unobserved social unrest, so we control for this by including BOP_{it} in our regressions. Similarly, per-capita GDP can be seen as a broad outcome variable that reflects institutions broadly defined (Lipset 1960; Hall and Jones 1999; Dollar and Kraay 2003; Easterly and Levine 2003; Glaeser, La Porta, Lopez-de-Silanes, and Shleifer 2004), and we have controlled for per-capita GDP in the regressions.

Country-specific fixed effects account for arbitrary persistent idiosyncratic effects on the incidence of social unrest. Since one might believe the observed correlation between vulnerability to revolution

Table 8.6
Social unrest and vulnerability to revolution: Adding country effects, control variables, GDP and GDP per capita

	(1)	(2)	(3)	(4)	(5)	(6)	(7)	(8)
v_{it}	0.316***	0.212***	0.265***	0.110*	0.240***	0.244***	0.203***	-0.049
	(0.022)	(0.026)	(0.025)	(0.051)	(0.056)	(0.032)	(0.045)	(0.075)
BOP_{it}	0.700***	0.229	1.235*	0.118	0.166	0.513*	0.912**	0.452
	(0.115)	(0.289)	(0.593)	(0.405)	(0.230)	(0.211)	(0.261)	(0.436)
C_{it}	0.328	0.028	0.323	-0.272	0.292	0.102	0.098	0.511
	(0.191)	(0.382)	(0.305)	(0.145)	(0.255)	(0.294)	(0.307)	(0.381)
B_{it}	0.055	-0.063	-0.032	-0.122**	0.022	0.009	-0.009	0.084
	(0.124)	(0.102)	(0.063)	(0.044)	(0.120)	(0.093)	(0.118)	(0.082)
O_{it}	0.228	-0.017	-0.115	-0.664***	0.138	0.124	-0.109	0.370
	(0.262)	(0.432)	(0.219)	(0.140)	(0.318)	(0.379)	(0.217)	(0.386)
GDP_{it}	-0.034	-0.051	-0.105	0.083	0.034	0.006	0.003	-0.072
	(0.108)	(0.084)	(0.078)	(0.045)	(0.132)	(0.089)	(0.108)	(0.050)
GDP_{it}/N_{it}	0.007	0.032	0.172	-0.075	0.057	0.147	-0.085	0.027
	(0.076)	(0.029)	(0.098)	(0.072)	(0.048)	(0.086)	(0.045)	(0.106)
Year effects	Yes	Yes	Yes	Yes	Yes	Yes	Yes	Yes
Nation effects	Yes	Yes	Yes	Yes	Yes	Yes	Yes	Yes
Interaction vector	Yes	Yes	Yes	Yes	Yes	Yes	Yes	Yes
Observations	1,459	1,459	1,459	1,459	1,459	1,459	1,459	1,459
Number of id	83	83	83	83	83	83	83	83

Note: The dependent variable takes a value of one for country i in year t if there is a politically motivated murder or attempted murder of a high government official or politician (column 1), if there is a strike of 1,000 or more industrial or service workers (column 2), if there is any armed activity, sabotage, or bombings carried on by independent bands of citizens or irregular forces and aimed at the overthrow of the present regime (column 3), if there is any rapidly developing situation that threatens to bring the downfall of the present regime (column 4), if there is any systematic elimination within the ranks of the regime or the opposition (column 5), if the country experiences a violent demonstration or clash of more than 100 citizens involving force (column 6), if there is any illegal or forced change in the top government elite, any attempt at such a change, or any successful or unsuccessful armed rebellion whose aim is independence from the central government (column 7), and if there is any peaceful public gathering of at least 100 people opposing the government (column 8). All equations include year and country-specific fixed effects. Cluster-robust standard errors at the region level are in parentheses below the estimated coefficients. *, **, and *** denote statistical significance at the 10 percent, 5 percent, and 1 percent levels.

and unrest to be driven by intertemporal changes in the propensity of social unrest, we have included year effects in all regressions. Additionally, there are in principle many complementary effects on social unrest driven by interactions among the components of v_{it}, such as the possibility that natural resource intensive countries that receive SAPs are more unrest-prone relative to others. To account for these types of influences we have included the full set of interaction permutations between the components of v_{it} and $\{O_{it}, B_{it}, C_i, BOP_{it}\}$.

Our having controlled for these factors implies that an alternative theory (i.e., an omitted variable simultaneously positively correlated with v_{it} and social unrest) would need to simultaneously influence openness, comparative advantage, government spending on wages and salaries, and the offering of an SAP to the country concerned while at the same time not being captured by persistent country-specific or time-specific factors. At the same time, without a persuasive structural model or instruments for all of $\{O_{it}, B_{it}, C_i, BOP_{it}\}$, one cannot rule out the possibility that arbitrary omitted variables do not drive the observed correlation between v_{it} and unrest. Nevertheless, we believe that by controlling for these extraneous factors, and thus eliminating them as viable candidates to explain the estimates we obtained, we have increased the probability that the result is driven by the main channel on which we have been focusing.

8.6 Conclusions

This chapter has proposed a way of understanding the link between the imposition of SAPs in response to BOP crises and the occurrence of social unrest. In response to the greater inequality brought about by deeper trade integration, if a country has a comparative advantage in primary products, the rest of society has an incentive to mount a revolution whereby it expropriates the elite's assets. In the absence of an SAP, the elite would face no constraints in making transfers to the rest of society in order to restore the status quo. But under the constraints imposed by the SAP, it is not immediately able to do this. Consequently social unrest breaks out as individuals signal to one another that they would be prepared to mount a revolution. If the elite did nothing the social unrest would escalate to the point where it would culminate in a revolution. But generally speaking, before that point is reached the elite acquiesce and break the conditionality of the SAP, making the transfers required to restore the status quo.

Our empirical approach has been to show that there is a positive correlation between a country's vulnerability to revolution and the actual incidence of social unrest using a variety of measures. To check the robustness of these correlations, they were conditioned on variables capturing salient alternative hypotheses. Our results provide empirical support for the framework we have laid out. Moreover, they suggest that accounting for institutions through which the elite make transfers to the rest of society in order to restore the status quo, such as the government civil service, is potentially important for understanding the effectiveness of IMF conditionality at inducing policy compliance. Prior accounts of such failure to comply had been attributed to 'lack of commitment by those responsible for implementing the programs'. The present framework goes further in providing a concrete set of circumstances under which such lack of commitment would be rational. In future work it would be useful to test comprehensively for the causality of 'vulnerability to revolution' for the outbreak of social conflict, either by constructing and estimating a structural model of social conflict in this context, or by obtaining instruments for all four components of the vulnerability measure.

A particular concern, both in academic and policy circles, has been why some countries have been provided SAP support for an extended period without any apparent improvement in their macroeconomic situation. As an illustration of this, Easterly (2005) shows in table 1 of his paper that the average outcome across a range of macroeconomic indicators for the top twenty recipients of SAP support over the period 1980 to 1999 was the same as those for a broad sample of developing countries. His claim is that if SAPs are intended to promote growth, then we should expect to see better performance from countries with SAPs. A second concern is that these countries were supported by SAPs for such a long time without any discernible improvement in performance. The present chapter provides a way of understanding this situation. For countries with a comparative advantage in primary products, deeper trade integration (which is mandated under an SAP) may actually cause a country to have to exit from the program due to the social unrest that it provokes, presumably without any resolution to the underlying problems. Repeated attempts to address current account imbalances in this way will repeatedly be met by the same outcome. Until this set of interactions is taken full account of in IMF policy initiatives, further progress on this issue is unlikely to be made.

Acknowledgments

We would like to thank Emily Blanchard, Rick Bond, Arye Hillman, and Isleide Zissimos for useful conversations about this chapter. We are grateful for comments from two anonymous referees that greatly improved the exposition. This chapter also benefitted from comments on a progenitor by participants at the CESifo conference on The Economics of Conflict—Theory and Policy Lessons. Financial support from CESifo is gratefully acknowledged.

Notes

1. SAPs have two components. One is the extension of loans, coupled with possible multilateral renegotiation to reduce a country's total debt obligations. The second is the adjustment of a country's policies which is aimed at increasing economic efficiency and growth, and with it a country's ability to meet its debt obligations (Boughton 2001). Elsewhere in the literature, the term 'Structural Adjustment Loan' (SAL) is used equivalently to our use of the term SAP.

2. Increasing the size of government may not be the most efficient way to make transfers aimed at maintaining political stability, with alternative more far-reaching measures such as land reforms likely to be more efficient. However, there appears to be anecdotal evidence to suggest that government employment is a relatively manipulable device through which transfers can be made quickly if the need arises, in contrast to land reforms which tend to proceed relatively slowly. For example, *The Economist* (2011) documents several instances where ruling elites rapidly made transfers to the rest of society through government employment in their attempts to quell the wave of uprisings in the Middle East known as the Arab Spring.

3. SAPs also typically require stabilization of the macroeconomic environment, principally through the use of monetary policy. That aspect of SAPs is beyond the scope of the present analysis. See Williamson (1989) for the original statement of the "Washington Consensus" on policy reform.

4. The interpretation that social unrest indicates vulnerability to revolution may seem extreme given that we have developed countries in our dataset where revolution is rarely observed. Here we are taking the position that these countries can in principle be vulnerable to revolution but that a well-functioning democracy has better mechanisms for defusing this vulnerability including, as a final backstop, transfer of power through the ballot box.

5. Structural adjustment loans from the World Bank also have conditionalities attached to them and there is a literature evaluating these as well. We focus on IMF SAPs because they are associated more closely with the occurrence of social conflict. This is perhaps because IMF SAPs are tied more tightly to balance of payments crises which are likely to require immediate constraints on entitlement spending that in turn increase inequality and provoke social unrest. World Bank lending has been more associated with long term structural adjustment, although since the 1980s IMF and World Bank lending have been used in conjunction with one another, the former maintaining its focus on adjustments

to recover from balance of payments crises, the latter on longer term objectives of policy reform (Boughton 2001; Easterly 2005).

6. For the purposes of our econometric implementation, trade integration is treated as exogenous. See the next section for details.

7. In fact there exist extreme conditions under which the elite will not be able to use government employment to maintain the status quo. We abstract from them here but discuss them at length in SZ.

8. Although a large literature takes the incidence of BOP crises and SAPs as given, there is a growing literature that attempts to instrument SAPs conditional on BOP incidence. While this approach may be useful for studying, for example, the relationship between SAPs and growth, it would not, in our context, fully address the identification concern since the usual instruments (e.g., political proximity to major shareholders at the IMF, voting behavior at the United Nations) will also be correlated with any potentially time-varying country-specific institution. For further discussion, see, for example, Bird and Rowlands (1991, 2002), World Bank (1992, 1998), Conway (1994), Alesina and Dollar (2000), Burnside and Dollar (2000), Barro and Lee (2005), Dreher and Jensen (2007), and Kilby (2009).

9. See the footnote of table 8.3 for more extensive descriptions of each of the measures of social conflict.

10. Since our estimation procedure identifies parameters using only within-variation, we need a sample whose variables exhibit significant variation across time. Fortunately, both trade integration and central government employment varied significantly during our sample period for many countries. An alternative would have been to employ data from the International Labor Organization. However, for our purposes, these data are not nearly as comprehensive in their coverage across countries as the IMF series, especially prior to 1995.

11. Let X_{ikt} be country i's exports of product category k to the rest of the world in period t, and let $X_{i\omega t}$ be total exports from country i to the rest of the world within a set of product categories ω. X_{nkt} is the sum of all other countries' (i.e., $j \neq i$) exports in product category k, and $X_{n\omega t}$ are total world exports in the set of product categories. Then RCA_{ikt} = $(X_{ikt}/X_{i\omega t})/(X_{nkt}/X_{n\omega t})$. Following the standard approach, country i has a revealed comparative advantage in product k if and only if $RCA_{ikt} > 1$. In our sample, RCA is stable over time, allowing use of the mode across years as our measure of a country's comparative advantage. Given that we are making cross-country sector comparisons, we also require a correspondence between the Balassa index and pre-trade relative prices; the Hillman condition must hold (see Hillman 1980). In a dataset of 165 countries from 1970 to 1998, Hinloopen and van Marrewijk (2008) have shown that violations of the Hillman condition are rare after 1984 but prior to 1984 violations do occur relatively frequently for countries whose exports are concentrated on a small number of sectors. Our main results are slightly stronger when we truncate the data in 1984, which provides support for our hypothesis and for the empirical relevance of the Hillman condition.

12. Goldberg, Khandelwal, Pavcnik, and Topalova (2010) argue in their study of India that in the event of an unanticipated BOP crisis and SAP, the tariff reforms mandated by the program may be regarded as exogenous. However, this argument would only apply in our dataset to the minority of countries in any given period that were constrained by SAPs. Therefore we cannot use the approach advocated by Goldberg et al.

References

Alesina, A., and D. Dollar. 2000. Who Gives Foreign Aid to Whom and Why? *Journal of Economic Growth* 5: 33–64.

Balassa, B. 1965. Trade liberalization and revealed comparative advantage. *Manchester School of Economic and Social Studies* 33: 99–123.

Barro, R. J., and J. W. Lee. 2005. IMF-Programs: Who Is Chosen and What are the Effects? *Journal of Monetary Economics* 52 (7): 1245–1269.

Bird, G., and D. Rowlands. 1991. IMF Lending: How is it Affected by Economic, Political, and Institutional Factors? *Journal of Policy Reform* 4 (3): 243–270.

Bird, G., and D. Rowlands. 2002. The pattern of IMF lending: An analysis of prediction failures. *Journal of Policy Reform.* Conference on the Role of Multinational Institutions in the International Monetary System, Miami.

Boughton, J. 2001. *Silent Revolution: The International Monetary Fund, 1979–1989.* Washington, DC: International Monetary Fund.

Burnside, C., and D. Dollar. 2000. Aid, policies, and growth. *American Economic Review* 90 (4): 847–68.

Conway, P. 1994. IMF lending programs: Participation and impact. *Journal of Development Economics* 45: 365–91.

Dollar, David, and Aart Kraay. 2003. Institutions, trade and growth. *Journal of Monetary Economics* 50 (1): 133–62.

Dreher, A., and N. M. Jensen. 2007. Independent actor or agent? An empirical analysis of the impact of US interests on IMF conditions. *Journal of Law and Economics* 50 (1): 105–24.

Easterly, W. 2005. What did structural adjustment adjust? The association of policies and growth with repeated IMF and World Bank adjustment loans. *Journal of Development Economics* 76 (1): 1–22.

Easterly, W., and R. Levine. 2003. Tropics, germs, and crops: How endowments influence economic development. *Journal of Monetary Economics* 50 (1): 3–39.

Economist, The. 2011. Throwing money at the street. March 12: 32.

Ellis, C. J., and J. Fender. 2010. Information cascades and revolutionary regime transitions. *Economic Journal* 121 (553): 763–92.

Glaeser, E., R. La Porta, F. Lopez-de-Silanes, and A. Shleifer. 2004. Do institutions cause growth? *Journal of Economic Growth* 9 (3): 271–303.

Goldberg, P. K., A. Khandelwal, N. Pavcnik, and P. Topalova. 2010. Imported intermediate inputs and domestic product growth: Evidence from India. *Quarterly. Journal of Economics* 125 (4): 1727–67.

Gorg, H., A. Hijzen, and M. Manchin. 2008. Cross-border mergers and acquisitions and the role of trade costs. *European Economic Review* 52: 849–66.

Guimond, M.-F. 2007. Structural adjustment and peace building. International Development Research Centre, Conflict and Development Program Initiative.

Hall, R. E., and C. I. Jones. 1999. Why do some countries produce so much more output per worker than others? *Quarterly Journal of Economics* 114 (1): 83–116.

Hartzell, C. A., M. Hoddie, and M. Bauer. 2010. Economic liberalization via IMF structural adjustment: Sowing the seeds of civil war? *International Organization* 64: 339–56.

Hillman, A. L. 1980. Observations on the relation between "revealed comparative advantage" and comparative advantage as indicated by pre-trade relative prices. *Weltwirtschaftliches Archiv* 116: 315–21.

Hinloopen, J., and C. van Marrewijk. 2008. Empirical evidence of the Hillman condition for revealed comparative advantage: 10 stylized facts. *Applied Economics* 40: 2313–28.

Kilby, C. 2009. The political economy of conditionality: An empirical analysis of World Bank loan disbursements. *Journal of Development Economics* 89 (1): 51–61.

Killick, T., R. Gunatilaka, and A. Marr. 1998. *Aid and the Political Economy of Policy Change*. London: Routledge.

Lipset, S. M. 1960. *Political Man: The Social Basis of Modern Politics*. New York: Doubleday.

Rose, A. 2004. Do WTO members have more liberal trade policy? *Journal of International Economics* 63: 209–35.

Stiglitz, J. 2002. *Globalization and Its Discontents*. London: Penguin Books.

Stroup, J. C., and B. C. Zissimos. 2011. Pampered bureaucracy, political stability, and trade integration. Working paper 11–W05. Department of Economics, Vanderbilt University.

Williamson, J. 1989. What Washington means by policy reform. In J. Williamson, ed., *Latin American Adjustment: How Much Has Happened?* Washington, DC: Institute for International Economics.

Walton, J., and D. Seddon. 1994. *Free Markets and Food Riots: The Politics of Global Adjustment*. Cambridge, MA: Blackwell.

World Bank. 1992. *Adjustment Lending and Mobilization of Private and Public Resources for Growth*. Country Economics Department, Policy and Research Series. vol. 22. Washington, DC: World Bank.

World Bank. 1998. *Assessing Aid: What Works, What Doesn't, and Why*. Oxford: Oxford University Press.

9 Social Preferences of Ex-Combatants: Survey and Experimental Evidence from Postwar Tajikistan

Alessandra Cassar, Pauline Grosjean, and Sam Whitt

9.1 Introduction

This chapter uses unique game-behavioral and survey evidence collected in postwar Tajikistan with the goal of better understanding the relationship between violence and pro-social behavior and, ultimately, the implications of violent conflicts for market development and institution building.

Recent studies have found surprising increases in pro-social behavior following exposure to violence, providing micro-level explanations for how societies might recover and develop even after devastating experiences (Bauer et al. 2011; Bellows and Miguel 2009; Blattman 2009; Voors et al. 2011). War has also been suggested to play a critical role in many macro-historical accounts of how nations develop and how political order and institutions are established within complex societies (Tilly and Ardant 1975; Tilly 1985; North, Wallis, and Weingast 2009; Fukuyama 2011). In some cases, however, the prospects of recovery from violence are not as promising. Some states appear deeply mired in poverty and stagnation, and in the worst cases, succumb to recurrent conflict and insurgencies (Collier et al. 2003; Collier and Hoeffler 2004).

The main hypothesis defended in this chapter and in a companion paper (Cassar, Grosjean, and Whitt, forthcoming) is that violence creates *long-lasting* divisions in pro-social preferences of individuals diversely affected by the war toward different groups—which we call the *conflict gap*. From a theoretical perspective, an important foundation for our hypothesis comes from the culture/gene evolutionary approach to understanding human cooperation. A fascinating hypothesis is that intergroup conflict, like evolutionary pressures, fuels antipathy toward outsiders but reinforces cooperation toward insiders, a behavior known as parochial altruism (Bowles 2008; 2009; Choi and Bowles 2007; Boyd and Richerson 2005). Pro-social behavior may thus be enhanced among the in-group, while the reverse result is expected toward the out-group. The conflict gap is easier to identify when clear lines can be drawn between friends and enemies, but less so when the conflict is contained within a common social community, as in some civil wars. These are cases where the conflict gap may be much more complex and challenging to reveal, especially when friends and enemies have been intermixed in local communities and not readily identifiable from one another. We turn our attention here to the problems of social cooperation posed by these circumstances.

We report here the results of behavioral experiments and a survey designed to capture pro-social norms and attitudes toward different groups. Our behavioral experiments use a simplified version of the Trust Game and the Dictator Game under two treatment conditions: Same Village, in which both of the players participating in the game live in the same village, and Distant Village, in which the recipient player might come from anywhere in the country. In the survey, we assess trust toward different groups, defined by varying levels of social proximity (i.e., family vs. someone from another nationality). We also introduce questions aimed at capturing the strength of kinship ties. Since, ultimately, we are interested in the implications of pro-sociality for market development and institution building, we also try and elucidate preferences for market development through survey questions.

Using the case of Tajikistan, we find evidence of long-term conflict gaps after violence. In our companion paper, we find that victimization has opened a significant gap between norms people apply to others in their local communities compared to distant others. Our results show how victimization undermines trust and fairness *within* local communities, decreases the willingness to engage in impersonal exchange, and reinforces kinship-based norms of morality. This chapter completes this result by reporting the relationship between *direct participation in combat* and pro-social behavior. We find that ex-combatants are much less trusting, less trustworthy, and less generous in our behavioral experiments. Lower generosity is exacerbated when the experimental treatment matches individuals with anonymous others from their local community. Survey results confirm that combatants trust all groups but their immediate family less compared to non-combatants. Consistent with such decrease in trust, ex-combatants have a lower willingness to engage in an economic transaction with an anonymous partner. Reflecting on results of previous studies, we find that ex-combatants are more likely to participate in groups and collective action as in Blattman (2009), but we caution that this may only be capturing political opposition, just as participating in combat has. Our research on the gap between pro-social behavior of combatants and non-combatants could help explain findings by Humphreys and Weinstein (2007) of the difficulties of re-integrating former combatants into society in Sierra Leone.

We interpret from our results that violence reinforces social cohesion and cooperation along kinship and network lines, but also undermines them along other dimensions which we believe are critical for institution building and market development, such as generalized trust and sense of fairness toward anonymous others.

Our contribution to the literature, which we review in more detail in section 9.2, is twofold. First, our experimental treatment, which distinguishes between Same and Distant Village partners, allows us to analyze the relationship between violence and pro-social behavior (trust and a sense of fairness) toward different groups: people from the same village, with whom the respondent may have directly interacted during the conflict, and others from further away (a more abstract concept). We complement our experimental results with survey evidence of trust toward different groups (from the family, to neighbors, to those with a different religion, etc.). We aim to test the hypothesis that war opens a gap between pro-social behavior toward different groups, as a function of an individual social distance to an anonymous other and of his/her likely role in the conflict, that is, parochial altruism. These results have implications for market development: markets need traders to go beyond personalized interactions and engage in trust with anonymous counterparts, at the very least at the local level. Second, to the best of our knowledge, this study is the first to provide game-behavioral evidence on combatants' other-regarding and trust preferences.

Our research is motivated by concerns about postconflict stabilization, institution building and economic development. We find important and intricate linkages between violence and pro-social behavior, social capital, and preferences for market development. If violence undermines foundations for social cooperation at the local level, as we see in some areas of Tajikistan, then building functional democratic and market institutions in those areas will present greater challenges than in societies where norms are more conducive to growth and development. The long-lasting differences we observe between ex-combatants and non-combatants also point to the challenges of postconflict reintegration, which may in turn have some implications for long-term stability. Even though ex-combatants are consistently less pro-social (less trusting, less generous), they are more likely to participate in collective action and in groups, and in particular, in religious groups. Participation in religious groups, in the Tajik context, may be perceived as a form of political opposition to the regime in place.

To be sure, this chapter only offers a case study of a particular conflict, but many civil conflicts share the "not readily identifiable" aspect of the Tajik civil conflict, which, we believe, drives our main results. Preliminary evidence from the legacy of World War II in France, Poland, Ukraine, and Belarus, where indistinguishable if not ethnically homogeneous groups fought one other at the local level on the basis of—unidentifiable political allegiances, point to similarly destructive legacies of violence on social capital (Grosjean 2013).

Studying the effect of conflict participation with cross-sectional data is mired with econometric identification problems, including self-selection bias, sample selection bias, and attrition bias inherent to combat death, as well as small sample issues to name a few. In section 9.4, we describe in detail how we deal with such identification challenges, but we claim by no means to be able to fully overcome them. The results we report in this chapter should be taken as reflective of mere correlations between participation in civil war and pro-social preferences and behavior. Still, these correlations are indicators of the gap in pro-social preferences and behavior between ex-combatants and non-combatants and are, as such, useful for policies that aim at combatant reintegration and postconflict stability.

Section 9.2 discusses relevant literature. Section 9.3 provides some background on the Tajik civil war. The empirical strategy and its limitation are discussed in section 9.4, and the research design, sampling, and subject recruitments in section 9.5. Section 9.6 presents the results. Section 9.7 concludes.

9.2　Relevant Literature

Our research focuses on pro-social preferences such as trust and fairness, because they have been found critical to solving cooperation and coordination problems and therefore crucial for economic and social development. Individual preferences toward others (e.g., trust, reciprocity, altruism, egalitarianism, parochialism, fairness) are key component of many economic decisions, are often associated with social capital, and are considered necessary for growth and development. Societal trust and preferences for fairness have been positively associated with growth and market development (e.g., Knack and Keefer 1997, 2001; Knack and Zack 2001; Henrich et al. 2010). The successful development of market economies requires agents to depart from closed group and personal interactions toward exchanges with anonymous others (Fafchamps 2006; Algan and Cahuc 2010). In this regard, generalized trust appears as a keystone for successful market development, and it is often included in the various definitions of "social capital" as one of its main elements. Generosity, egalitarianism, and a sense of fairness, instead of spitefulness, may also help sustain trade, cooperation, and development especially in countries when institutional contract enforcement is weak, by letting individual engage in profitable trades that are beneficial to the individual and others and by preventing the violation of contracts. Given the necessarily incomplete nature of contracts, a sense of fairness and trust may support trade even in countries with well-functioning institutions. Inside societies in which generosity and fairness are anticipated, more individuals may be willing to participate in impersonal trade, while the opposite definitely may work as a trade deterrent (Fehr, Hoff, and Kshetramade 2008).

If trust, a sense of fairness, and other pro-social preferences are so important for the development of markets and growth, the question we address here and in the companion paper (Cassar, Grosjean, and Whitt, forthcoming) is whether they can be affected in a predictable manner by the violence brought about by wars and civil conflicts. Very recent literature, like our work, is addressing this macro issue through micro studies of the differences between individuals adversely affected by war. This approach is based on the implicit assumption that a macro effect is a product of war's impact on social preferences at the individual level, and in principle, these should be observable. It is an attempt to assess a war's consequences when a macro study or a counterfactual is not readily identifiable. It is a conservative approach in the sense that a lack of a significant difference in behavior between individuals doesn't necessarily mean that the war brought about no effects. Mechanisms that, on the contrary, work at the macro level or spill over from directly affected individuals to the unaffected might have implications for everyone. Especially in-long-lasting civil wars it is hard to imagine anyone not being affected. In all of these cases, we would not

find differences at the individual level, yet at the macro level a significant effect would still be possible. On the contrary, significant differences at the individual level could reveal a mechanism through which
a war may exert its effects. Several studies specifically focus on the
behavioral legacies of conflicts and find evidence of increased pro-
social actions among those more affected by conflict, leading to possibly positive interpretations of some of the effects of wars for social
capital building. In particular, Bauer et al. (2011) provide evidence of
higher in-group egalitarianism and parochialism among victimized
children in the Republic of Georgia in the immediate aftermath of the
war with Russia and among those that were children and teens during
the civil war in Sierra Leone. Bellows and Miguel (2009) also find a
significant increase in collective action in Sierra Leone among the
affected. Blattman (2009) reports higher voting and political action in
Uganda. Voors et al. (2011) conducted an experiment in Burundi to
examine the impact of exposure to conflict on social, risk, and time
preferences and find that individuals that have been exposed to greater
levels of violence during the war display more altruistic behavior
toward their neighbors, are more risk seeking, and have higher discount rates. Becchetti et al. (2011) report higher trustworthiness in
Kenya after the postelection civil unrest. Gilligan et al. (2011) provide
additional evidence of a positive legacy of conflict on norms of cooperation at the community level by finding higher levels of trust and
contribution to public goods in villages that were affected by the Maoist
insurgency in Nepal.

A less positive result on the interplay of trust with violence has been
found by Nunn and Wantchekon (2011) who show that a history of
violence, even going as far back as the slave trade in Africa, can impact
contemporaneous trust negatively and strongly. Their hypothesis is
that the negative legacy of slave trade on general trust is mainly due
to the destruction of social ties through inter-ethnic slave raiding. In
the same vein, in the companion paper Cassar, Grosjean, and Whitt
(forthcoming), we find that more than a decade after the Tajik civil war,
which was characterized by insurgency and community infighting,
exposure to conflict has opened a significant gap between norms people
apply to others in their local communities compared to distant others.
We do find evidence of increasing pro-social behavior, but only when
subjects are matched with very distant others—an abstract concept.
More important, our results show how conflict exposure undermines
trust and fairness *within* local communities, decreases the willingness

to engage in impersonal exchange, and reinforces kinship-based norms of morality, all pointing to negative implications for market development and growth.

Most of the literature is concerned with the effects of victimization—receiving acts of violence—on preferences. Studies of the effect of *participation* in violence, as is the object of this chapter, are much scarcer. Impediments to the investigation of the effects of participation in violence are sample size and the issue of causal identification. Most of the literature on the effects of conflict on preferences reviewed above relies on survey data. Ex-combatants may not only be few and hard to find, but may also be reluctant to truthfully reveal their participation in violence. Furthermore combatants may be different from non-combatants in observable and unobservable ways, so any comparison of combatants to non-combatants will conflate the impacts of violence with preexisting differences that led some people to become perpetrators. On the issue of selection into combat, although most theoretical models of conflict and crime suggest that the individuals most likely to engage in fighting (or crime) are the ones with the smallest opportunities in the productive sector (Becker 1968; Grossman and Kim 1995), empirical studies find otherwise. Friedman (2011) uses data from postwar tribunals (*Gacaca*) and documents the characteristics of violence perpetrators in the Rwandan genocide. She finds that higher levels of education are associated with higher participation in violence among Hutu, especially in areas with high local unemployment. This echoes findings by Krueger and Maleckova (2003) and Berrebi (2007), who find that terrorist bombers come disproportionately from wealthy families, and have above average income and education levels. An interpretation by Azam (2005) is that the behavior of participants in violent terrorist acts, and in particular, of suicide bombers, is explained by their altruism toward future generations. A more general interpretation is that participation in violent and terrorist acts is an act of political participation.

Concerning the impact of combat on later life outcomes, a small empirical literature focuses on the economic reintegration of combatants. Angrist (1990) overcomes both issues of small sample size and unobservable bias by exploiting random drafts for the Vietnam War. He finds evidence of large and persistent earning gaps between male veterans and non-veterans. Annan et al. (2011) document economic gaps for male ex-combatants in Uganda, but not for female. The interpretation of the latter result is that the only channel through which combat affects earning gap is not through psychological shocks—or preferences—but by time spent away from civilian education and labor markets. Indeed the authors find no evidence of a legacy of combat on psychological distress, such as depression or traumatic stress. They also do not find any evidence that ex-combatants face difficulty in gaining social acceptance upon their return to their local communities, or that they display higher levels of hostility. The main strength of this study comes from causal identification. The sample of ex-combatants consists of returnee child soldiers who were forcibly recruited by the Lord's Resistance Army, which, the authors convincingly argue, conducted abduction in a random and indiscriminate fashion. The main weakness is that the analysis relies on survey data and self-reported symptoms of psychological distress and self-reported hostility level. Self-reported data are subject to a self- and social-desirability bias that could bias their results toward zero. Blattman (2009) uses the same identification strategy and a similar sample of former child soldiers in Uganda and finds evidence of increased voting and participation in groups, which he attributes to higher pro-sociality. The link to pro-sociality is only conjectural however, since preferences are not directly elicited through behavioral experiments. By focusing exclusively on ex-combatants, Humphreys and Weinstein (2007) analyze the impact of the disarmament, demobilization, and reintegration (DDR) program in Sierra Leone. Their results from a sample of over 1,000 ex-combatants indicate that contrary to what is usually expected, women or young people do not exhibit more difficulties reintegrating to civilian life than men or adults; higher ranking officers are less trusting of democratic processes, and the abusiveness of the unit in which a combatant fought is a strong predictor of regaining acceptance in a combatant' community. Overall, the authors find very little evidence of any positive impact of the DDR program at the individual level. In contrast to their work, we compare combatants to non-combatants to assess ex-combatant postconflict social cooperation and support for market institutions. Importantly, in addition to survey measures, our study provides one of the first datasets of behavioral measures of social cooperation obtained through participation in incentivized games.

9.3 Background on the Tajik Civil War and Postconflict

The Tajik conflict erupted after the fall of the Soviet Union in 1992 and ended with a negotiated settlement in 1997. It is estimated that between

50,000 and 100,000 people died and over 1 million people were displaced (out of a population of 5 million in 1992). A variety of interpretations of the conflict can be found in the literature based on regionalism, ideology, elite instrumentalism, and conflict over resources (see Jawad and Tadjbaksh 1995; Hiro 1995; Akiner 2001; Chatterjee 2002; Heathershaw 2009 for detailed accounts of the Tajik civil war and aftermath). From a regional perspective, the war is often described as a struggle between a pro-government alliance of northern and southern factions against eastern opposition groups, out of which the southern faction emerged as dominant. Ideologically, the conflict is often characterized as former communists against a highly fractionalized group of challengers comprised of Islamic revivalists, ethnic nationalists, and pro-democratic reformers. Most of the conflict took place in central and southern low-lying areas where these population groups were intermixed. What makes the Tajik conflict particularly intriguing for our main hypothesis is the complex networks of rivalries that emerged within local communities during the fighting. With the exception of Russians and Uzbeks, the Tajik civil war was fought along intra-Tajik divisions, and it was often difficult to make simple shorthand predictions about who was fighting whom. The various warring factions were not easily identifiable, and fighting often took place across networks of rival groups for control of the same local communities (Tuncer-Kilavuz 2009, 2011). We believe this should have important implications for the long-term development of trust and other pro-social preferences in local communities, especially for those who actively participated in the violence.

Since the war, Tajikistan is still in a process of economic recovery. According to the World Bank, Tajikistan's GDP fell 60 percent during the war, which also corresponded to the period of transition after the dislocation of the Soviet Union, and has yet to recover to pre-war levels. Based on the Human Development Index (HDI), the UNDP has estimated that Tajikistan will not recover to its 1990 HDI levels until 2015—over twenty years since the start of the conflict. Today, over half of Tajiks live in poverty according to the UNDP, which has estimated real unemployment as high as 35 to 40 percent. This led anywhere from 400,000 to 1.5 million Tajiks to emigrate abroad (mainly to Russia) for work and remittances account for nearly half of Tajikistan's GDP.

Politically, a host of monitoring organizations has cited Tajikistan's vulnerabilities on democracy, human rights, and prospects for instability. According to Polity IV data as well as the "Failed State" and "State

Fragility" indexes, Tajikistan is considered "especially vulnerable to the onset of new political instability events, such as outbreaks of armed conflict, unexpected changes in leadership, or adverse regime changes" (Marshall and Cole 2009, p. 9). Freedom House and Transparency International rank Tajikistan low on freedom and high on corruption. Finally, Tajikistan has never experienced a transition of power since the conflict ended. Although the government of Emomalii Rahmon has managed to keep peace, many have raised concerns about Tajikistan's long-term stability and have suggested that a destabilizing political or economic shock to President Rahmon's regime could initiating another intra-Tajik power struggle similar to the one that provoked the 1992 civil war (Akiner 2001; Jonson 2006; Heathershaw 2009).

9.4 Empirical Strategy

We investigate how having directly participated in the conflict as a combatant affects individual behavior and social, economic and political preferences. The general form of the estimation equation is as follows:

$$Y_{ij} = \beta_0 + \beta_1 C_{ij} + \beta_2 X_{ij} + \beta_3 R_j + \varepsilon_{ij}, \tag{9.1}$$

where our outcome variable Y_{ij} includes different measures of elicited social preferences, market orientation, and economic and political preferences of respondent i in region or village j; C_{ij} is a measure of whether the respondent participated directly in combats during or since the civil war, X_{ij} is a set of pre-war individual and household controls, and R_j is a set of region or village fixed effects. For participation in combat we use a dummy variable (*Fight*) taking value 1 if the respondent declares direct participation in combat during the civil war or after the peace agreement was signed.

In all regressions, using experimental data, we additionally include controls for the different experimental treatments. Since we are also interested in the different behaviors of combatants across the different experimental treatments, we include an interaction term between our combat proxies and the experimental treatment in the following way:

$$Y_{ij} = \beta_0 + \beta_1 C_{ij} * SV_{ij} + \beta_2 X_{ij} + \beta_3 R_j + \varepsilon_{ij}, \tag{9.2}$$

where SV_{ij} is a dummy variable taking value 1 in the "Same Village" experimental treatment. Standard errors are clustered at the village level in all specifications. Specifications control alternatively for region and village dummies.

The main weakness of our study has to do with causal identification. Combatants may be different from non-combatants in observable and unobservable ways and so any comparison of combatants and non-combatants will conflate the impacts of violence with preexisting differences that led some people to become perpetrators. This is especially problematic if the characteristics associated with participation in combat are also those associated with the outcomes that we want to observe. For example, the literature reviewed in section 9.2 suggests that participation in violence is akin to political participation and should therefore correlate with higher levels of altruism. In other words, one would expect ex-combatants to be more pro-social, and this would bias our results upward. Also combat requires high trust among members of the fighting unit, so combat experience, again, may bias our results in the Trust Game upward. On way to deal with the potential selection and omitted variable bias is to control for individual characteristics, but we are limited by our small sample size in the number of variables we can control for. Still, we include in the regression framework some pre-war individual characteristics that are unlikely to have changed as the outcome of participation in combat but may be related with our outcome variables, such as age or gender. We also check that the results of all specifications are robust to the inclusion of village fixed effects. Because of the regional nature of the conflict, all specifications include regional fixed effects, but the use of village fixed effects goes a step further and enables us to remove factors that are common to a given village and that might have led to higher participation in violence. In addition to omitted variable and self-selection bias, attrition and displacement are problematic for the identification of causal effects of participation in violent acts. Attrition bias due to combat death is inherent to cross-sectional studies of this kind and we have no means to address this issue. Endogenous displacement of combatants also poses a challenge for the purpose of econometric identification. Combatants may self-select to specific regions or villages precisely because of local—not necessarily observable—characteristics that may conflate the estimated impact of violence. In order to deal with this issue, we re-run our analysis on the subsample of combatants who have always lived in the same village. Nevertheless, we are aware that none of these strategies fully eliminates concerns about self-selection, omitted variables and sample selection bias so that we should only regard coefficients as suggestive correlations. Still, these correlations are indicators of the gap in pro-social preferences and behavior between ex-combatants and non-combatants and are, as such, useful for policies that aim at combatant reintegration and postconflict stability.

9.5   Research Design, Sampling, and Recruitment

Our inferences are based on survey and experimental evidence from a random sample of the Tajik population conducted between June and July 2010. Within the sample, we compare attitudes and behavior of subgroups with varying experiences in direct fighting during the 1992 to 1997 civil war. Specifically, we ask whether those who participated in fighting are markedly different in attitudes and behavior from those who did not.

The survey covers broad themes of employment and market activity, political preferences and views on democracy, social engagement and trust, and finally, questions related to violence during the civil war. Participation in combat is elicited by the survey question: "Did you personally fight in the civil conflict in Tajikistan from 1992 to 1997?" In addition we want to capture respondents who might have participated in combat after 1997, since clashes continued after the official end to the conflict. We also ask: "Did you personally take part in armed clashes or fight in Tajikistan since the peace agreement in 1997?" In accord with our indicator of participation in combat, *Fight* takes value one if respondents answer yes to either question. The main limitation to this question is that we are unable to identify whether combatants were on the side of the government or of opposition forces. This question was too sensitive to ask. Nevertheless, we are pretty confident that all respondents were on the side of the insurgency due in part to the locations where they were sampled. Indeed the survey also inquires about economic occupations, and no respondent who reports having participated in combat reports being a member of military forces. Instead, our sample of combatants consist of people either unemployed or employed in the education, health, or construction sector. Moreover the majority of respondents in our sample of combatants is from the Gharm area of the Rasht Valley (66.67 percent), which was the hotbed of insurgency. We therefore strongly believe that our *Fight* variable measures participation in insurgency.

In selecting our sample, we use a three-stage random selection method. First, villages within four regions (Khatlon, Dushanbe, Rasht, and Pamir) were selected with probability proportional to size, based on the latest census. Most of the violence during and since the conflict took place in Khatlon, Dushanbe, and Rasht valley regions. The Pamir and northern Sughd regions remained peaceful during the civil war, and we selected the Pamir to include for comparison. Consistent with accounts of the war, the people in our sample who were involved in fighting are located in the Khatlon, Dushanbe, and, especially, the Rasht valley. Second, households were randomly selected within each location, using the random route method. Urban locations were further subdivided into administrative districts if necessary, and interviewers were assigned random routes by the research team. No more than five interviews were obtained from a single random route, which consisted of contacting every fifth numbered house or apartment in an apartment block from the initial starting point. We used schools as starting points in most cases because housing and apartment blocks were typically clustered nearby. In the event of multiple schools in a district, we randomly selected a school as a starting point. Interviewers began their random routes at different distances and in different directions from the school. We trained twelve Tajik, Uzbek, and Pamiri interviewers, both male and female. Once interviewers made contact with a household, they completed a roster of every member of the household where one adult member of the household was randomly selected to participate in the study, as the third stage of the selection procedure. Interviews were typically conducted in a private location, either in the home if possible or outside in a quiet location. Once the survey was completed, the interviewer would accompany the subject to the school or other designated location to take part in the experimental component of the study.

The experiments took place usually in a large schoolroom with each person seated at a separate desk or when space was limited, subjects completed the study in small groups. The experiments were conducted by a local administrator who read from a standard set of instructions. All subjects completed three experiments commonly referred to as Dictator, Ultimatum, and Trust "games."[1] The Dictator Game is a one-shot experiment where subjects are given a fixed sum of money (in this case 40 Somoni, or approximately $9) and must decide how much to keep for themselves and how much to send to an anonymous recipient. In our experiment, the anonymous recipient was either someone locally—but not in the room—(Same Village treatment) or someone from another location in Tajikistan (Distant Village treatment). We randomized the treatments to sessions (see the experimental instructions for more details). Following the Dictator Game, subjects completed an Ultimatum Game and finally a Trust Game with the same local/non-local treatments. In the Ultimatum Game, subjects must again decide how to divide 40 Somoni between themselves and an anonymous recipient, but this time, the recipient may reject an allocation that they do not like. If the recipient rejects the allocation, neither the subject nor the recipient receives any money.[2] Finally, in the Trust Game, all subjects start with 20 Somoni, and playing as first players, they have to decide how much to keep for themselves and how much (if any) to send to an anonymous recipient. Senders don't know anything about these possible receivers except that they are coming either from the Same Village or from a Distant Village (our treatment variable). Whatever they give to the recipient is tripled in value, and the recipient decides how much (if any) to send back to the subject. All subjects played both parts, first as senders and then as receivers and, since the actual matching between senders and receivers depended on the treatment (Same Village or Distant Village), receiver preferences were elicited through the strategy method. After completing all three experiments, one experiment is chosen randomly for payment in which all the subjects in the group are paid based on whether their individual decision matched randomly with that of an anonymous recipient.

Before making their incentivized decisions, subjects were given the opportunity to ask questions and administrators used many examples (and a quiz) to ensure that the subjects understood the instructions clearly. During the actual experiment, no talking was allowed. Each person made a decision privately so that neither the administrator nor anyone else in the group could see what that person had decided to do. At the end of the experiment, forms were collected and subjects were paid according to the decision randomly chosen for payment plus a small show-up fee for their time traveling to and from the experimental location.

In total, 426 subjects took part in the survey and experiments in 17 locations in groups of 10 to 20 subjects per location. Subjects' earnings ranged between 0 and 60 Somoni ($0 to $13.50), with an average earning of 24 Somoni (SD 10.9) or $5.40 (SD $2.46) for their participation in the experiments.[3]

9.6 Results

9.6.1 Determinants of Participation in Violence

As can be seen in table 9.1, only a small minority of respondents to our survey had participated in combat (or admits to it). Less than 3 percent of our sample declares having fought in or since the civil conflict. In order to study the determinants of participation in combat, the same table reports the results of regressions where declaring being a combatant is regressed on a number of observable individual characteristics. Gender, education, and ethnicity are significant individual predictors of participation in combat. The data mirror the results of earlier literature (Friedman 2011; Krueger and Maleckova 2003; Berrebi 2007), as the combatants tend to be more educated, although the only significant result is obtained for those who completed compulsory education versus those who have not. Members of the Uzbek minority are more likely to have participated. Region of residence is, as expected, a significant predictor, with inhabitants from Gharm, the region most affected by the conflict and by postconflict troubles, more likely to have participated in combat. Income is negatively correlated with participation in combat, although the results are not statistically significant. An important caveat here is that income is measured at the time of the survey and may therefore be an outcome of the conflict. Nevertheless, the lack of statistical significance denotes the absence of significant earning gaps between combatants and non-combatants in our sample.

9.6.2 Fighting and Pro-social Preferences: Experimental Results

Dictator Game   Figure 9.1 and the regressions results displayed in table 9.2 show that combatants are less generous than non-combatants. Combatants give much less in the Dictator Game, and particularly so in the "Same Village" experimental treatment in which they know that the amount they are about to give will go to a person (anonymous) coming from the same village as theirs. These results are quantitatively significant. The mean offer in the Dictator Game is 10.26 somoni[4] out of a maximum of 40 somoni, an estimate lower than the ones often found in US laboratory studies. Having personally fought is associated with a roughly 40 percent lower Dictator Game donation (columns 1 and 2, average coefficient), although the effect is statistically significant at the 10 percent level only when village dummies are included. The magnitude of the drop in generosity is larger when respondents are

Table 9.1
Determinants of fighting

OLS regression

Dependent variable	Fight	
	(1)	(2)
Age	0.001	0.001
	[0.175]	[0.324]
Gender	0.036**	0.038*
	[0.049]	[0.068]
Pamiri		0.016
		[0.396]
Uzbek	0.031**	0.047**
	[0.016]	[0.019]
Dushanbe	−0.009	0.016
	[0.559]	[0.361]
Gharm	0.034**	0.097
	[0.018]	[0.188]
Khatlon	0.006	0.012
	[0.639]	[0.607]
Any member of Communist Party	−0.006	−0.003
	[0.518]	[0.687]
Displaced by communist regime.	−0.001	0.004
	[0.922]	[0.671]
Urban	0.002	−0.007
	[0.761]	[0.698]
Compulsory education	0.044*	0.048*
	[0.073]	[0.052]
Secondary education	0.013	0.012
	[0.346]	[0.441]
Higher education	0.011	0.019
	[0.522]	[0.318]
Middle income	−0.029	−0.033
	[0.199]	[0.228]
Rich	−0.026	−0.023
	[0.284]	[0.387]
FE	Region	Village
Observations	377	377
R-squared	0.07	0.11
Mean dependent variable	0.026	
Standard deviation dependent variable	0.159	

Note: Robust standard errors are clustered at the village level. All regressions include a constant; *P*-values are in brackets. The excluded ethnicity is Tajik; the excluded 1992 region is Pamir; the excluded education is compulsory education not completed; the excluded income is poor (lower third of the income distribution).

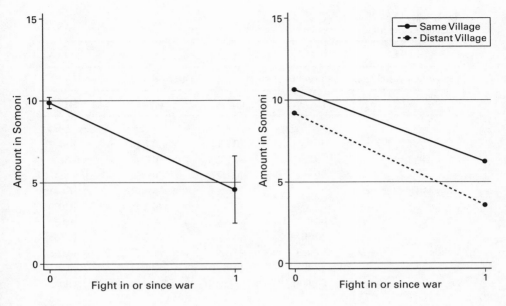

Figure 9.1
Average amount sent in the Dictator Game (range between 0 and 40 Somoni) by experimental treatment

matched with someone from the same village. Ex-combatants give between 76 percent (column 3: $[(-1.125 - 6.627)/10.26] \times 100$) and 87 percent (column 4: $[-2.981-5.841)/10.26]) \times 100$) less than non-combatants to someone from the same village. The coefficient on the interaction between *Same Village* and *Fight*, which measures the additional effect, for a combatant, of being matched to someone from the same village, is statistically significant at the 5 percent (with region dummies) to 10 percent (with village dummies) level. By contrast, the main effect of *Fight* is no longer statistically significant. The lower generosity of combatants compared to non-combatants observed in columns 1 and 2 thus mainly comes from the drop in generosity of combatants toward the members of their own village. Other results indicate that non-combatants also tend to be less generous toward members of their village. The coefficient on the *Same Village* treatment is essentially zero when only regional dummies are included and becomes negative, although just short of standard levels of statistical significance, when village dummies are included. In our companion paper (Cassar, Grosjean, and Whitt forthcoming), we find that respondents who were victimized during the conflict are less generous toward their fellow

Table 9.2
Dictator Game regression results

OLS regression

Dependent variable: Amount sent by first-mover in the Dictator Game

	(1)	(2)	(3)	(4)
Fight	−3.354	−4.940*	−1.125	−2.981
	[0.236]	[0.100]	[0.736]	[0.412]
Same village	−0.066	−2.432	0.068	−2.269
	[0.961]	[0.117]	[0.960]	[0.146]
Same village*fight			−6.627**	−5.841*
			[0.028]	[0.070]
Age	−0.033	−0.042	−0.030	−0.039
	[0.309]	[0.210]	[0.355]	[0.238]
Gender	−1.083	−0.049	−1.133	−0.098
	[0.425]	[0.970]	[0.414]	[0.941]
FE	Region	Village	Region	Village
Observations	418	418	418	418
R-squared	0.103	0.173	0.105	0.174

Note: *P*-values are in brackets (robust standard errors clustered by sampling village). All regressions include a constant.

village members than toward distant others. The fact that such victims are included here as part of the control group could explain the negative sign of the *Same Village* treatment coefficient.

Trust and Trustworthiness Figures 9.2 and 9.3 and the regression results reported in tables 9.3 and 9.4 show that combatants are both less trusting and less trustworthy than non-combatants. Table 9.3 reports regression results where the dependent variable is the amount sent by the sender in the Trust Game, a proxy for trust. Table 9.4 reports regression results where the dependent variable is the amount returned (average amount estimated using the strategy method—the mean of the respondent final returns to all the possible amounts that the sender could have sent) by the receiver in the Trust Game, a proxy for trustworthiness. Specifications alternatively include region and village fixed effects. In the whole sample, the average amount sent in the Trust Game is 6.97[5] (out of 20 somoni) and the average amount returned is 13.5.[6]

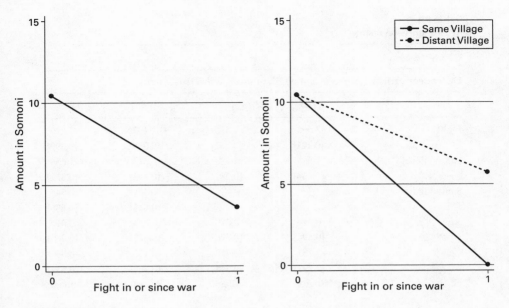

Figure 9.2
Average amount sent in the Trust Game (range between 0 and 20 Somoni) by experimental treatment

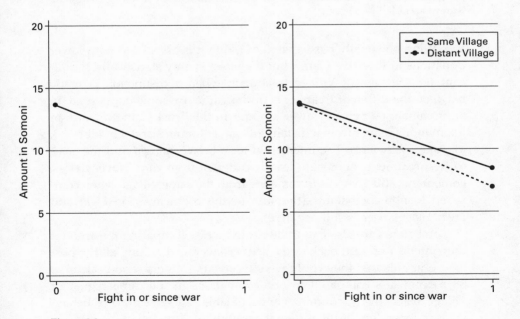

Figure 9.3
Average amount returned in the Trust Game (strategy method) by experimental treatment

Table 9.3
Trust regression results

OLS regression

Dependent variable: Amount sent by first-mover in the Trust Game

	(1)	(2)	(3)	(4)
Fight	−3.693	−3.375	−4.497*	−4.229*
	[0.224]	[0.265]	[0.088]	[0.099]
Same village	1.565	1.727	1.517	1.656
	[0.164]	[0.282]	[0.193]	[0.322]
Same village*fight			2.391	2.545
			[0.643]	[0.656]
Age	0.014	0.019	0.013	0.017
	[0.594]	[0.526]	[0.628]	[0.560]
Gender	−0.151	−0.372	−0.133	−0.350
	[0.771]	[0.544]	[0.790]	[0.559]
FE	Region	Village	Region	Village
Observations	418	418	418	418
R-squared	0.042	0.093	0.043	0.094

Note: *P*-values are in brackets (robust standard error clustered by sampling village). All regressions include a constant.

Having personally participated in fighting is associated with lower donations in the Trust Game, but the effect is only statistically significant for the Distant Village treatment, when a distinction is made between the different treatments of the game. Ex-combatants send an approximate 60 percent lower amount in the Trust Game toward an anonymous player from a distant village (columns 3 and 4 of table 9.3, average coefficient). The interaction term between *Fight* and the *Same Village* treatment is not significantly different from zero. Nevertheless, combatants still give less to someone from the same village when compared to non-combatants (the sum of the coefficients on *Fight* and *Fight*Same Village* is still negative).

Combatants are also less trustworthy: when comparing the amount they intend to return back to the sender (averaged among all the possible amounts that they could have received), fighters send back 26 to 38 percent less compared to non-combatants in the same region or village, respectively (columns 1 and 2 of table 9.4). Here players' behavior is independent of the different experimental treatments.

Table 9.4
Trustworthiness regression results

OLS regression

Dependent variable: Mean returned by second-mover in the Trust Game

	(1)	(2)	(3)	(4)
Fight	−3.574*	−5.188**	−4.092	−5.639
	[0.094]	[0.028]	[0.230]	[0.129]
Same village	0.381	−0.324	0.350	−0.361
	[0.724]	[0.812]	[0.742]	[0.786]
Same village*fight			1.539	1.346
			[0.741]	[0.777]
Age	−0.031	−0.042	−0.032	−0.043
	[0.419]	[0.284]	[0.417]	[0.287]
Gender	0.957	1.271	0.969	1.282
	[0.284]	[0.163]	[0.273]	[0.159]
FE	Region	Village	Region	Village
Observations	418	418	418	418
R-squared	0.075	0.152	0.075	0.152

Note: *P*-values in brackets (robust standard errors clustered by sampling village). All regressions include a constant.

Summary and Robustness   Taken together, these results suggest some negative legacy of combat on pro-social behavior, such as trust, trustworthiness, and a sense of fairness. An important caveat of our results has to do with a bias due to self-selection into fighting and with the presence of omitted variables that may be correlated both with the probability to engage in violent combat and with the behavior in the Dictator and Trust games. However, previous literature reviewed in section 9.2 suggests that such a selection bias should, if anything and at least for the Dictator Game, affect our results upward: combatants are expected to be *more* altruistic, whereas our results point to *lower* levels of altruism among combatants. Another bias has to do with selective migration. However, when, in an attempt to overcome this issue, we only consider the sample of people who have never moved (see appendix tables 9A.1 to 9A.3), all results but those related to trustworthiness are not only robust but actually become stronger. The subsample of combatants who have never moved are significantly less trusting and less generous, and particularly so when matched to someone from their own village. Indeed, in this subsample, the interaction term between *Same Village* and *Fight* is negative in all specifications for all our behavioral measures: generosity (Dictator Game offers), trust (Trust Game offers), and trustworthiness (Trust Game amount returned). However, the coefficient on this interaction is only statistically significantly different from zero when it comes to the Dictator Game offers.

Survey Results   We first check the robustness and relevance of our experimental evidence by looking at the combatants' responses to the traditional survey questions on trust toward different groups of people defined by their level of social distance to the respondent. The results, which we describe below in more detail, corroborate our experimental findings that combatants are much less trusting toward any group to whom they are not directly related to or that they do not know personally. These results are suggestive of two things, which we investigate next. First, in light of the literature on the role of trust in sustaining impersonal exchange (see section 9.2), lower levels of impersonal trust may have negative implication for market development. To test such implications, we examine directly the respondents' stated preferences on participation in impersonal exchange. Second, the fact that trust toward any group but family members is lower among combatants suggests that participation in combat may be associated with the reinforcement of kinship ties and clannishness. Combatants might have learned that they can trust no other but their clan and immediate family. To test this hypothesis, we try and investigate the strength of kinship-based norms. Our results confirm that combat is associated with the reinforcement of such norms, suggesting further negative consequences of insurgency and civil war on the development of impersonal exchange (Greif and Tabellini 2010). Third, we investigate participation in combat as a determinant of collective action and group participation.

Trust toward Different Groups   Our survey included questions on trust toward different groups, which are defined by their level of social distance to the respondent. This question is formulated as follows: "I'd like to ask you how much you trust people from various groups. Could you tell me for each whether you trust people from this group completely, somewhat, not very much or not at all (on a scale of 1 to 5)?" This question is asked for each of the following groups: your family, people in your neighborhood, people you meet for the first time, people of another religion, and people of another nationality. The survey also included a traditional question on trust, the so-called general trust question, which asks: "Generally speaking, would you say that most people can be trusted, or that you can't be too careful in dealing with people? Please answer on a scale of 1 to 5, where 1 means that you have complete distrust and 5 means that you have complete trust."

Table 9.5 reports regression results where the response to each trust question is regressed on combat experience, controlling for age, gender, and, alternatively, region and village fixed effects. Results are very clear: combat is associated with lower trust toward any other group but the immediate circle of kin and friends. Levels of trust toward the family or people the respondent knows personally are not significantly associated with combat experience. By contrast, combatants trust neighbors, people from another religion, and people from another nationality significantly less.

However, turning to the general trust question—formulated in the same way as in the GSS questionnaire: "Generally speaking, would you say that most people can be trusted, or that you can't be too careful in dealing with people (on a scale of 1 to 5)?—the coefficient on fighting is positive, although it is not significant when regional fixed effects are included. We find this result—which contradicts the ones with both our other survey questions on trust and the experimental measures—particularly interesting in light of the existing debate on whether such GSS questions correlate with experimental measures (e.g., Glaeser et al. 2000). Our results indicate that this question might not be a valid instrument for eliciting a measure of trust that correlates with either stated trust in specific groups or behavioral measures when the other party is a "concrete" other person living in the same community. We expect this to be due to the fact that the GSS formulation is so generic that a respondent interprets it in an abstract context and therefore replies in terms of "how should one behave" and not in a more specific "how one actually behaves" in concrete contexts.

Market Integration and Participation   Lower levels of impersonal trust may have negative implication for market development (see literature in section 9.2). We investigate directly the respondents' stated preferences on participation in impersonal exchange with the following survey question: "When you go to the market, how important is it to buy from a seller that you know personally?"—with a four-point scale

Table 9.5
Trust in different groups, market, and group participation

OLS regression

Dependent variable (1 = positive reply):	Fight	Age	Gender	FE	Observed	R-squared
Trust family members	−0.061	0.000	−0.048	Region	417	0.024
	[0.554]	[0.694]	[0.459]			
	−0.062	0.001	−0.031	Village	417	0.067
	[0.548]	[0.591]	[0.609]			
Trust personal acquaintances	−0.233	0.012*	−0.054	Region	413	0.035
	[0.442]	[0.086]	[0.720]			
	−0.170	0.012*	−0.018	Village	413	0.095
	[0.558]	[0.087]	[0.904]			
Trust neighbors	−0.721**	0.004	−0.107	Region	416	0.083
	[0.031]	[0.304]	[0.402]			
	−0.660**	0.006	−0.083	Village	416	0.156
	[0.040]	[0.242]	[0.416]			
Trust people met for first time	−1.411***	0.003	−0.122	Region	414	0.168
	[0.001]	[0.613]	[0.447]			
	−1.559***	0.002	−0.062	Village	414	0.208
	[0.000]	[0.744]	[0.710]			
Trust people of another religion	−1.454***	0.002	−0.024	Region	416	0.184
	[0.000]	[0.697]	[0.873]			
	−1.656***	0.001	−0.048	Village	416	0.245
	[0.000]	[0.863]	[0.782]			
Trust people of another nationality	−1.196***	0.002	−0.033	Region	416	0.146
	[0.004]	[0.684]	[0.828]			
	−1.390***	0.001	−0.081	Village	416	0.220
	[0.001]	[0.851]	[0.607]			

Table 9.5
(continued)

OLS regression

Dependent variable (1 = positive reply):	Fight	Age	Gender	FE	Observed	R-squared
General trust (GSS question)	0.355 [0.223]	−0.004 [0.449]	−0.053 [0.760]	Region	396	0.081
	0.600* [0.073]	−0.002 [0.730]	−0.036 [0.844]	Village	396	0.131
Important to personally know trader	1.186** [0.013]	−0.004 [0.275]	−0.088 [0.495]	Region	418	0.067
	1.125** [0.023]	−0.005* [0.097]	−0.030 [0.805]	Village	418	0.123
Freedom to marry	−0.059 [0.306]	0.001 [0.564]	0.047 [0.244]	Region	345	0.492
	−0.094** [0.046]	0.001 [0.670]	0.063 [0.123]	Village	345	0.538
Participation in groups	0.364*** [0.000]	−0.000 [0.913]	0.155 [0.226]	Region	404	0.184
	0.363*** [0.000]	−0.000 [0.979]	0.174 [0.193]	Village	404	0.216
Community meetings	0.296* [0.061]	0.002 [0.256]	0.085 [0.106]	Region	407	0.064
	0.304* [0.072]	0.001 [0.533]	0.095 [0.114]	Village	407	0.120
Religious groups	0.647*** [0.000]	−0.000 [0.955]	0.067 [0.377]	Region	339	0.064
	0.615*** [0.000]	0.000 [0.881]	0.102 [0.178]	Village	339	0.115

Note: *P*-values are in brackets (robust standard errors clustered by sampling village). Regressions include a constant.

answer from "not important at all" to "essential." We interpret a higher response on that scale as signaling a lower willingness to participate in an anonymous economic exchange. The effect of personal involvement in fighting is positive, statistically significantly different from zero at the 5 percent level and robust to the inclusion of village fixed effects, indicating that combatants are less willing to participate in exchange with anonymous traders. This is consistent with the observed decrease in the offers in the Trust Game.

Strength of Kinship Ties　The result that trust toward any group but one's family members is lower among combatants suggests that participation in combat may be associated with the reinforcement of kinship ties and clannishness. Combatants may have learned that they can trust no other but their clan and immediate family. The variable that we use to measure the strength of kinship ties is the respondent's opinion about the freedom to marry. As stressed by Greif (2006), restricted and consanguineous marriages have historically provided one means of creating and maintaining kinship groups. We ask in the survey whether the respondent supports freedom to marry or rather thinks best for parents to choose a spouse for their children. The results displayed in table 9.5 show that active combat is associated with a significant decrease in the support for free marriage, even when we control for whether the respondent herself married freely.

Participation in Groups　Several survey questions aim at capturing participation in groups and association. First, we ask respondents whether they had participated in any community meetings during the week preceding our team's visit. Second, we build an index variable that sums the number of groups and associations the respondents belongs to. We ask about a variety of groups, such as mosque and religious organization, NGOs, neighborhood groups, labor unions, fraternal groups, and youth associations. This index takes values from 0 to 5. Group participation is low on average in our sample, which is consistent with the literature documenting evidence of low levels of civil society development in post–Soviet Republics (Howard 2003). The mean of the group participation index is 0.79 and 40 percent of respondents who do not participate in any group. However, combat experience in the civil war is significantly and positively associated with group participation. Regression results displayed in table 9.5 show that combatants are more likely to have attended community meetings. This mirrors the result by Blattman (2009) who finds a link between fighting in a civil war and local collective action in Uganda. However, taken together with the rest of our results, this may not be a positive sign of inclusive social capital development. Even though group membership and civic participation have been widely used in the literature as measures of social capital and, as such, associated with positive development outcomes (for a recent review, see Guiso, Sapienza, and Zingales 2010), this acceptance of social capital may also have negative connotation if it leads to the exclusion of outsiders (Bourdieu 1985; Portes 1998). We also investigate which particular group and association combatants are more likely to join. It is specifically religious groups, which in Tajikistan are associated with political opposition to the regime in place, that receive a boost in membership among war combatants.

9.7 Conclusion

This chapter considered the relationship between fighting in a civil war and pro-social behavior and, to the best of our knowledge, provides the first experimental measures of pro-sociality among former (and possibly current) combatants in a civil conflict. More than ten years after the official end of the Tajik civil war, we find persistent behavioral and attitudinal differences between combatants and noncombatants. Game-behavioral evidence points to ex-combatants being much less generous, less trusting, and less trustworthy than non-combatants. Survey evidence confirms that combat is associated with lower trust toward any other group but the immediate circle of kin and friends.

These results bode ill both for the economic and political reintegration of combatants. Trust is an important dimension of economic exchange, and we find indeed that combatants are less willing to participate in anonymous market transactions. Consistently with recent literature, we find that combatants are more likely to participate in groups and collective action, but we caution that such behavior signals political opposition rather than civil society revitalizing and political reintegration. The kind of groups that combatants are more likely to participate in are religious groups, which, in Tajikistan, may be perceived as a form of political opposition to the regime that is in place currently, as it was to the regime that was in place during the civil war.

To conclude, we find in this chapter and in a companion paper that looks into the effects of victimization during the Tajik civil conflict important linkages between violence, pro-social behavior, and the formation of social capital. We find lasting negative consequences of increasing exposure to violence (as victims and combatants) on cooperative social norms, especially at the local level, where most of the fighting took place. We consider this a serious gap opened by the conflict. If violence undermines foundations for social cooperation, as we see in some areas of Tajikistan, then building functional democratic and market institutions in those areas may present very serious challenges.

Appendix

Table 9A.1
Dictator Game results—Subsample of non-movers

OLS regression

Dependent variable: Amount sent by first-mover in the Dictator Game

	(1)	(2)	(3)	(4)
Fight	−4.136	−7.025*	−1.948	−4.410
	[0.218]	[0.082]	[0.557]	[0.176]
Same village	0.830	−1.037	0.916	−0.903
	[0.610]	[0.615]	[0.571]	[0.659]
Same village*fight			−6.490*	−7.853**
			[0.060]	[0.022]
Age	−0.053	−0.054	−0.052	−0.052
	[0.369]	[0.433]	[0.389]	[0.456]
Gender	−0.465	0.059	−0.457	0.057
	[0.834]	[0.981]	[0.837]	[0.982]
FE	region	village	region	village
Observations	199	199	199	199
R-squared	0.080	0.150	0.081	0.152

Note: *P*-values in brackets (robust standard errors clustered by sampling village). All regressions include a constant.

Table 9A.2
Trust results—Subsample of non-movers

OLS regression

Dependent variable: Amount sent by first-mover in the Trust Game

	(1)	(2)	(3)	(4)
Fight	−5.346***	−4.758***	−5.105**	−4.216*
	[0.003]	[0.005]	[0.024]	[0.052]
Same village	1.703	1.917	1.712	1.945
	[0.156]	[0.346]	[0.156]	[0.343]
Same village*fight			−0.712	−1.628
			[0.754]	[0.473]
Age	0.020	0.019	0.020	0.020
	[0.641]	[0.686]	[0.640]	[0.679]
Gender	−0.263	−0.587	−0.262	−0.588
	[0.740]	[0.467]	[0.741]	[0.468]
FE	Region	Village	Region	Village
Observations	199	199	199	199
R-squared	0.075	0.128	0.075	0.128

Note: P-values in brackets (robust standard errors clustered by sampling village). All regressions include a constant.

Table 9A.3
Trustworthiness results—Subsample of non-movers

OLS regression

Dependent variable: Mean returned by second-mover in the Trust Game

	(1)	(2)	(3)	(4)
Fight	−0.056	−2.002	1.143	−1.166
	[0.993]	[0.786]	[0.910]	[0.915]
Same village	0.521	−0.281	0.568	−0.238
	[0.641]	[0.847]	[0.605]	[0.862]
Same village*fight			−3.558	−2.514
			[0.732]	[0.818]
Age	−0.041	−0.038	−0.041	−0.038
	[0.392]	[0.475]	[0.413]	[0.495]
Gender	2.169*	2.151	2.173*	2.150
	[0.086]	[0.143]	[0.087]	[0.144]
FE	Region	Village	Region	Village
Observations	199	199	199	199
R-squared	0.068	0.139	0.069	0.139

Note: P-values in brakets (robust standard errors clustered by sampling village). All regressions include a constant.

Notes

1. See the online appendix for a description and explanation of each game. The online appendix can be found at http://p8.storage.canalblog.com/84/30/1099015/88940496.pdf.

2. Since we didn't find any significant result for the Ultimatum Game, we do not discuss them in this chapter for space consideration, but we make them available upon request.

3. For comparison, the average monthly salary at the beginning of 2011 was around USD100 and the minimum wage around USD18.

4. 10.10 in the Same Village treatment, 10.31 in the Distant Village treatment.

5. 10.56 in the Same Village treatment, 9.04 in the Distant Village treatment.

6. 13.62 in the Same Village treatment, 13.39 in the Distant Village treatment.

References

Akiner 2001. *Tajikistan: Disintegration or Reconciliation?* London: Royal Institute of International Affairs.

Algan, Yann, and Pierre Cahuc. 2010. Inherited trust and growth. *American Economic Review* 100 (5): 2060–92.

Angrist, Josh D. 1990. Lifetime earnings and the Vietnam era draft lottery: Evidence from Social Security Administrative records. *American Economic Review* 80 (3): 313–36.

Annan, Jeannie, Christopher Blattman, Dyan Mazurana, and Khristopher Carlson. 2011. Civil war, reintegration, and gender in northern Uganda. *Journal of Conflict Resolution* 55 (6): 877–908.

Azam, Jean-Paul. 2005. Suicide-bombing as inter-generational investment. *Public Choice* 122 (1–2): 177–98.

Becker, Gary. 1968. Crime and punishment: An economic approach. *Journal of Political Economy* 76 (2): 169–217

Bauer, Michal, Alessandra Cassar, Julia Chytilová, and Joseph Henrich. (Forthcoming). War's enduring effects on the development of egalitarian motivations and in-group biases. *Psychological Science*.

Becchetti, Leonardo, Pierluigi Conzo, and Alessandro Romeo. 2011. Violence and social capital: Evidence of a microeconomic vicious circle. Working paper 197. ECINEQ, Palma de Mallorca.

Bellows John and Edward Miguel. 2009. War and collective action in Sierra Leone. *Journal of Public Economics* 93 (11–12): 1144–57.

Berrebi, Claude. 2007. Evidence about the link between education, poverty and terrorism among Palestinians. *Peace Economics, Peace Science and Public Policy* 13 (1): 38 pp.

Blattman, Christopher. 2009. From violence to voting: War and political participation in Uganda. *American Political Science Review* 103: 231.

Bourdieu, Pierre. 1985. The social space and the genesis of groups. *Social Science Information* 24 (2): 195–220.

Bowles, Samuel. 2008. Conflict: Altruism's midwife. *Nature* 456: 326–27.

Bowles, Samuel. 2009. Did warfare among ancestral hunter-gatherers affect the evolution of human social behaviors? *Science* 324: 1293.

Cassar, Alessandra, Pauline Grosjean, and Sam Whitt. 2013. Legacies of violence: Trust and market development. *Journal of Economic Growth* 18 (3): 285–318.

Chatterjee, S. 2002. *Society and Politics in Tajikistan: In the Aftermath of the Civil War.* London: Greenwich Millenium Press.

Choi, Jung-Kyoo, and Samuel Bowles. 2007. The coevolution of parochial altruism and war. *Science* 318: 636–40.

Collier, Paul, Lani Elliot, Håvard Hegre, Anke Hoeffler, Marta Reynal-Querol and Nicholas Sambanis. 2003. Breaking the conflict trap: Civil war and development policy, vol. 1. Policy research report. World Bank, Washington, DC.

Collier, Paul, and Anke Hoeffler. 2004. Greed and grievance in civil war. *Oxford Economic Papers* 56 (4): 563–95.

Fafchamps, Marcel. 2006. Development and social capital. *Journal of Development Studies* 42 (7): 1180–98.

Fehr, Ernst, Karla Hoff, and Mayuresh Kshetramade. 2008. Spite and development. *American Economic Review* 98 (2): 494–99.

Friedman, Willa. 2011. Local economic conditions and participation in the Rwandan genocide. Working paper. APSA 2011 Annual Meeting.

Fukuyama, Francis. 2011. *The Origins of Political Order.* New York: Farrar, Straus, Giroux.

Gilligan, Michael J., Benjmain J. Pasquale, and Cyrus D. Samii. 2011. Civil war and social capital: Behavioral-game evidence from Nepal. Working paper. Available at SSRN: http://ssrn.com/abstract=1911969 or http://dx.doi.org/10.2139/ssrn.1911969.

Glaeser, L., L. Laibson, A. Scheinkman, and L. Soutter. 2000. Measuring trust. *Quarterly Journal of Economics* 115: 811–46.

Greif, Avner. 2006. Family structure, institutions, and growth: The origins and implications of Western corporations. *American Economic Review* 96 (2): 308–12.

Greif, Avner, and Guido Tabellini. 2010. Cultural and institutional bifurcation: China and Europe compared. *American Economic Review* 100 (2): 135–40.

Grosjean, Pauline. 2013. Conflict and social and political preferences: Evidence from World War II and civil conflict in 35 European countries. Working paper. University of New South Wales.

Grossman, Hershchel, and Minseong Kim. 1995. Swords or plowshares? A theory of security of claims to property. *Journal of Political Economy* 103 (6): 1275–88

Guiso, Luigi, Paula Sapienza, and Luigi Zingales. 2010. Civic capital as the missing link. Working paper 15845. NBER, Cambridge, MA.

Heathershaw, J. 2009. *Post-Conflict Tajikistan: The Politics of Peacebuilding and the Emergence of Legitimate Order.* London: Routledge.

Henrich, Joseph, Jean Ensminger, Richard McElreath, Abigail Barr, Clark Barrett, Alexander Bolyanatz, Juan Camilo Cardenas, et al. 2010. Markets, religion, community size, and the evolution of fairness and punishment. *Science* 327: 1480–84.

Hiro, Dilip. 1995. *Between Marx and Muhammad: The Changing Face of Central Asia*. London: Harper Collins.

Howard, Marc. 2003. *The Weakness of Civil Society in Post-Communist Europe*. Cambridge: Cambridge University Press.

Humphreys, M., and J. M. Weinstein. 2007. Demobilization and reintegration. *Journal of Conflict Resolution* 51 (4): 531–67.

Jawad, Nassim, and Shahrbanou Tadjbakhsh. 1995. *Tajikistan: A Forgotten Civil War*. London: Minority Rights Group.

Jonson, L. 2006. *Tajikistan in the New Central Asia: Geopolitics, Great Power Rivalry, and Radical Islam*. London: Taurus.

Knack, Steven, and Philip Keefer. 1997. Does social capital have an economic payoff? A cross-country investigation. *Quarterly Journal of Economics* 112 (4): 1251–88.

Knack, Steven, and Philip Keefer. 2001. Trust and growth. *Economic Journal* 111: 295–321.

Knack, Stephen, and Paul J. Zack. 2001. Trust and growth. *Economic Journal, Royal Economic Society* 111 (470): 295–321.

Krueger, Alan B., and Jitka Maleckova. 2003. Education, poverty and terrorism: Is there a causal connection? *Journal of Economic Perspectives* 17 (4): 119–44.

Marshall, M., and B. Cole. 2009. Global report 2009: Conflict, governance, and state fragility. Center for Systemic Peace, Vienna, VA.

North, Douglass C., Joseph Wallis, and Barry Weingast. 2009. *Violence and Social Orders: A Conceptual Framework For Interpreting Recorded Human History*. New York: Cambridge University Press.

Nunn, Nathan, and Leonard Wantchekon. 2011. The slave trade and the origins of mistrust in Africa. *American Economic Review* 11 (7): 5221–52.

Portes, Alejandro. 1998. Social capital: Its origins and applications in modern sociology. *Annual Review of Sociology* 24: 1–24.

Richerson, Peter, and Robert Boyd. 2005. *Not by Genes Alone: How Culture Transformed Human Evolution*. Chicago: University of Chicago Press.

Tilly, Charles, and Gabriel Ardant. 1975. *The Formation of National States in Western Europe*. Princeton: Princeton University Press.

Tilly, Charles. 1985. War making and state making as organized crime. In Peter Evans, Dietrich Rueschemeyer, and Theda Skocpol, eds., *Bringing the State Back*. Cambridge: Cambridge University Press.

Tuncer-Kilavuz, Idil. 2009. The role of networks in Tajikistan's civil war: Network activation and violence specialists. *Nationalities Papers* 37 (5): 693–725.

Tuncer-Kilavuz, Idil. 2011. Understanding civil war: A comparison of Tajikistan and Uzbekistan. *Europe–Asia Studies* 63 (2): 263–90.

Voors, Marteen, Eleonora Nillesen, Philip Verwimp, Erwin Bulte, Robert Lensink, and Daan van Soest. 2011. Does conflict affect preferences? Results from field experiments in Burundi. *American Economic Review* 102 (2): 941–64.

Contributors

Vincenzo Bove, University of Essex

Raul Caruso, Catholic University of the Sacred Heart

Alessandra Cassar, University of San Francisco

Jacopo Costa, University of Florence

Maria Cubel, University of Barcelona & IEB

Leandro Elia, Institute for the Protection and Security of the Citizen, European Commission—Joint Research Centre, Ispra

Jose Luis Evia, Catholic University of Bolivia and Andean University "Simon Bolivar" of Bolivia

Davide Fiaschi, University of Pisa

Pauline Grosjean, Australian School of Business, The University of New South Wales

Ruixue Jia, IIES, Stockholm University

Kai A. Konrad, Max Planck Institute for Tax Law and Public Finance

Roberto Laserna, CERES, Bolivia

Pinghan Liang, RIEM, Southwestern University of Finance and Economics

Roberto Ricciuti, University of Verona and CESifo

Stergios Skaperdas, University of California, Irvine

Caleb Stroup, Grinnell College

Karl Wärneryd, Stockholm School of Economics and CESifo

Sam Whitt, High Point University

Ben Zissimos, University of Exeter

Index